Sustainable Rural Development

Addressing Natural Resources, Agriculture, Human Development, Health and Energy for Sustainable Development in Assam and North-East India

Shamintra Ghosh

Preface

Sustainable development is the buzz word today used in all development strategies and policy formulations. The book aims to study the development that is taking place in remote regions of the country, whether it takes really to growth or something else. The growth and development strategy must be people centric, it must promote the living standard, reduce the gap between the rich and the poor and most importantly it should keep the environment intact otherwise the development is not going to sustain. The poor human life is more dependent on the environmental resources. Thus the development policy must keep strict eye on agriculture which is the mainstay of 75% people, human development and environment. Developing countries need not follow the conventional path to development with regard to technologies but must use to their advantage the cutting edge technology options now available to 'leapfrog', and put the tools of modern technology to use. Mechanisms must be put in place to make available to developing countries the latest technologies at reasonable cost.

Author

Shamintra Ghosh

Asst. Prof. Silchar College

Dept. Economics

Chapter 3

An Interlinked Role of Agriculture and Human Development in Assam 46

3.1 Productivity in various districts along with other salient characteristics 47

3.2 Regression Analysis of Agriculture and Poverty 48

3.3 Human Development Characteristics of Assam 49

3.4 Regression Analysis between Human Development and Agriculture 52

Appendix on Agriculture and Sustainability 56

Chapter 4

Energy: A Major Determinant of Sustainable Development 68

4.1 Power Infrastructure in Assam: Essential Need for Human Development 69

4.2 Renewable Energy Sector in Assam 78

4.2.1 Solar Electrification in Villages of Assam 81

4.2.2 Wind Energy 83

4.2.3 Hydel Energy 87

4.2.4 Bio-Mass 89

Chapter 5

Major Issues of Sustainable Development in Barak Valley Zone of Assam 91

5.1 An Introduction to Geography and Climate 92

5.2 Gross Domestic Product of Barak Valley 94

5.3 Demographic Profile 96

5.4 Agriculture in Barak Valley 98

5.5 Human Development Profile 107

Contents	Page No.
Chapter 1	
Sustainable Development and Water in Assam	7
1.1 An Introduction to Sustainable Development	8
1.2 An Introduction to the Water Resource	11
1.3 Water on Surface	11
1.4 River System of Brahmaputra	13
1.5 River System of Barak	16
1.6 Wetlands	16
1.6.1 Lakes and Ponds	17
1.6.2 Swampy/ Marshy	21
1.6.3 Reservoirs	22
1.6.4 Tanks	22
1.7 Ground Water	23
Chapter 2	
Sustainability and Land Resources in Assam	27
2.1 An Introduction to Land Resources	28
2.2 Land Use Pattern	29
2.3 Agricultural Land	32
2.4 Forest-Land	35
2.5 Wastelands	37
2.6 Soils and Fertility	40
2.7 Soil Erosion	43

5.6 An Analysis of Agro-Human Development Linkage	**110**

Chapter 6	
Health and Sustainable Development in Assam	**115**
6.1 Health Performance in Assam: A Comparison with other North-Eastern states and India	116
6.1.1 Introduction to Health and Development	116
6.1.2 Socio-economic and Health profile of North-East States as compared to India	118
6.1.3 Comparison on the Basis of Major Health Outcomes	121
6.1.4 Disparity on the basis of nutrition, women and child health	128
6.2 Women, Child and Reproductive Health: A Comparative Study of Rural-Urban Development in Assam	131
6.2.1 Introduction to the Issue	131
6.2.2 Assam - Key Indicators of Rural Development and Health Environment	132

Chapter 7	
A Cross Sectional Data Analysis on Sustainability of Rural Development -A Study in Barak Valley	**145**
7.1 Agriculture and Human Development Performance	146
7.2 Study of Inter-linkage among Variables	192
7.3 ADO Circle Wise Performance	209
7.4 Agriculture and Poverty Interface	250

Chapter 8 **Findings and Policy Recommendation**	262
An Epilogue	282
Bibliography	302
Technical Appendix	305

Chapter 1

Sustainable Development and Water in Assam

1.1 An Introduction to Sustainable Development

1.2 An Introduction to the Water Resource

1.3 Water on Surface

1.4 River System of Brahmaputra

1.5 River System of Barak

1.6 Wetlands

1.6.1 Lakes and Ponds

1.6.2 Swampy/ Marshy

1.6.3 Reservoirs

1.6.4 Tanks

1.7 Ground Water

1.1 An Introduction to Sustainable Development

Sustainable development is a major issue today in all development dialogues. United Nations say's "Investment is critical to the ability of developing countries to achieve needed economic growth to improve the welfare of their populations and to meet their basic needs in a sustainable manner, all without deteriorating or depleting the resource base that underpins development. Sustainable development requires increased investment, for which domestic and external financial resources are needed. Foreign private investment and the return of flight capital, which depend on a healthy investment climate, are an important source of financial resources. Many developing countries have experienced a decade-long situation of negative net transfer of financial resources, during which their financial receipts were exceeded by payments they had to make, in particular for debt-servicing. As a result, domestically mobilized resources had to be transferred abroad instead of being invested locally in order to promote sustainable economic development". The developments of those regions of the world which are more endowed with resource require planned utilization otherwise it may lead to depletion at such a rate which will endanger the upcoming generation. Assam is endowed with several natural resources, thus their consumption requires more precautions so that sustainable development can be ascertained.

The prime objectives of the study are –

1. To evaluate the various determinants of sustainable rural development
2. To study the importance of natural resource in sustainable livelihood of the people
3. To study the inter-relationship of agriculture, environment and human development
   To study the performance of health sector in North-East as compared to India
4. To analyse the inter-state disparity of health status among North-East states.
5. To analyse the health environment and living conditions that determine rural development.
6. To analyze the multidimensional poverty in relation to sustainable agriculture and human development
7. To analyse the rural-urban disparity that exists in women and reproductive health care.
8. To study the rural-urban disparity in child health care.

The prime hypotheses are

1. There exists a positive relation between sustainable rural development and sustainable farming
2. Public health care is a major determinant of sustainable rural development
3. There exists a positive relation between agro-human development linkage and sustainable development
4. Multidimensional Poverty is inversely related with agro-human development linkage

Data Source and Methodology

For 1st and 2nd chapters, data has been collected from various government journals and reports of Ministry of Environment & Forests, Govt. of India.

For 3rd, 4th and 5th chapters, data for the study was taken from secondary sources. Energy statistics has been collected from Assam Power Distribution Company (APDCL) and ASEB. Data on crop wise area and production, land use statistics, rainfall, irrigation, fertiliser use was taken from Statistical Abstract of the state, Directorate of Agriculture/Horticulture, CSO, Directorate of Economics and Statistics, Human Development Report at national and state level etc. Physical output was converted into value term by using state level prices of various agricultural crops. These prices were generated by dividing state level value of output of each crop estimated by CSO by the output of the crop for the year 2003-04 and 2004-05. According to CSO methodology such prices represent farm gate prices. Agricultural Development Index (ADI) is prepared based on six factors of yield, irrigation, fertiliser, HYV seeds, rainfall and infrastructure as done by Barah et al(2001) and K.Singh(2010).

For 6th chapter, data has been taken from the Census of India (2001, and 2011), National Family Health Survey 2 (NFHS 2) (1998–9) and NFHS 3 (2005–6), data on health statistics from the Ministry of Health and Family Welfare and the National Sample Survey (NSS) 58th (2002) and 65th (2008–9) rounds-2. Further, India Human Development Report (2011), State HDRs of North-East, NRHM report etc have been used to analyse the data.

For 7th chapter, data has been collected from both primary and secondary sources. Multistage sampling has been followed. In the Barak Valley region there are six agricultural subdivisions—(1) Cachar district (3 subdivisions), (2) Karimganj district (2 subdivisions) (3)

Hailakandi (1 subdivisions). From each subdivision one ADO circle has been selected subject to the condition that the selected circle will represent the entire subdivision. From each ADO circle two villages (one agriculturally developed having at least some marketing network and other agriculturally underdeveloped) has been selected in consultation with Agricultural Development Officer. From the selected villages 450 sample of farming households has been selected for the study.

A number of indices have been constructed to address the objectives of the study which includes: (a) Agricultural Performance Index (API), (b) Human development by Quality of Life (c) Wealth Index, (d) Health Index, (e) Education Index and (f) Multidimensional Poverty Index. All these indices have been constructed at the household level. Moreover, suitable statistical and regression techniques will be used to analyze the relationship among concerned variables of the study.

1.2 An Introduction to the Water Resource

Assam is endowed with enormous water resources. The large perennial rivers and other water bodies with the rich aquifer speak about vastness of its water resource. Surface water is available in the forms of river, stream, lake, swamps, pond etc. The ground water is available at low to moderate depth almost in entire state. Although there is seasonal and regional variation in the availability of water resources, the annual availability of water resource remain almost same. In the last few decades the use of water has been growing at a fast rate, which is more than twice the rate of the increase of human population. The consumption of water has increased due to the increase of human population as well as the diversification of human activities. With the increase of per capita consumption of water in domestic, agricultural and industrial sectors, cause the reduction of potential per capita availability of water. Moreover, it may cause the deterioration of water quality to a great extent.

1.3 Water on Surface

Apart from the rain water received, the state is endowed with number of perennial rivers and lake locally known as beel. The state is drained by the dance networks of two river system, viz the Brahmaputra and the Barak. These rivers have large number of tributaries joining them from both the banks. There are about 73 important tributaries of the Brahmaputra river and 11 tributaries of Barak river. The vast potential surface water resource of the state is not yet properly utilized in the state. In the last few decades, the rate of consumption of water in the agricultural sector, industrial sector and in the urban centres has been increased significantly. The discharges of untreated domestic wastewater, industrial wastewater, run of from the agricultural fields and the urban sewage water posing threat to the water bodies of state.

Agriculture constitutes the largest share of water consumption amongst various uses followed by the domestic and industrial uses. The gross irrigation potential created up to March 2002 through govt. irrigation schemes in Assam was 5,13,341.00 hectare (includes both irrigation from surface water and ground water) against the irrigation potential of 240406.17 hectare in 1987. This indicates the increasing trend of water utilization in agricultural sector. Apart from irrigation, the second most beneficial uses of water are drinking, cooking, bathing, washing, etc. – domestic use. More than 75 per cent population of the state are living in the rural area and due to certain factors the direct use of river water is limited in the state. The ground water is the main source of water for most of the rural population of the state. The per capita abstraction would therefore be small and may be estimated at 25 litres per day.

Urban areas are generally provided with organized water supply. Cities and town located near the river usually depend on the river for their source of water. This hold good for the Brahmaputra basin too. With the steady growth of urban centres in the river basins of the state, the water abstraction for the domestic consumption is one of the major constituents of the water consumption. The table no 3.2 show the district wise water consumption by the urban people in the state. It may be mentioned here that there is usually combination sources i. e. directly from river or through tube wells. The estimate is based on a gross of per capita average demand of 150 litres per day, although local variation and variation among the various groups of users are expected. The share of water consume in the industrial sector is increasing in last two decades with the growth of industries in the state. Water is mainly use in the industries for cooling and washing purposes and after use it is generally drained out to the natural water bodies either after treatment or without treatment.

Besides the river, another important source of surface water is the wetlands of the state. There are about 3513 numbers of wetlands of different size and shape in the state. The total area under different categories of wetland in Assam is about 1012.32 sq km during the pre monsoon season. It constitutes 1.29 percent of the total geographical area of the state. Of the total wetlands, 1367 inland wetlands suffer due to the problem of invasion by aquatic weeds and need ameliorative steps for conservation. Out of this, 656 are swampy/marshy areas, 366 ox-bow lakes/cut-off meanders, 193 lakes/ponds, 133 water-logged, 13 tanks and 3 reservoirs. The wetlands of the state are facing serious threat from the human society. The large-scale encroachment, over fishing in wetlands, filing up of wetlands for other uses and dumping of wastes in the wetlands are some of the human activities causing serious damage. Like the surface water bodies, the pressure on the ground water is increasing in the state. The rate of groundwater extraction in the state has been increase by many folds in last decade of for irrigation through shallow tube wells. Unscientific dumping of municipal solid and industrial wastes on the ground and in the water body is increasing with the population growth. The excessive extraction of ground water especially for the irrigation and in densely settled areas for the domestic consumption the water table in winter season goes down beyond the reach of low and medium depth dug wells and tube wells and thereby causing water crises in some areas of the state.

1.4 River System of Brahmaputra

The Brahmaputra is one of the biggest rivers of the world. The Brahmaputra basin covers an area of 5, 80,000 Sq. Km of which 1, 94,413 Sq. Km falls in India. In India, the basin lies in the states of Arunachal Pradesh, Assam, Nagaland, Meghalaya, Sikkim and West Bengal. Brahmaputra is a perennial river, feed by snow as well as by rain. The Brahmaputra rolls down the plain of Assam east to west for a distance of 640 km up to Bangladesh border. Through its course, the river receives innumerable tributaries (about 73) coming out of the northern, north eastern and the southern hill ranges. The mighty river with a well-knit network of tributaries drains an area of 56,480 Sq. Km of the state accounting for 72 per cent of its total geographical area. Most of the right bank tributaries of Brahmaputra are snow as well rain feed and are perennial. It is the fourth largest river in the world in term of average water discharge at the mouth with a flow of 19,830 m3s-1. The river carries 82 per cent of its annual flow during the rainy season (May through October). The maximum discharge of the river at Pandu (in Guwahati) on 23-08-62 was 72794 m3s-1 and the minimum discharge at the same point on 20-02-68 was 1757 m3s-1. The mean annual flood discharge and dry season discharge of the river at Pandu is 51156 m3s-1 and 4420 m3s-1 respectively. The discharge per unit area of basin at Pandu is 0.03m3s-1. The principal tributaries of Brahmaputra River and their annual discharge are given in table below.

Table-1: Right Bank Tributaries of the Brahmaputra River and their annual discharge

Sl. No.	Rivers	Length (km)	Average annual discharge (m^3 s^{-1})
1	Subansiri	442	7,55,771
2	Ranganadi	150	74,309
3	Baroi	64	20,800
4	Bargang	42	16,000
5	Jia Bharali	247	3,49,487
6	Gabharu	61	8,450
7	Balsiri	110	9,300
8	Dhansiri	123	26,577
9	Noa-Nadi	75	4,450
10	Nanoi	105	10,281
11	Barnadi	112	5,756
12	Puthimari	190	26,324
13	Pagladiya	197	15,201
14	Manas-Aie-Beki	215	3,07,947
15	Champamati	135	32548
16	Gaurang	98	22263

| 17 | Tipkai | 108 | 61786 |
| 18 | Godadhar | 50 | 7000 |

Source:-ENVIS

Table-2: Left Bank Tributaries of the Brahmaputra River and their annual discharge

Sl. No.	Rivers	Length (km)	Average annual discharge ($m^3 s^{-1}$)
1	Buridihing	360	141539
2	Desang	230	55101
3	Dikhow	200	41892
4	Jhanji	108	8797
5	Bhogdoi	160	6072
6	Dhansiri	352	68746
7	Kopili	297	90046
8	Krishna	81	22452
9	Kulsi	93	11643
10	Jinari	60	7783

Source:-ENVIS

1.5 River System of Barak

Barak is the second largest river system in the North East India as well as in Assam. The river with a total length of 900 km from source to mouth drains an area of 52,000 sq. km. In India and traverses a distance of 532 km up to the Indo-Bangla border. Like Brahmaputra, the Barak is also a perennial river of the state. The important north bank tributaries of Barak River are Jiri, Siri, Madhura, Jatinga and Larang, while the important south bank tributaries include sonai, Ghagra, katakhal, Dhaleswari, Singla and Longai. The flows of the rivers in Assam decrease considerably during the dry season. They maintained pick flow in summer rainy months.

1.6 Wetlands

The valley of the river Brahmaputra with its innumerable fresh water lakes (locally called beel), or ox-bow lakes (era suti), marshy tracts and seasonally flooded plains and hundreds of riverine sandbars and islands was, till recently, an ideal wetland eco-system which contained specialised wetland animals like the fresh water dolphin, dugong and the great Indian one-horned rhino and reptiles like the crocodile, the winter monitor lizard and few species of turtles. All these creatures are either extinct or highly endangered at present. With the progressive destruction of the Brahmaputra valley wetlands since the advent of the British, along with these animals and others, we have lost yet another spectacular natural beauty - the hundreds of thousands of water birds all along the 800 km. of the river. The destruction of the Brahmaputra valley wetland system started with the arrival of the water hyacinth from Central America more than a century ago. Extensive growth of this fast growing weed can cut out sun light from the micro flora and also produces faster eutrophication by slowing down water current and depositing debris at the bottom. The second phase of enhanced eutrophication took place with the raising of earthen bunds along the banks of almost the entire length of the river and many of its tributaries after the 1950 earthquake. These artificial levees cut off, to a great extent, the periodic flushing out of the wetlands by the monsoon flood. The third and the final onslaught on the wetlands has taken place with the arrival of the human settlers in the sand bars and the minor river islands, mostly in the lower Assam. This has turned the wetlands into agricultural zones rich in rice and vegetables but totally denuded of wild-life. With the vanished wetlands, gone also are the rich supplies of fish, a compulsory item of the Assamese menu and a good source of protein for the rural mass. In spite of the presence of the mighty Brahmaputra, its numerous tributaries, and the large number of wetlands, Assam today imports 0.20 lakh tonnes of fish an anually to satisfy the domestic market. Out of this, 0.14 lakh tonnes is consumed in Assam. The total fish production from Assam's wetlands is 1.55 lakh tonnes per year. Thus, a total of 1.69 lakh tonnes of fish is supplied from imports as well as local wetlands. The total demand for fish in the state, on the other hand, is estimated at 2.21 lakh tonnes per year, 6.68 percent of which met by imports from other states (source : Directorate of Fisheries, Government of Assam). As a result, there is a deficit of 0.52 lakh tonnes of fish every year and consequently the price of fish has rocketed up to such a height that the poor man simply cannot afford to buy it even once in a week. The production potential of wetlands in the state is estimated at 400-500 kg/ha/year after development. The progressive short supply of fish in Assam is a direct consequence of mismanagement and neglect of its wetland eco-system.

It is therefore felt to be an imperative need to conserve these wetlands and protect their unique biodiversity. If properly managed, the wetlands are going to be a source of immense wealth for this state leading also to enrichment of the quality of its environment.

1.6.1 Lakes and Ponds

In Assam, there are 690 lakes and ponds as recorded through the study. These lakes /ponds cover an area of 15494.00 ha which constitutes 0.20 percent of the total geographical area of the state and 15.30 percent of the total area under wetlands. The smallest of them measures 2.50 ha while the largest one has 882.50 ha of areal coverage. Majority of this type of wetlands have water with low turbidity. An analysis of aquatic vegetation in these lakes / ponds indicates that most of them have no vegetation or are partially vegetated. Highest number of lakes / ponds are observed in Golaghat district (113 number) followed by Dhubri (73 number) and Nagaon (68 number) districts. But areawise, the highest area under this category is observed in Kamrup district (15705.00 ha) followed by Nagaon (2175.50 ha) and Dhubri (1816.50 ha) districts. Some of the important wetlands under this category are Deepar beel in Kamrup district, Dhir beel in Dhubri district, Tamaranga beel and Dalani beel in Bongaigaon.

Table-3: District-wise Wetlands

District	Number	Area (ha)
Barpeta	97	3301.00
Bongaigaon	100	3158.50
Cachar	340	7188.00
Darrang	103	3515.00
Dhemaji	139	3960.00
Dhubri	233	6459.70
Dibrugarh	86	2752.50
Goalpara	165	3832.50
Golaghat	330	5467.50
Hailakandi	47	840.00
Jorhat	109	2108.50
Kamrup	352	11407.00
Karbi Anglong	77	897.00
Karimganja	70	5719.50
Kokrajhar	85	1578.40
Lakhimpur	151	3033.50

Morigaon	183	11658.00
Nagaon	379	11295.50
N.C. Hills	10	2552.50
Nalbari	68	1988.00
Sibsagar	109	2135.00
Sonitpur	206	3651.00
Tinsukia	74	2732.50
Total	3513	101231.60

Source: Assam Remote sensing research centre.

Fig-1

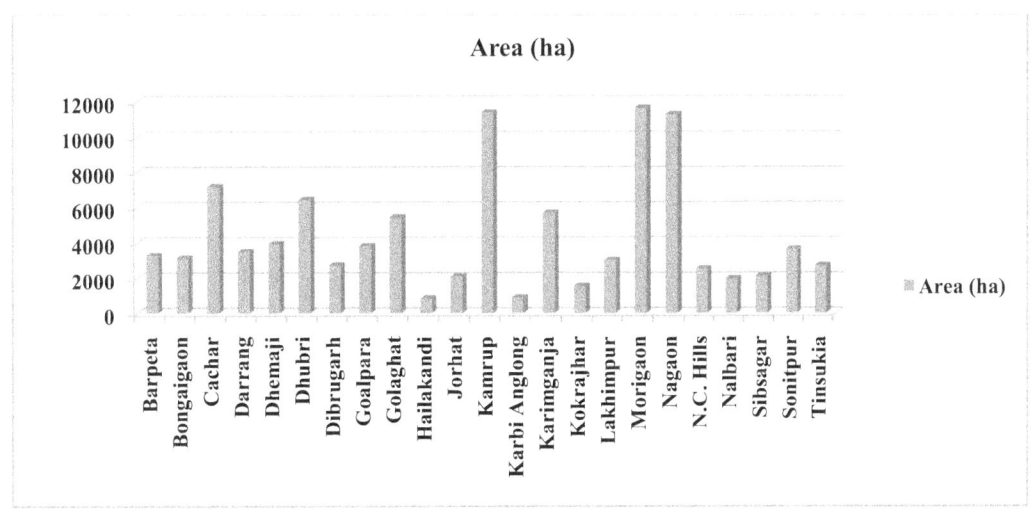

Table-4: Size wise distribution of wetlands in Assam

Area Class (Ha)	Total Number	Total Waterspred Area (Ha)	Total Vegetation Area (Ha)	Total Wetland Area (Ha)
1.0-100.0	3341	52878.1	1920.5	55821.5
100.1-200.0	100	12921.5	947.5	13869.0
200.1-300.0	36	7979.5	537.0	8527.0
300.1-400.0	14	4505.0	328.0	4823.0
400.1-500.0	4	1815.0	0.0	1815.0
500.1-600.0	6	2625.0	602.5	3227.5
>600.1	12	13068.0	70.0	13148.0
TOTAL	3513	96818.10	4405.5	101231.6

Source:-ARSAC

A total 861 number of ox-bow lakes/cut-off meanders is observed throughout the state of Assam, covering an area of 15460.60 ha which constitutes 0.20 percent of the total geographical area of the state and 15.27 percent of the total area under wetlands. The smallest of them measures 5.0 ha while the largest one has 582.50 ha of areal coverage. Majority of this type of wetlands have water with low turbidity. An analysis of aquatic vegetation in these ox-bow lakes / cut-off meanders indicates that most of them are either without vegetation or partially vegetated. Highest number of ox-bow lakes / cut-off meanders are observed in Golaghat district (104 number) followed by Nagaon district (71 number) and Dhubri district (68 number). But area wise, the highest area under this category is observed in Morigaon district (2143.00 ha) followed by Nagaon (1746.00 ha) and Golaghat (1563.00 ha) districts. Some of the important wetlands under this category are Morikolong and Patoli beel in Nagaon district, Mer beel in Golaghat district and Guruajan in Morigaon district.

In Assam, a total of 1125 number of waterlogged areas are observed which are distributed unevenly covering an area of 23431.50 ha which constitutes 0.30 percent of the total geographical area of the state and 23.15 percent of the total area under wetlands. The smallest of them is 2.5 ha while the largest one has 3010.00 ha of areal coverage. Majority of this type of wetlands have low turbidity. An analysis of aquatic vegetation in these wate-logged areas indicates that most of them are free from aquatic vegetation. Highest number of water(c)logged areas are observed in Cachar district (231 number) followed by Nagaon district (138 number) and Sonitpur district (110 number). But area wise, the highest area under this category is observed in Cachar district (4869.50 ha) followed by Karimganj (4667.00 ha) and Nagaon (2559.50 ha) districts. Some of the important wetlands under this category are Son beel in Karimganj district and Raumari beel in Darrang district. These water-logged areas play significant role in the region's economy as they are present in large numbers in the rural areas containing good amount of fishes and other aquatic fauna and providing habitat to a variety of migratory as well as domestic birds. Besides they have remarkable potential for supplying irrigation water to the nearby agricultural fields during the dry periods. There are some waterlogged areas which can be developed for recreational purposes and as tourist spots such as the Son beel in Karimganj district.

1.6.2 Swampy/Marshy

These swampy/marshy areas constitute another major group of wetlands in Assam. These are identifiable on satellite imagery by their reddish tone indicating the presence of vegetation, associated with dark blue tone inferring to the presence of water and their occurrence in the low lying areas. Due to the presence of varied quantities of minerals in the water, these swampy/marshy areas are either moderately or highly turbid. In most cases, there is no feeder channel to control the inflow or outflow of water. In Assam, as many as 712 number of swampy/marshy areas have been identified from satellite data which cover an area of 43433.50 ha constituting 0.55 percent of the total geographical area of the state and 42.91 percent of the total area under wetlands. The smallest of them is 2.5 ha while the largest one has 1350.00 ha of areal coverage. Majority of this type of wetlands are with low turbidity. An analysis of aquatic vegetation in these lakes / ponds indicates that most of them are partially vegetated. Highest number of swampy/marshy areas are observed in Kamrup district (155 number) followed by Nagaon (92 number) and Goalpara (68 number) districts. But area wise, the highest area under this category is observed in Kamrup district (8109.50 ha) followed by Morigaon (7051.00 ha) and Nagaon (4764.50 ha) districts. Some of the important wetlands under this category are Nandan-Sonai beel in Morigaon district, Batha beel in Darrang district and Urpad beel in Goalpara district. Unlike the water-logged areas, the swampy/marshy areas don't have much contribution to the state's economy. But with the help of proper developmental schemes by converting them into utilizable form, these may boost up the economy of the state to a significant level.

1.6.3 Reservoirs

Reservoirs are artificial impoundments of water for irrigation, flood control, municipal water supplies, hydro-electric power generation and so forth. There are as many as 10 numbers of reservoirs covering an area of 2662.5 ha which constitutes 0.03 percent of the total geographical area of the state and 2.63 percent of the total area under wetlands. The smallest of them covers 17.50 ha while the largest one has 930.00 ha of areal coverage. Majority of this type of wetlands contains water with low turbidity. An analysis of aquatic vegetation in these reservoirs indicates that most of them are either free from vegetation or partially vegetated. Highest number of reservoirs is observed in N.C.Hills district (4 nos.) followed by Golaghat and Nalbari districts (2 nos. each). But area wise, the highest area under this category is observed in N.C.Hills district (2365.00 ha) followed by Kamrup (220.00 ha) and Golaghat (37.50 ha) districts.

1.6.4 Tanks

Assam has several thousands of family owned small size tanks, these have not entered into reckoning as far as this report is concerned because of the scale factor. In Assam, a total of 115 numbers of tanks are identified from satellite data. These tanks occupy an area of 749.00 ha which constitutes 0.01 percent of the total geographical area of the state and 0.74 percent of the total area under wetlands. The smallest of them covers 2.5 ha while the largest one has 55.00 ha of areal coverage. Majority of this type of wetlands have low turbidity. An analysis of aquatic vegetation in these tanks indicates that most of them are free from vegetation. Highest number of tanks are observed in Sibsagar district (20 number) followed by Kamrup (18 number) and Sonitpur (16 number). But area wise, the highest area under this category is observed in Sibsagar district (267.00 ha) followed by Sonitpur (83.50 ha) and Kamrup (80.00 ha) districts. Some of the important wetlands under this category are Gaurisagar Pukhuri, Sibsagar Pukhuri and Joysagar Pukhuri in Sibsagar district. Besides providing water to the people of the nearby areas, these tanks can also be used for rearing fishes and raising plantation crops like coconut, arecanut, cashewnut etc. along the sides of the ponds. Ornamental gardens can also be developed on the banks of the ponds.

1.7 Ground-Water

Assam is one of the rich states of the country in term of the ground water development potentiality. The entire Brahmaputra valley, covering more than 70 per cent of the total geographical area of the state, contains prolific aquifer system with water table lying within 5 m of land surface. The Barak valley also has a good potentiality for the development of ground water. The present stage ground water development even in the Brahmaputra valley, the most populous part of the state, is nothing but in a nascent stage. Based on the recommendation of the Ground Water Estimation Committee, Ministry of Irrigation, March 1984, the recoverable recharge of ground water in Assam as worked out by the Central Ground Water Board, to about 2 million hectare metre per year. With the present ground water resource available to be utilized, it is estimated that an additional area of about 14 lakh hectare of net area sown can be brought under irrigation. Besides the irrigational use, ground water forms the most common form source of domestic use water in the state. The lifting of ground water through dug wells, tube wells, shallow tube wells and deep tube wells for irrigation, domestic and industrial use is very common in the state.

Table-5: Ground water distribution in Assam

District	GW resource dynamic (MCM)	Utilisable GW resource for irrigation (MCM)	Utilisable GW resource for drinking and allied (MCM)	Gross draft (MCM)	Balance available (MCM)	State of GW development (%)
Barpeta	1161	987	74	56	931	5.68
Bongaigaon	591	502	89	25	477	4.98
Cachar	817	694	123	1	693	0.15
Darrang	1407	1196	211	73	1123	6.10
Dhemaji	1660	1411	249	44	1367	3.11
Dhubri	1300	1105	195	64	1041	5.79
Dibrugarh	1635	1390	245	41	1349	2.94
Goalpara	495	421	74	20	401	4.75
Golaghat	1794	1525	269	42	1483	2.75
Hailakandi	98	83	15	3	80	3.61
Jorhat	1461	1242	219	35	1207	2.81
Karbi Anglong	584	496	88	1	495	0.20
Anglong						

Kamrup	1229	1045	184	71	974	6.80
Karimganj	133	113	20	4	109	3.54
Kokrajhar	1580	1343	237	35	1308	2.60
Morigaon	321	273	48	43	230	15.75
Nagaon	935	795	140	126	669	15.84
Nalbari	639	543	96	37	506	6.81
N.C. Hills	607	516	91	1	515	0.19
Lakhimpur	1167	992	175	31	961	3.12
Sonitpur	1615	1373	242	110	1263	8.01
Sibsagar	1658	1409	249	35	1374	2.48
Tinsukia	1832	1557	275	46	1511	2.95

Source: Central Ground Water Board

Pollution of Water

The problem of water pollution is rampant in all thickly populated areas. Water does possess a self-cleaning property. The problem intensifies with the addition of pollutants in our water-ways from many sources like wastes from reactors, laboratories, hospitals and fallout from nuclear explosions, domestic wastes from the cities and towns, chemical wastes from factories and industrial units, etc. 90% of water pollution is due to human waste, which gives rise to such diseases as intestinal infection, hookworms, cholera, typhoid, infectious hepatitis, etc. chemicals like DDT, Parathion, linden, etc contribute a great deal to water pollution. To prevent water pollution, the discharge of effluents from the industries as well as the use of DDT should be controlled. All domestic waste should be properly treated before discharging it into the water bodies. Acid rain can be prevented by reducing the emission of oxides of sulphur-nitrogen.

Chapter 2

Sustainability and Land Resources in Assam

2.1 An Introduction to Land Resources

2.2 Land Use Pattern

2.3 Agricultural Land

2.4 Forest-Land

2.5 Wastelands

2.6 Soils and Fertility

2.7 Soil Erosion

2.1 An Introduction to Land Resources

The 'land' is a very precious gift of nature. His relatively thin cover on the continental surface serving as a medium for plant growth is a product of thousands and million year's natural activity. It is true that nothing can be achieved without using the elements of nature, but misuse and over utilization causes serious damage to the natural system. The level of utilization of land depends on the socio-cultural and economic achievement of people living under different nature environment. Accordingly, people have developed different land use techniques and the land use pattern. Thus, land utilization is a dynamic process, varied spatially and temporally. Land use pattern has a long drawn effect on the economy as well as on the ecology of any area. Assam with a total geographical area of 78438 sq. km is very rich in land resources. Its vast fertile alluvial tracts and low hills with suitable climatic condition offer excellent condition for utilization of for different uses. The land use pattern of the state witnessed a change in last few decades. The fast growing population aided with the modern technology lead to rapid change in the land use pattern of the state. The effects such an unwise change is well reflected in the forms of ecological imbalance and land degradation through soil erosion. The forest area has been decreasing due to the encroachment for agricultural. There are already conflicting report regarding areas under forests as well as degraded land as claimed by the govt. and as brought out by the other national agencies. The area under forest in Assam as legally notified is 3071 sq. km accounting for about 39.1 per cent of the total geographical area of the state. But the actual forest cover based on the imagery (1990) is only 21.9 per cent of the total area. These differences clearly indicate the nature of land use changes in the state. The horizontal growth of settlement in the last few decades due the rapid growth of population and the resultant growth of other developmental activities also leading to a slow but continual change to the land use pattern at different scale.

2.2 Land Use Pattern

The land use classification scheme developed by the National Remote Sensing Agency (Dept. of Space, Govt. of India) has been adopted for the State of Assam. The Major classes of land use as identified by the Assam Remote Sensing Application Centre are built-up land, agricultural land, forest land, wasteland, water bodies and others.

Table-6: Land use Pattern in Assam, Satellite base data, 2004 (area in hectares)

Sl. No.	Land use class	Total area (in hectare)	% to total area
1	Built-up land	21147	0.27
2	Agricultural land	4248639	54.11
3	Forest land	1726387	21.9
4	Wastelands	1060602	13.50
5	Water bodies	557180	7.10
6	Others	238346	3.02

Source: Assam Remote Sensing Application Centre

Assam is basically an agriculture dependent state. More than 65 per cent of its total area is under agriculture. The increasing pressure of population and the lack of employment opportunity in other sectors, the pressure on agricultural sector is increasing alarmingly. This situation leads to the intensification of agricultural sector and the fragmentation of land holdings. Such situations cause serious damage to the land and the economy of the state.

Table-7: Estimated number of operational holdings by size classes and types, Assam

Sl. No	Size class (area in hectare)	Number of Operational holding		Institutional	Total
		Individual	Joint		
1	Below 0.5	1027193	8587	1073	1036853
2	0.5 - 1.0	623929	7570	900	632399
3	1.0 - 2.0	551203	7834	2041	561078
4	2.0 - 3.0	237703	3507	405	241615
5	3.0 - 4.0	107786	1640	204	109630
6	4.0 - 5.0	49509	876	97	50482
7	5.0 - 7.5	37861	911	142	38914
8	7.5 - 10.0	6629	261	112	7022
9	10.0 - 20.0	2589	164	298	3051
10	20.0 and above	369	74	1510	1953
11	All size	2644771	31444	6782	2682997

Source: Statistical Handbook of Assam, 2011

The above table shows that the individual land holders are the most in number while small land holders are the highest in the state. 1036853 are very small or marginal land owners in the sate which depicts the inequality in the distribution of land in the state. The skewed distribution of land in the state is a formidable obstacle for the human development and sustainable development of the sate as well.

Table-8: District wise distribution of Built up land, Assam

Sl. No.	District	Built up land (in he.)
1	Barpeta	3255
2	Bongaigaon	138
3	Cachar	592
4	Darrang	191
5	Dhemaji	208
6	Dhubri	513
7	Dibrugarh	911
8	Goalpara	175
9	Golaghat	395
10	Hailakandi	486
11	Jorhat	404
12	Kamrup	7960
13	Karbi Anglong	129
14	Karimganj	1434
15	Kokrajhar	703
16	Lakhimpur	338

17	Morigaon	278
18	Nalbari	229
19	N.C. Hills	187
20	Nagaon	590
21	Sibsagar	924
22	Sonitpur	135
23	Tinsukia	972
	Total	21147 (0.20%)

Source: Assam Remote Sensing Application Centre

2.3 Agricultural Land

Agriculture is the dominant land use category in the state. It account for about for about 54.11 per cent of the total geographical area of the state. Including persons dependent on plantation, more than 80 per cent of the total population of Assam is dependent on agriculture. With the increase of population and the development of agro-technology, lots of changes take place in the agricultural scenario of the state. The net area sown as well as the gross cropped area increased significantly in the last few decades. This decreases the area under other uses especially area under forest. Although, the development in agriculture has tremendous important in the economy of the state but the ecological impacts of the changing land use pattern need to be considered.

Table-9: District wise distribution of Agricultural land, Assam

Sl. No.	District	Agricultural Land (area in hectare)							
		Area	Kharif	Rabi	Double crop	Net area sown	Plantation	Fallow land	Total
1	Barpeta	330730	173206	194003	139345	227864	12892	837	241593
2	Bongaigaon	31335	22099	--	18277	3822	11389	--	15211
3	Cachar	377927	103035	57878	38894	122019	34558	--	156577
4	Darrang	346530	180497	99298	82835	196960	57239	952	255151
5	Dhemaji	314312	212991	25000	119061	118930	55805	--	174735
6	Dhubri	274550	135906	126398	110167	152137	573	21306	174016
7	Dibrugarh	346763	117253	43695	20969	139979	80156	--	220135
8	Goalpara	253045	130363	43850	25573	148640	969	3340	152949
9	Golaghat	35410	12284	57555	33102	14729	93898	1186	24238

		0	4			7			1
10	Hailakandi	132293	98270	--	1723	96547	38640	--	135187
11	Jorhat	291470	21293	60998	43886	38405	61100	4815	104320
12	Kamrup	473380	235840	156516	145867	246489	25894	1939	274322
13	Karbi Anglong	1033200	135612	129280	12980	251912	8722	--	260634
14	Karimganj	183900	48938	28596	24658	52876	36093	1121	90090
15	Kokrajhar	471650	264186	243137	238979	268344	15435	3709	287488
16	Lakhimpur	250328	92985	90875	110499	73361	47365	--	120726
17	Morigaon	121966	67968	18972	33914	53026	646	9868	63540
18	Nalbari	202480	137161	89445	82122	144484	20989	7892	173365
19	N.C. Hills	489000	6290	1748	1748	6290	--	--	6290
20	Nagaon	431905	283772	202479	154659	331592	30431	3281	365304

21	Sibsagar	260290	105068	23278	15304	113042	100455	--	213497
22	Sonitpur	525520	215966	51059	29498	237527	55682	3937	297146
23	Tinsukia	355626	46752	451	2981	44222	179760	--	223982
Total		7852300	2958295 (37.6%)	1744511 (22.3%)	1487041 (18.9%)	3215765 (40.96%)	686913 (12.3%)	64183 (0.8%)	4248639 (54.1%)

Source: Assam Remote Sensing Application Centre

2.4 Forest-Land

As per the land use data, the total area under different types of forest is only 17,26,387 ha. which is about 21.9 per cent of the total area of the state. The actual area under forest in the state is less than the area under it should be as per its location i. e. 33.3 per cent to the total area. Out of the total (21.9 %) forest area 12.47 per cent is under evergreen/semi evergreen forest, 5.7 per cent under deciduous forest, 2.72 per cent in degraded forest and 1.01 per cent is under forest plantation. The over exploitation of forests and the large-scale encroachment of forest lands, the forest resources of the state has been depleting very fast. The shifting cultivation especially in the hill districts is one of the principal causes of the forest lost in the state.

Table-10: District wise distribution of Forestland, Assam

Sl. No.	District	Forest Land (in Hectare)				
		Evergreen/ semi evergreen	Deciduous	Degraded/ Degrade land	Forest Plantation	Total
1	Barpeta	--	19413	--	3998	23411
2	Bongaigaon	--	2062	3292	--	5354
3	Cachar	128651	--	14302	--	142953
4	Darrang	12149	--	10368	698	23215
5	Dhemaji	45096	--	1806	--	46902
6	Dhubri	8535	37990	--	--	46525
7	Dibrugarh	29036	12452	3787	--	45275
8	Goalpara	--	4935	9732	8183	22850
9	Golaghat	17084	--	13521	--	30605
10	Hailakandi	35165	--	15289	--	50454
11	Jorhat	25221	--	2403	--	27624
12	Kamrup	--	64281	37839	15140	1172600
13	Karbi Anglong	247640	169661	6844	26748	450893

14	Karimganj	18697	--	27494	137	46328
15	Kokrajhar	68862	80930	4604	1483	155879
16	Lakhimpur	4543	--	1033	--	5576
17	Morigaon	--	36694	1946	1042	39682
18	Nalbari	2918	8008	1602	--	12528
19	N.C. Hills	179132	--	7938	--	187070
20	Nagaon	5671	3491	10071	15136	34369
21	Sibsagar	17456	1047	9394	800	28697
22	Sonitpur	81401	333	23657	2470	107861
23	Tinsukia	52512	12436	6862	3266	75076
	Total	979769 (12.40%)	453733 (5.70%)	213784 (2.70%)	79101 (7.00%)	1726387 (21.90%)

Source: Assam Remote Sensing Application Centre

2.5 Wastelands

Among the most potential sector of land uses for development is the wastelands. The total area under different types of wasteland in the state is 10606020ha. which account for about 13.5 per cent of the geographical area of Assam. The different types of wasteland seen in the districts are – water logged area, swamps and marshes, gullied and ravinous land, land with or with out scrub and the area under shifting cultivation. Shifting cultivation constituted the most dominant class accounting about 9.48 per cent state's area. The two hill districts namely Karbi

Anglong and the N.C.Hills have 42.37 per cent and 59.65 per cent areas respectively under shifting cultivation. The swamps and the marshes of the state are ecologically very important as these areas having rich aquatic biodiversity. But due lack of proper conservation and development, most of them are now being filled up and converted to agricultural land. The over and uncontrolled exploitation of these swamps and marshes, the aquatic biodiversity of these areas have lost to greater extent. The degradation of forest in the upper catchments of the rivers intensify the problem of gully erosion, which already reach to unmanageable proportion. Thus an integrated wasteland development strategy is the need of the time.

Table-11: District wise distribution of Wasteland, Assam

Sl. No.	District	Wasteland (in Hectare)					
		Water logged	Marshy/Swampy	Gullied/Revinous	Land with or without scrub	Shifting cultivation	Total
1	Barpeta	--	901	--	193	--	1094
2	Bongaigaon	--	278	--	5281	--	5559
3	Cachar	2713	4974	--	60656	7771	76114
4	Darrang	--	1142	1142	13289	--	15573
5	Dhemaji	--	5459	--	13282	--	18741
6	Dhubri	--	960	--	3144	--	4104
7	Dibrugarh	4432	--	--	--	--	4432

8	Goalpara	--	1722	--	24765	--	26487
9	Golaghat	--	988	--	4549	--	5537
10	Hailakandi	903	1876	--	28369	3726	34874
11	Jorhat	318	1871	--	--	2147	4336
12	Kamrup	--	4012	--	38218	1221	43451
13	Karbi Anglong	--	--	--	--	437844	437844
14	Karimganj	--	1174	--	33709	391	35274
15	Kokrajhar	--	192	--	127	--	319
16	Lakhimpur	--	2601	--	1185	--	3786
17	Morigaon	--	785	--	139	--	924
18	Nalbari	--	3142	--	--	--	3142
19	N.C. Hills	--	--	--	--	291837	291837
20	Nagaon	--	12128	--	3927	--	16055
21	Sibsagar	7388	2524	--	--	--	9912
22	Sonitpur	--	8209	--	8343	--	16552
23	Tinsukia	1459	3196	--	--	--	4655

Total	17213 (0.2%)	58134 (0.7%)	1142 (0.01)	239176 (3.00%)	744937 (9.4 %)	1060602 (13.5%)

Source: Assam Remote Sensing Application Centre

Among the other categories of land use, the grassland/grazing land and mining area are seen in Assam. The grasslands claim 3.00 per cent of the total area of the state whereas the mining covers only 0.02 per cent of the total area. Mining area is mainly seen in the Tinsukia district of the state. The grasslands are widely distributed in the state

2.6 Soils and Fertility

The diversified geological conditions, topographical characteristics, climatic situations and vegetation types have favour the formation of different types of soil in the state. The soils of Assam can broadly be divided into four main groups, viz. Alluvial soils, Piedmont soils, Hill soils and Sand-lateritic.

The alluvial soils are extensively distributed over the Brahmaputra and Barak plain and are very fertile. The alluvial soils can further be divided into two main sub types-young alluvial and old alluvial soils. The young alluvial soils is characterized by modern alluvium deposits. The colour of these soils is generally gray to molted gray. On the other hand, the old alluvial soils occurs in some patches of Kokrajgar, Barpeta, Nalbari, Kamrup, darrang, Sonitpur, Lakhimpuir and Dhemaji district. Generally, the old alluvial soils are very deep with fine loams to coarce loams in texture. The piedmont soils are confined to the northern narrow zone along the piedmont zone of the Himalayan foothills. The soils are very deep and fine to coarse loamy in texture. The hill soils are generally found in the southern hill regions of the state. These soils are deep, dark grayish brown in colour and fine to coarse loamy in texture. The lateritic soils are extensively occurring in N.C. Hills district and in some parts of the southern Karbi Plateau. These soils are dark and finely textured with heavy loams.

Soil is the most valuable nature resource and serves as one of the prime requisite of life. Soils and in its turn the land through their relative fertility support all agricultural activity ant the plant growth and thereby the most important element of the natural ecosystem. As regards the soils of Assam, geology (parent material), topography and climate seem to play vital role in their formations. Therefore, under varying geological conditions, topographical characteristics and agro-climatic situations different types of soils are found to occur in the hills, piedmonts, plateaus and plains. The soils of Assam may thus generally be divided into four groups, viz.

1. Alluvial soils
2. Piedmont soils
3. Hill soils
4. Lateritic soils.

a) Alluvial Soils:

The alluvial soils are extensively distributed over the Brahmaoutra and Barak plain. These soils are very fertileas they formed from the alluvium deposits, deposited by the rivers Brahmaputra, Barak and their tributaries. The alluvial soils of Assam can be further be divided into two sub-types base on some micro differences in character such as – younger alluvium and old alluvium. The younger alluvial soil occurs in an extensive belt of the north-bank and south-bank plains including the active flood plains of the Brahmaputra and the Barak rivers. This soil characterized by recent deposition of alluvium, moderately deep to very deep with grey to melted grey colour. It is mostly composed of sandy to silly loams and slightly acidic in nature. On the riverbanks it is less acidic and sometimes nutral or slightly alkaline. The soil lack in profile development and is deficient in phosphoric acid, nitrogen and humus. The old alluvial soil occurs in some patches of Kokrajhar, Barpeta, Nalbari, Kamrup, Darrang, Sonitpur, Lakhimpur and dhemaji districts between the northern piedmont soil belt and the southern new alluvial soils of the Brahmaputra valley. In the south bank districts of the valley it occurs in a narrow belt bounded between the southern hill soils and northern new alluvial soils. In the Kopili plain covering Nagaon district the old alluvium finds wider extension. The Barak plain, on the other hand, has some elongated patches of old alluvial soil confined between the new alluvial soils of the active floodplain and the hill soils boardering Mizoram. Generally the old alluvial soil is very deep, brownish to yellowish brown with texture of fine loams to coarse loams and is slightly to moderately acidic.

b) Piedmont Soils:

The piedmont soils are confined to the northern narrow zone along the piedmont zone of the Himalayan foothills. These soils comprise the Bhabar soil and the Tarai soil, covering respectively the Bhabar and the Tarai belt of the Brahmaputra valley. The Bhabar soil occurs in the narrow belt along the Assam-Arunachal boarder extending east up to the river Subansiri' is characterized by unassorted detritus of boulders, pebbles, cobbles, sand and silts. This soil is deep and fine to clay loamy in texture. The Tarai soil occurring just south of the Bhabar soil extends up to Dihang river in some discontinuous narrow patches. This soil varies from sandy to silty loams that remain saturated and support tall grasses in a series of swamps.

c) Hill Soils:

The hill soils are generally found in the southern hilly terrains of the state. The fertility of these soils defers greatly in different regions. These soils are rich in nitrogen and organic matters. On the basis of the physical texture and chemical composition, the hill soils may be divided into –red sandy soils and red loamy soils. The red sandy soils are distributed covering as narrow belt along the Assam- Meghalaya border, the Karbi Plateau, southern part of Barail range of the N.C.Hill district and some parts of the foothills along the eastern border of the Cachar district. This soil is very deep and well drained, brownish to yellowish in colour, strongly to moderately acidic with high organic content. The red loamy soils, on the other hand, occurs in the narrow southern foothill belt running along the Assam's boarder with Arunachal and Nagaland and also in the southern fringes of the Karbi Plateau and the Barail hills of N.C.Hills district.

d) Lateritic Soils:

The lateritic soils in the state extensively occurs almost entirely over the N.C.Hills district covering some parts of southern Karbi Plateau while few patches are confined to eastern margin of the Hamren sub-division of Karbe Anglong district, southern boarder of Golaghat district and the northern part of the Barak plain along the foothills of the Barail range. These soils are dark and finely texture with heavy loams and deficient in nitrogen, potash, phosphoric acid and lime. The soils of Assam are very rich in content of nitrogen and organic matter. The alluvial soils of the Brahmaputra and the Barak valley are highly fertile and are very much suitable for rising of varieties of crops round the year such as cereals, pulses, oilseeds, plantation crops etc. The well drained, deep, acidic alluvial soils of upper Assam with good proportion of phosphoric content are mostly for the plantation. New alluvial soils occurring in the char lands of the Brahmaputra are most suitable for growing oilseeds, pulses and rabi crops. The alluvium of the plains offers excellent opportunity for cultivating rice and vegetable. The soils occurring in the upper reaches of the hill slopes are very suitable for horticulture and plantation crops.

2.7 Soil Erosion

Riverbank erosion during high flood period in the valley is a regular annual feature. Over bank flood due to breaches in the embankment render the fertile cultivable land unsuitable for crop production due to deposition of coarse sand on the surface to a variable depth. As per Assam Government Revenue Dept. records, an area of 6116 hectares of land was affected by soil erosion in Upper Brahmaputra Valley and North Bank Plain zone during 1994.

Table12: Soil Erosion Statistics of Assam:

a) Total Cultivable area in Assam	34,60,082 ha
b) Area affected by Soil Erosion	1,93,000 ha
c) Area under Wasteland & Degraded Land	2,71,556 ha
d) Area affected by shifting cultivation	1,70,000 ha
e) Average area being eroded due to flood and soil erosion problems	6,500 ha
f) Average area affected by Flood annually	4,50,000 ha
g) Average annual rainfall in Assam	2,4000 mm
h) Total Annual Silt Load of Brahmaputra (1990)	3,59,241 Cu.M

At Bhurbandha At Pandu	4,94,357 Cu.M
i) Annual Soil Erosion rate (1990) Jia Bharali River Puthimari River	4,721 Tonnes per Sq.Km 2,887 Tonnes per Sq.Km

(Source Directorate of Soil Conservation Ulubari, Guwahati-7)

The highly productive and fertile soils of Assam are now facing the serious problem of soil erosion like other parts of the country. Under heavy precipitation and humid climate loss of topsoil through surface run-off is the most common type of soil erosion in the entire state. The problem of topsoil erosion is severe in the plain during the flood season. It is estimated that nearly 3.2 million hectares of land of the plain districts of the state are vulnerable to topsoil erosion with varying intensity. Terrain deformation through mass movement is another type of soil degradation, which is primarily confined to the hill districts of Karbi Anglong and N.C. Hills covering an area of about 1.53 million hectares. Another important type of soil erosion in the state, which assumed serious proportion in the recent time, is the bank erosion by the rivers. It is observed that at some places, a few kilometers of bank along the villages, fertile agricultural lands and roads are being eroded by the rivers. Majuli, the largest river island of the world is now seriously affected by the erosion and virtually facing the threat to existence. The extent of loss to the bank erosion varies from year to year depending on the severity of floods in the state.

Table-13: Estimated area affected by soil erosion in Assam under special problems

Sl. No.	Land utilization classes	Area in hectares
1	Shifting cultivation	1,70,000
2	Surface flooding	4,50,000

Source: Soil Conservation Directorate, Govt. of Assam

Table-14: Estimated area affected by soil erosion in Assam by various land utilization classes

Sl. No.	Land utilization classes	Area in hectares
1	Cultivable land	7,70,000
2	Forest land	8,83,000
3	Pasture and grazing land	74,000
4	Non-agricultural land	1,82,000
5	Barren land	3,08,000

Source: Soil Conservation Directorate, Govt. of Assam

Land is laid waste by destructive means of plantation and polluted by the disposal of domestic and industrial waste. Jhum cultivation, new habitations and settlements, big reservoirs and dams made for various uses such as irrigation, water supply and power, etc. play a role is destroying and adversely changing the land surface. Unscientific mining and extraction of raw materials from the ground have lasting damage on land. Sludge from the sewage plant is deposited on the land surface and which affect the fertility of the soil. They are harmful to human beings and the plant kingdom alike. The growth in population has cascaded land acquisition by man. Land full of vegetation and forest were cut down to make way for its agriculture, habitation and business. The land surface is now under strenuous strain with its forest cover depleting and land covered with poisonous wastes. The effort for afforestation must be given utmost priority by different government agencies, NGOs and institution to increase forest cover. All schemes will have to adhere strictly to the environmental guidelines set and existing industrial houses should set aside sufficient funds to treat waste products from their factories.

Chapter 3

An Interlinked Role of Agriculture and Human Development in Assam

3.1 Productivity in various districts along with other salient characteristics

3.2 Regression Analysis of Agriculture and Poverty

3.3 Human Development Characteristics of Assam

3.4 Regression Analysis between Human Development and Agriculture

Appendix on Agriculture and Sustainability

3.1 Productivity in various districts along with other salient characteristics

Table-15

District	Production per hectare (value in RS.)	Production per worker (value in RS.)	Fertiliser-NPK per hectare (NSA)	AFV %	Crop Intensity %	Worker per hectare	Rainfall: mm	NSA: 000 ha	Rural poor %
Jorhat	29632	18585	59	12.6	143	1.59	1803.7	120	27.50
Kamrup	25674	16338	81	9.3	140	1.57	1428.6	180	22.30
Golaghat	33595	17444	31	14.2	128	1.93	2118.6	117	25.50
Karbi Anglong	24433	12779	6	5.0	154	1.91	1121.5	126	26.50
Morigaon	19645	9468	65	4.3	135	2.07	1165.8	92	21.50
Dibrugarh	24931	19667	55	9.1	129	1.27	2249.7	138	19.20
Sibsagar	26683	19728	11	7.4	111	1.35	1900.8	138	20.30
Cachar	29728	21491	44	14.8	127	1.38	2366.1	115	33.50
Hailakandi	34515	17890	30	11.7	141	1.93	3094.2	46	37.00
Karimganj	29037	16638	60	9.2	140	1.75	4559.9	69	40.90
Barpeta	26316	16148	93	11.3	154	1.63	1909.1	180	39.90
Tinsukia	27805	15765	54	13.8	142	1.76	2609.6	99	14.40
Dima Hasao	43716	32482	2	30.2	127	1.35	1144.9	28	16.10
Sonitpur	26405	14776	29	9.4	147	1.79	1646.1	166	23.60
Nagaon	31306	17289	109	9.3	151	1.81	1541.7	235	23.50
Kokrajhar	25176	9419	70	7.8	160	2.67	3767.7	85	35.70
Nalbari	23830	18504	74	10.1	137	1.29	1904.4	154	15.00
Lakhimpur	22188	5913	17	7.7	172	3.75	1544.6	100	24.40
Goalpara	26513	13930	116	10.3	137	1.90	2458.7	79	33.90
Dhemaji	20099	6200	4	7.8	162	3.24	3471.7	63	40.00

Bongaigaon	24856	14181	106	8.5	165	1.75	3219.4	95	33.00
Darrang	23248	14343	87	10.2	143	1.62	1796.6	205	30.10
Dhubri	23955	11983	118	7.7	153	2.00	3225.2	144	42.40

Data source: Statistical Abstract, CSO, Directorate of Economics and Statistics, CMIE.

Production per hectare and Production per worker in Assam is Rs.27099.39 and Rs. 15693.96 respectively. Though Dima Hasao district tops with Rs. 32482 but it happens mainly due to low density of population. Productivity level in different districts of Assam did show large variation. Value of crop output per hectare was close to Rs. 20 thousand in district Morigon and Dhemaji. Dima Hasao came at the top with per hectare productivity of Rs. 43.7 thousand. Hailakandi ranked second though its productivity was much lower than North Cachar Hills district. Fertiliser-NPK per kg per hectare of net sown area in Assam, Area under fruits and vegetables, Cropping intensity, Worker per hectare, Rainfall in Assam, Net sown area and % of Rural poor have high level causal relationship among them.

3.2 Regression Analysis of Agriculture and Poverty

A linear regression model is prepared to analyse the factors of agricultural development and rural poverty.

Table-16

Model	R	R Square	Adjusted R Square	Std. Error of the Estimate
1	.873	.763	.652	3072.570

a. Predictors: (Constant), Rural poor, NSA(net sown area), WPH(worker per hectare), AFV(area under fruits and vegetables), NPK, Rainfall, CI(cropping intensity)

b. Dependent Variable: PPH(production per hectare)

In the Model Summary, we see that the coefficient of multiple correlation r(R) is .873, indicating a strong positive linear relationship between the predictors and the dependent variable. The coefficient of determination r2 (R Square) of .763 indicates that for the sample, 76% of the variation of production per hectare can be explained by the variation in Rural poor, NSA, WPH, AFV, NPK, Rainfall, CI. But this may be an overestimate for the population from which the sample is drawn, so we use the Adjusted R Square as a better estimate for the population i.e. .652. Finally, the Standard Error of the Estimate is 3072.570.

3.3 Human Development Characteristics of Assam

Table-17

District	HDI value	Income index	Education index	Health index	Urban population (in %)	Rural population (in %)	HDI Rank	Income Rank	Education Rank	Health Rank
Jorhat	0.65	0.564	0.722	0.664	13.94	86.06	1	2	1	1
Kamrup	0.574	0.573	0.701	0.45	7.27	92.73	2	1	3	7
Golaghat	0.54	0.409	0.65	0.564	8.29	91.71	3	5	6	3
Karbi Anglong	0.494	0.491	0.535	0.547	35.79	64.21	4	4	19	6
Morigaon	0.494	0.562	0.551	0.371	12.01	87.99	4	3	17	10
Dibrugarh	0.483	0.162	0.564	0.636	18.17	81.23	6	12	5	2
Sibsagar	0.469	0.242	0.702	0.464	11.62	88.38	7	8	2	5
Cachar	0.402	0.266	0.634	0.307	19.45	80.52	8	7	9	12

Hailakandi	0.363	0.234	0.563	0.293	16.95	83.05	11	9	14	14
Karimganj	0.301	0.078	0.62	0.207	8.82	91.18	19	19	11	18
Barpeta	0.396	0.385	0.527	0.279	7.61	92.39	9	6	20	15
Tinsukia	0.377	0.082	0.571	0.479	12.14	87.86	10	18	13	4
N.C.Hills	0.363	0.211	0.65	0.229	11.45	88.55	11	10	6	17
Sonitpur	0.357	0.071	0.552	0.45	9.21	90.79	13	21	16	7
Nagaon	0.356	0.179	0.583	0.307	4.92	95.08	14	11	12	12
Kokrajhar	0.354	0.145	0.474	0.443	8.75	91.85	15	14	22	9
Nalbari	0.343	0.076	0.641	0.314	6.77	93.23	16	20	8	11
Lakhimpur	0.337	0.154	0.657	0.2	7.31	92.69	17	13	4	20
Goalpara	0.308	0.146	0.536	0.243	8.35	91.65	18	14	18	16
Dhemaji	0.277	0.026	0.622	0.186	31.18	68.82	20	23	10	21
Bongaigaon	0.263	0.103	0.557	0.129	4.90	95.10	21	16	15	22
Darrang	0.259	0.057	0.514	0.207	2.37	97.63	22	22	21	18
Dhubri	0.214	0.102	0.454	0.086	6.85	93.15	23	17	23	23

Data source: Assam HDR-2003

The HDI value derived for the State as whole was 0.407. Jorhat, the district that is ranked first, has a HDI value which is more than three times that of Dhubri, the lowest ranked district. The figures for the income index are very skewed. Only six districts (Kamrup, Jorhat, Morigaon, Karbi Anglong, Golaghat, and Barpeta) have income index values higher than the State average; the remaining 17 districts have income index values lower than the State average. The income index for Kamrup is more than twice the State average.

Educational attainments measured by the education index are more evenly spread through the State with 11 districts ranked above the State average and 12 districts with educational index values below the State average. The highest ranked district, Jorhat has an education index value a little over one and a half times that of Dhubri, which is ranked lowest. Ten districts have health index18 values higher than the average for the State, and thirteen districts have health index values lower than the State average. The highest ranked district, Jorhat has a health index value nearly twice the State average.

Urbanization is regarded as one of the most important factor in the human development of any area. In this category once again upper Assam districts are ahead of others. Barak Valley is lagging behind here too. Cachar has 2 towns and 13.94% population in urban area while Karimganj has 3 towns and 7.27% population. Hailakandi has 2 towns and 8.29% population having access to urban amenities of life. The Kamrup district has the highest position in this regard with 7 towns and 35.79% population having access to urban amenities of life, Ngaon has 7 towns with 12.01% population, Dibrugarh with 6 towns and 18.17% population. Lower Assam districts are also lagging behind and flood affected district of Dhemaji is at the lowest.

3.4 Regression Analysis between Human Development and Agriculture

A linear regression model was prepared on the basis of Productivity, Agricultural Development Index, Human Development Index and Human Poverty Index in Assam to study their interrelationship and interlinked role for sustainable development.

Table-18

Districts	HDI	HPI	HPI Rank	ADI	Output per worker
Jorhat	0.65	31.33	6	0.15	18585
Kamrup	0.574	24.72	3	0.19	16338
Golaghat	0.54	30.84	5	0.15	17444
Karbi Anglong	0.494	44.44	23	0.09	12779
Morigaon	0.494	34.06	10	0.11	9468
Dibrugarh	0.483	24.30	2	0.14	19667
Sibsagar	0.469	24.28	1	0.15	19728
Cachar	0.402	39.71	17	0.18	21491
Hailakandi	0.363	41.02	19	0.17	17890
Karimganj	0.301	40.22	18	0.14	16638
Barpeta	0.396	35.22	13	0.15	16148
Tinsukia	0.377	33.71	9	0.10	15765
N.C.Hills	0.363	42.66	21	0.17	32482
Sonitpur	0.357	34.60	12	0.13	14776
Nagaon	0.356	30.33	4	0.20	17289
Kokrajhar	0.354	42.73	22	0.15	9419
Nalbari	0.343	33.04	8	0.14	18504
Lakhimpur	0.337	32.81	7	0.07	5913
Goalpara	0.308	39.55	16	0.14	13930
Dhemaji	0.277	37.03	15	0.06	6200
Bongaigaon	0.263	35.37	14	0.12	14181

Darrang	0.259	34.43	11	0.18	14343
Dhubri	0.214	41.92	20	0.18	11983
Assam	**0.407**	**34.30**		**0.14**	**15693.9565**

Data source: HDR-2003, CSO, CMIE and Statistical abstract.

Agricultural Development Index, Human Development Index and Human Poverty Index have are largely varied in Assam.

The above table shows that upper Assam is on the top regarding the human development in the state. Jorhat, Dibrugarh, Kamrup etc are having very high level in income, education, and health. The condition of the Barak Valley is not at all satisfactory in HDI value. All the three districts of the valley are having lower HDI value the state average. Regarding income, education and health the same picture is found. According to the ranking of the districts, it can be easily perceived that Barak Valley exists in the medium category of the human development zone. Not only lagging behind in all over HDI value but also in all parameters i.e. income, education and health as well. Jorhat tops in the overall value along with education and health. Kamrup is the first regarding the income. Cachar is 8th in HDI ranking, Hailakandi is 11th and Karimganj is formidably at the 19th position. The income, education and health ranking of Cachar district is at 7th, 9th and 12th while that of Hailakandi district is at 9th, 14th and 14th respectively. The condition of Karimganj district is the most terrible in the valley. It is at the 19th, 11th and 18th position in income, education and health respectively. The districts of lower Assam and hill districts of N.C.Hills and Karbi Anglong are at low human development zone.

Relation between Human Development, Agriculture and Poverty-

Model Summary-1   Table-19

Model	R	R Square	Adjusted R Square	Std. Error of the Estimate
1	.532	.283	.170	.09954

a. Predictors: (Constant), agricultural development index, % of rural poor, human poverty index

b. Dependent variable – human development index

Relation between Human Development, Productivity and Poverty-

Model Summary-2 Table-20

Model	R	R Square	Adjusted R Square	Std. Error of the Estimate
1	.546	.298	.187	.09851

a. Predictors: (Constant), productivity- output per worker, human poverty index, % of rural poor

b. Dependent Variable: human development index

In the Model Summary-1, we see that the coefficient of multiple correlation r(R) is .532, indicating a good positive linear relationship between the predictors and the dependent variable. The coefficient of determination r^2 (R Square) of .283 indicates that for the sample, 28% of the variation of Human Development can be explained by the variation in agricultural development index, % of rural poor i.e. income poverty and human poverty index. In the model summary-2, we see the coefficient of multiple correlation r(R) is .546, indicating a good positive linear relationship between the predictors and the dependent variable. The coefficient of determination r^2 (R Square) of .298 indicates that for the sample, 29% of the variation of Human Development can be explained by the variation in productivity- output per worker, human poverty index, % of rural poor.

Relation between Agriculture, HDI and Poverty-

Table-21

Model	R	R Square	Adjusted R Square	Std. Error of the Estimate
1	.677	.459	.338	.03000

a. Predictors: (Constant), human development index, human labour , % of rural poor, human poverty index

b. dependent variable: agricultural development index.

In the Model Summary, we find that the coefficient of multiple correlation r(R) is .677, indicating a high level of positive linear relationship between the predictors and the dependent variable. The coefficient of determination r2 (R Square) of .459 indicates that for the sample, 45% of the variation of Agricultural Development can be explained by the variation in human development index, human labour , % of rural poor, human poverty index. But this may be an overestimate for the population from which the sample is drawn, so we use the Adjusted R Square as a better estimate for the population i.e. .338.

Appendix on Agriculture and Sustainability

Agro-Climate

Assam at present consists of two hill districts and twenty 25 plain districts. The climate of the hills is generally salubrious while that of the plains is comparatively warm in summer but cool in winter. Accordingly, the climate of Assam is characterised by alternate cool and warm periods with a highly humidity, Especially from May to November. Between March and May at the time when precipitation in Northern India is at the minimum, Assam gets some amount of rainfall from the Northwest which keep the temperature low in the season of spring. It happens to be so because of the extreme humidity which comes with the monsoon. In the plains of Assam, including the district of Cachar the temperatures in summer may be only about 38°C. But the humidity may be so high that one will perspire and feel very uneasy, especially during the period between two bouts of rainfall.

From the climatic point of view the year in Assam can broadly be divided in two, the cold season and the rainy season. However, there are two other short seasons namely spring and autumn representing the transition between cold and rainy seasons and that between rainy and cold seasons respectively. From the middle of November to the middle of February the cold season prevails with the sky becoming clear and temperature going down below 15°C. Fogs also appear during these months, especially in the morning and evening but they disappear during the daytime. From March temperature begins to rise, dust, storms begin to blow in western Assam and occasional Northwesters visit with thunder storms. The showers of this period prevent the temperatures from rising and they settle down the unwanted dusts which appear in the air. Besides, they also help to make the vegetation green after the dry winter. After the short spring the south west monsoon bursts in the third week of June and rains continue to pour with short spells of drought. The atmosphere there becomes sultry and temperature stands at 30°C to 35°C. Towards late September, the rains peter out and temperature also decreases and the short autumn sets in, while the sky begins to become clear mists appear in the horizon. With the farther fall of temperature, winter sets in from late November.

There is a slight variation of climate from region to region within the State. For instance, the climate of the region covering Kamrup, Nalbari and Barpeta in west-central Assam is characterised by plentiful rains and foggy winter. The cold season in this region is from

December to February and this is followed by the sand-storms and thunderstorms from March to May. The rainy season, as in rest of Assam begins in late June and continues upto late September. October and November constitute the post-monsoon period. In western Assam comprising the districts of Goalpara, Bongaigaon, Kokrajhar and Dhubri,the climate is intermediate between that of the North Bengal Plains and the west-central Assam Valley. In this region,the day temperatures in April and May are nearly the same as in the monsoon months. The climate of the Barak Valley districts is characterised by abundant rainfall, moderate temperatures and high humidity. The year may be divided into four seasons and the cold season is identical with Goalpara and Kamrup. The climate of the east central Assam comprising Darrang, Sonitpur, Marigaon and Nagaon is characterised by the absence of a dry hot summer season,the highest temperature being experienced during the period of south west monsoon along with abundant rains and a humid atmosphere throughout the year. The climate of the eastern Assam districts (Golaghat, Jorhat, Sibsagar, Tinsukia ,Dibrugarh, Dhemaji and Lakhimpur)is somewhat identical to Darrang and Nagaon with temperature remaining slightly lower than in the latter.

Agriculture is the dominant land use category in the state. It account for about for about 54.11 per cent of the total geographical area of the state. Including persons dependent on plantation, more than 80 per cent of the total population of Assam is dependent on agriculture. With the increase of population and the development of agro-technology, lots of changes take place in the agricultural scenario of the state. The net area sown as well as the gross cropped area increased significantly in the last few decades. This decreases the area under other uses especially area under forest. Although, the development in agriculture has tremendous important in the economy of the state but the ecological impacts of the changing land use pattern need to be considered.

Pollution:
Agricultural activities that cause pollution include confined animal facilities, grazing, pesticide spraying, irrigation, fertilizing, planting, and harvesting. The major agricultural pollutants that result from these activities are sediment, nutrients, pathogens, pesticides, and salts. Agricultural activities also can damage habitat and stream channels. Agricultural impacts on surface water and ground water can be minimized by properly managing activities

that can cause agricultural pollution. Nutrients such as phosphorus, nitrogen, and potassium in the form of fertilizers, manure, sludge, and crop residues are applied to enhance production. When they are applied in excess of plant needs the productivity of land reduces. Pesticides, herbicides, and fungicides are used to kill pests and control the growth of weeds and fungus. These chemicals can destroy the quality of agricultural land.

Agricultural Diversity

Assam is the centre of core for several field, horticultural and cash crops. It is known as the centre of diversity of rice. The Central Rice Research Institute at Cuttack maintained 2054 rice germ plasm stock from Assam. Assam possesses rich diversity in several grain legumes such as 61 lines of green gram, 59 lines of black gram, 44 lines of lentil, 12 lines of arhar and 29 lines of field pea which are maintained at the Regional Agricultural Research Station (RARS), Shillongani. 12 wild species of sugarcane are found in the state of Assam. 1074 germplasm of tea are maintained at Toklai Experimental Station, Jorhat. Among variety of fruits and vegetables, citrus and banana germ plasm are in rich state. Aquatic fruits like makhana or gorgon fruit (Eurale ferox) occur throughout the state. Almost all temperate, tropical and sub-tropical commercial vegetables are grown in the state. The state is rich in genetic resource of cucurbits, non-tuberiferous solanums and beans and tuber crops.

Agricultural Status

District wise distribution of Agricultural land, Assam, 2008

Sl. No.	District	Agricultural Land (area in hectare)							
		Area	Kharif	Rabi	Double crop	Net area sown	Plantation	Fallow land	Total
1	Barpeta	330730	173206	194003	139345	227864	12892	837	241593
2	Bongaigaon	31335	22099	-	18277	3822	11389	-	15211
3	Cachar	377927	103035	57878	38894	122019	34558	-	156577
4	Darrang	346530	180497	99298	82835	196960	57239	952	255151
5	Dhemaji	314312	212991	25000	119061	118930	55805	-	174735
6	Dhubri	274550	135906	126398	110167	152137	573	21306	174016
7	Dibrugarh	346763	117253	43695	20969	139979	80156	-	220135
8	Goalpara	253045	130363	43850	25573	148640	969	3340	152949
9	Golaghat	354100	122844	57555	33102	147297	93898	1186	242381

10	Hailakandi	132293	98270	-	1723	96547	38640	-	135187
11	Jorhat	291470	21293	60998	43886	38405	61100	4815	104320
12	Kamrup	473380	235840	156516	145867	246489	25894	1939	274322
13	Karbi Anglong	1033200	135612	129280	12980	251912	8722	-	260634
14	Karimganj	183900	48938	28596	24658	52876	36093	1121	90090
15	Kokrajhar	471650	264186	243137	238979	268344	15435	3709	287488
16	Lakhimpur	250328	92985	90875	110499	73361	47365	-	120726
17	Morigaon	121966	67968	18972	33914	53026	646	9868	63540
18	Nalbari	202480	137161	89445	82122	144484	20989	7892	173365
19	N.C. Hills	489000	6290	1748	1748	6290	-	-	6290
20	Nagaon	431905	283772	202479	154659	331592	30431	3281	365304
21	Sibsagar	260290	105068	23278	15304	113042	100455	-	213497

22	Sonitpur	525520	215966	51059	29498	237527	55682	3937	297146
23	Tinsukia	355626	46752	451	2981	44222	179760	-	223982
	Total	7852300	2958295 (37.6%)	1744511 (22.3%)	1487041 (18.9%)	3215765 (40.96%)	968691 (12.3%)	64183 (0.8%)	4248639 (54.1%)

Source: ARSAC

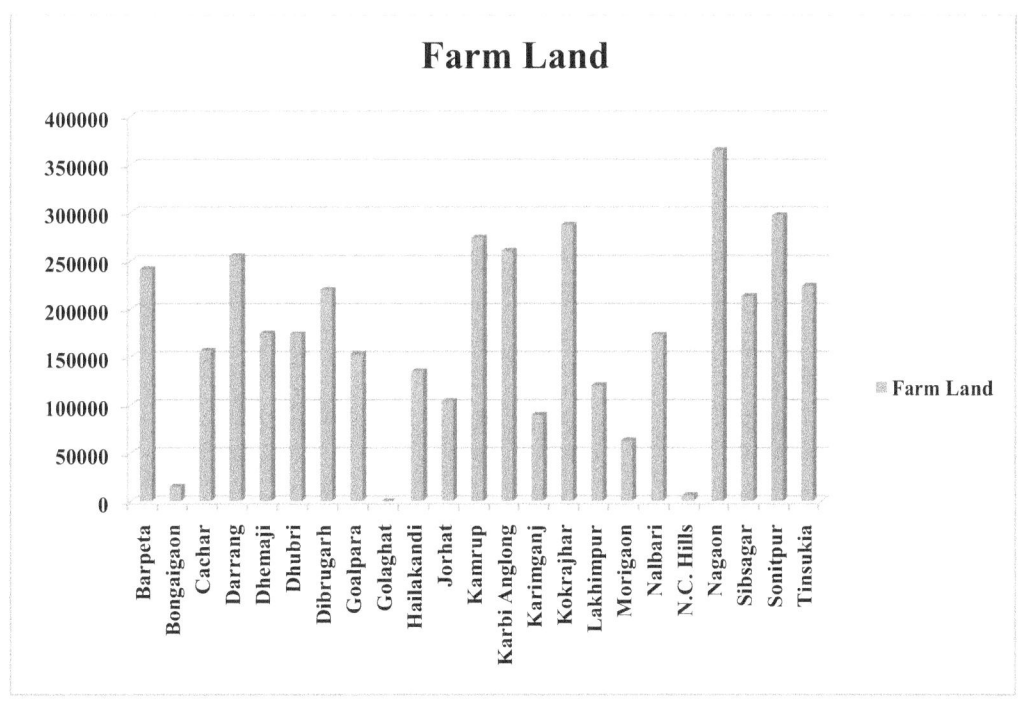

Index No. of Area, Production, Productivity for Food and Non-food Crops in Assam, 2008 - 2009

(Base - Triennium ending 1981 - 82 = 100)

Crops	Area	Production	Productivity
Total Rice	112.82	166.61	137.41
Total Cereals	110.71	164.02	136.69
Total Pulses	93.94	128.92	127.41
Total Food Grains	110.25	163.02	136.45
Total Oil Seeds	133.17	285.25	105.97
Total Fibres	60.28	78.21	125.93
Total Condiments & Spices	152.98	151.63	98.62
Total Fruits & Vegetables	192.95	220.47	118.62
Total Misc Crops	48.47	47.00	96.49
Total Non-food Grains	116.81	166.14	113.82
All Commodities	111.75	164.64	134.15

Source: Statistical Handbook Assam 2009

Area and Production of Horticultural Product in Assam (2008 - 2009)

Crop	Area (in Ha)	Production (in Tonne)
Banana	42631	589595
Orange	5960	66866
Jack fruit	17408	156091
Guava	3786	49781
Litchi	4123	18846
Mango	3698	28881
Papaya	6942	101528
Pineapple	13893	212561

Ha-Hectare

Source: Statistical Handbook Assam 2004

District-wise Irrigation Potential through Government Irrigation Schemes (upto 31.3.2008)

(Area in Hectare)

District	Minor	Major and Medium	Total
Dhubri	14593	-	14593
Kokrajhar	21249	6060	27309
Bongaigaon	6161	-	6161
Goalpara	12017	-	12017
Barpeta	18559	41453	60012
Nalbari	18360	300	18660
Kamrup	17555	15635	33190
Darrang	31830	24599	56429
Sonitpur	26003	31452	57455
Lakhimpur	10594	-	10594
Dhemaji	6208	-	6208
Morigaon	16527	-	16527
Nagaon	15716	76939	92655
Golaghat	16273	-	16273
Jorhat	12459	-	12459

Sibsagar	15970	-	15970
Dibrugarh	10754	2040	12794
Tinsukia	5982	-	5982
Karbi Anglong	18976	7661	26637
N.C.Hills	5571	-	5571
Karimganj	2892	-	2892
Hailakandi	3875	-	3875
Cachar	5780	-	5780
Assam	313904	206139	520043

Ha – Hectare

Source : Statistical Handbook Assam 2009

District-wise and Season-wise consumption of fertiliser in Assam, 2008 - 2009 (in tonnes)								
District	Kharif				Rabi			
	N	P	K	Total	N	P	K	Total
Dhubri	3340	1132	1893	6365	7081	2740	4985	14806
Kokrajhar	1758	962	934	3657	1041	649	726	2416
Bongaigaon	2528	1942	1612	6082	2278	1718	1511	5507
Goalpara	1635	1077	837	3551	1932	941	717	3590
Barpeta	3277	1858	1563	6698	4663	2493	2049	9205
Nalbari	2612	1314	1411	5337	3233	1601	1477	6311
Kamrup	4303	2069	2117	8490	2933	1835	1539	6307
Darrang	4140	2404	2176	8720	3848	2405	2244	8497
Sonitpur	918	712	514	2144	945	698	524	2167
Lakhimpur	415	99	239	753	278	87	107	472
Dhemaji	25	14	13	52	97	43	31	171
Morigaon	1668	929	484	3081	2103	1188	688	3979
Nagaon	7146	3615	2372	13133	5231	2186	1952	9369
Golaghat	587	636	559	1782	387	300	241	928
Jorhat	2421	885	1057	4363	829	474	574	1877
Sibsagar	461	403	207	1071	202	146	106	454

Dibrugarh	1473	1027	810	3310	1510	928	789	3227
Tinsukia	1608	793	878	3279	1550	962	619	3131
Karbi Anglong	228	168	20	416	223	95	52	370
N.C.Hills	8	6	4	18	11	9	5	25
Karimganj	1025	810	709	2544	619	487	326	1432
Hailakandi	680	211	54	945	447	175	72	694
Cachar	1462	522	404	2388	1129	386	272	1787
Assam	43721	23591	20867	88179	42570	22546	21606	86722

N - Nitrogen, P - Phosphorus, K - Potassium

Source : Statistical Handbook Assam 2009

Chapter 4

Energy: A Major Determinant of Sustainable Development

4.1 Power Infrastructure in Assam: Essential Need for Human Development

4.2 Renewable Energy Sector in Assam

4.2.1 Solar Electrification in Villages of Assam

4.2.2 Wind Energy

4.2.3 Hydel Energy

4.2.4 Bio-Mass

4.1 Power Infrastructure in Assam: Essential Need for Human Development

According to various empirical analysis, we know that electricity consumption per capita has a strong correlation to social development indices (HDI, life expectancy at birth, infant mortality rate, and maternal mortality) and especially to economic indices (such as GDP per capita). Increasing electricity consumption per capita can directly stimulate faster economic growth and indirectly achieve enhanced social development--especially for low and medium human development countries. In most cases, the threshold for moving from a low to a medium HDI economy transitions when 500kwh per capita is attained. When this minimal amount of electricity is used for pumping water, providing light and refrigerating food and medicines, a community can significantly improve their living conditions. Electricity plays a key role in both economic and social development. In Assam the consumption of energy per capita is very low and it depicts a lower level of human development in the state.

Status of Rural electrification

As per survey conducted and data collected during the year 2005 and taking into consideration the ongoing rural electrification works under MNP, PMGY, TSP and SCSP etc. the total un-electrified inhabited census villages as per Cencus-2001 is 8592 out of which 4045 numbers of villages, electrified earlier, have been found to be de-electrified due to various reasons viz. flood, storm, theft of conductor etc. Also, 2202 numbers of villages are identified as remote where connectivity with existing grid is either not feasible or not economically viable. A total 13205 numbers of grid connected electrified villages are found to require intensification in terms of length of lines and numbers of distribution sub-stations to provide access to electricity to all rural households.

Generating capacity of major plants

Table-22

Sl. No.	Name & Plant	Installed Capacity (MW)	Available Generation Capacity (MW)
1.	Namrup T.P.S	119.5	80
2.	Lakwa T.P.S*	120	100
3.	Karbi Longpi HEP	100	100
4.	Chandrapur T.P.S	60	-
5.	Lakwa Waste Heat Recovery Project	37.2	Commissioned on 13.01.2012
	Total	436.2	280

Source: ASEB

37.2 MW Lakwa waste Heat Recovery Project was test commissioned the STG with all three HSRGS in Service on 24.12.11 generating 32 MW of power and the unit was put on trial run thereafter. It has generated maxm load of 35.6 MW in the trial run period. The machine was inaugurated on 13.01.12 by Hon'ble CM but to be put into commercial run by 1.3.2012.

Assam has share-allocations from Central Power Generating Stations of NER which are at present as

Table-23

Sl. No.	Station	Installed Capacity (MW)	Share allocation	
			%	MW
1.	Loktak HEP	105	29.45	30
2.	Khandong HEP	50	56.29	28
3.	Kopilli HEP	200	53.46	106
4.	Kopilli Stg-II HEP	25	52.36	13
5.	AGBPP	291	56.50	164
6.	AGTPP	84	45.59	38
7.	DHEP	75	43.81	32
8.	RHEP	405	43.33	175
9.	Farakka	1600	3.41	545
10.	Kahalgaon-I	840	2.49	209
11.	Kahalgaon-II	1000	5.07	507
12.	Talcher	1000	2.73	273
13.	Unallocated Power (15%)	183	62.3	114
	Total	5858	-	2234

Source: ASEB

Assam also is having 162 MW shares from unallocated power from NTPC stations of Eastern region during peak hours. The above table depicts the share of the state of Assam in central govt's power projects in North-East region as well as in Eastern region. The entire allocation constitutes 2234 MW out of a total of 5858 MW i.e. 38.1% of the total generation. The demand for power in Assam has already surpassed the total supply while the new projects are being delayed due to many reasons. The slow progress of the office work along with protests from different environmental and social groups are obstructing the speedy execution of projects already undertaken by the govt.

Generation projects coming up during 12th plan period under state sector are as

Table-24

Sl. No.	Project	Capacity (MW)	Expected year of commissioning
1.	Namrup Replacement Project	100	December, 2012
2.	*Margharita Thermal Power Project	2x250	In 12th Plan
3.	Lower Kopilli HEP	3x50	In 12th Plan

* Coal linkage yet to be received

These will be developed either through IPP or through Joint Ventures to be formed by Govt. of Assam, APGCL & private players.

Small Hydro: APDCL has entered PPA for private participation for SHP.

1. Myntriang SHP (2x3+1x1.5) 9 MW, Lugnit SHP (2x3) 6 MW

2. Champawati SHP (3x1.33) MW (Already commissioned)

3. Pahumara SHP (2x1) MW (Under construction)

4. Bordikarai SHP 4.7 MW (Under construction)

5. Desang SHP 9 MW (Financial closure is in progress)

6. Kolong Stage I & Stage-II 4 MW each (Implementation agreement not signed with developer)

7. Dronpara SHP 2 MW (At DPR stage)

It is expected to cover eight villages by the above generating stations. In addition to above, the small Hydro Power Policy notified by the State Govt. includes 90 nos. of potential small hydro generating stations ranging from 0.1 MW to 20 MW and totalling 148.90 MW, in different parts of the state. These will be developed through IPPs/Users Societies/APGCL and are likely to be made operational by early part of 12th Plan. The short fall power is being met by purchase through short term bilateral agreements with power traders, purchase from power exchanges and from the Captive Power Plants of IOCL, Digboi. As such, the deficit scenario will prevail in Assam up to 2012-13, and considerable inflow of power from generations outside the region will be required till the Central Sector projects in NER become operational. The Govt. of Assam shall be taking up with the central Govt. for additional allocations from generators of E.R. and other regions to meet the shortfalls.

The existing 33/11 KV transformation capacities in each district for feeding rural leads and additional requirements are as

Table-25

Sl. No.	District	Existing 33/11 KV capacity(MVA)	Addl. Requirements (MVA)
1	Goalpara	33.8	5
2	Nalbari	30	5
3	Barpeta	47	5
4	Darrang	65	2.5
5	Kamrup	79	10
6	Bongaigaon	27	-
7	Dhubri	28	5
8	Kokrajhar	37	20
9	Tinsukia	103	5
10	Dibrugarh	76	10
11	Sibsagar	90	5
12	Jorhat	70	3
13	Golaghat	62	6
14	Lakhimpur	30	2.5
15	Dhemaji	15	2.5

16	Nagaon	110	17.5
17	Marigaon	36.3	-
18	Cachar	88.8	15
19	Hailakandi	28.8	10
20	Karimganj	28.8	5
21	Karbi-Anglong	27.5	5
22	N.C.Hills	18.5	-
23	Sonitpur	90.2	30
	Total	1221.45	164

Transmission Plan of the Government

The present transformation capacity at different voltage levels of Assam under AEGCL, a successor company of ASEB, is as below:-

(i) 220/132 KV = 910 MVA

(ii) 132/66 KV = 177.5 MVA

(iii) 132/33 KV = 967.5 MVA

(iv) 66/33 KV = 224 MVA

Source: APDCL

New 33/11 KV Substations and augmentation shall be developed in blocks where these do not exist. At the same time augmentation of 33/11 KV existing substation also become necessary either by increasing the capacity of power transformer or by commissioning new substations. Accordingly, some of the 11 KV feeders are also to be strengthened. The mapping of existing 11 KV lines superimposing proposed lines shall be done during execution of contracts for RGGVY. The Govt. has already notified the small Hydro Power Policy vide no. PEL. 196/2002/199 dtd- 19th March'2007. The policy envisages development of small hydro power stations specially in Karbi Anglong and N.C. Hills districts, through Independent Power Producers / Users Society, who shall be allowed either to sell the power to any HT consumer within Assam, to local rural grids within Assam, to local power distribution entities predominantly in rural areas. All sales will be approved, as may be required, by the Assam Electricity Regulatory Commission. A number of villages electrified earlier have been de-electrified due to various reasons viz.(i)damage due to storm, flood etc. (ii) Theft of conductors and other line materials by miscreants etc.

The district-wise numbers of such de-electrified villages as on year-2010-11 are

Table-26

District	Nos. of de-electrified villages
Dhubri	255
Kokrajhar	337
Bongaigaon	338
Goalpara	290
Barpeta	174
Nalbari	140
Kamrup	345
Darrang	159
Cachar	148
Karimganj	75
Nagaon	186
Sonitpur	140
Karbi-Anglong	126
N.C. Hills	129
Morigaon	163
Hailakandi	49
Tinsukia	99
Jorhat	183
Golaghat	117
Lakhimpur	174
Dhemaji	187
Dibrugarh	139
Sibsagar.	77
Total	4030

Source: APDCL

All these de-el-electrified villages have to be re-electrified to achieve 100% village electrification.

The total numbers of un-electrified villages in the state-excluding villages where ongoing schemes are being implemented are as on year 2010-11.

Table-27

Sl. No.	District	Nos. of un-electrified villages
1	Dhubri	138
2	Kokrajhar	94
3	Bongaigaon	21
4	Goalpara	33
5	Barpeta	126
6	Nalbari	5
7	Kamrup	44
8	Darrang	45
9	Cachar	82
10	Karimganj	135
11	Nagaon	172
12	Sonitpur	503
13	Karbi-AngIong	1254
14	N.C.Hills	113
15	Morigaon	91
16	Hailakandi	22
17	Tinsukia	263
18	Jorhat	60
19	Golaghat	367
20	Lakhimpur	373
21	Dhemaji	464
22	Dibrugarh	132
23	Sibsagar.	25
	Total	4562

Source: APDCL

All these un-electrified villages also shall be electrified by grid connectivity from conventional grid/stand alone systems. There are 2139 nos. of un-electrified remote census villages in Assam where grid connectivity is either not feasible or not economical, and as already cleared by REC Ltd. In most of these remote village the inhabitants not very sound. Also all such villages being mostly flood prone in plain area, establishment of bio-mass based or solar energy based power plants are not considered feasible. As such in villages in plain areas, solar photo voltaic have lighting systems shall be provided to each household with subsidy from Ministry of New and Renewable Energy Sources. State Govt. should also provide suitable funding for implementations of remote village electrification.

District-wise numbers of identified un-electrified remote census villages are-

Table-28

Name of District	Nos. of Remote villages	Name of District	Nos. of Remote villages
Barpeta	35	N.C. Hills	257
Darrang	29	Karimganj	45
Goalpara	77	Cachar	41
Kokrajhar	40	Hailakandi	14
Kamrup	36	Tinsukia	32
Bongaigaon	29	Lakhimpur	92
Dhubri	86	Sibsagar	3
Nagaon	3	Dibrugarh	6
Marigaon	14	Golaghat	74
Karbi Aaglong	818	Dhemaji	311
Sonitpur	35	Jorhat	62

Source: APDCL

4.2 Renewable Energy Sector in Assam

The scenario in energy consumption in India is no different. The per capita energy consumption figures are very low in spite of high rate of development now taking place. The per capita consumption of energy in India is in the region of 400 KWH per annum. The different sources of energy are-

- Solar Energy
- Wind Energy
- Hydel Energy
- Bio-Mass

Solar Energy and SPV Systems

Solar water heaters have proved the most popular and solar photovoltaic for decentralized power supply are fast becoming popular in rural and remote areas.

More than 700000 PV systems of capacity over 44MW for different applications are installed all over India. The market segment and usage is mainly for home lighting, street lighting, solar lanterns and water pumping for irrigation. Over 17 grid interactive solar photovoltaic generating more than 1400 KW are in operation in 8 states of India. As the demand for power grows exponentially and conventional fuel based power generating capacity grows arithmetically. Especially in rural, far-flung where the likelihood of conventional electric lines is remote, SPV power generation is the best alternative.

Environmental Benefits

- Solar water heaters do not pollute.
- By using solar water heater, we can get rid off carbon dioxide, nitrogen oxides, sulphur dioxide, and the other air pollution. When a solar water heater replaces an electric water heater, the electricity displaced over 20 years represents more than 50 tons of avoided carbon dioxide emissions alone. Carbon dioxide traps heat in the upper atmosphere, thus contributing to the "greenhouse effect."
- Solar water heaters can operate in any climate.

Solar Cookers

The box type solar cookers with a single reflecting mirror being promoted by the Ministry of Non-conventional Energy Sources became most popular throughout the country since 1982. These cookers are manufactured mainly by small/tiny industries to a set of specifications developed by MNES, later approved by Bureau of Indian Standards. These cookers become popular in the rural areas where women spend a lot of time foraging for firewood. A family size solar cooker is sufficient for 4 to 5 members and saves about 3 to 4 cylinders of LPG every year.

Wind Power

India now ranks as a "wind superpower" with an installed wind power capacity of 1167 MW and about 5 billion units of electricity have been fed to the national grid so far. Wind resource assessment programme, wind monitoring, wind mapping, covering 800 stations in 24 states with 193 wind monitoring stations are in operations.

Renewable Energy

Assam possesses immense potential for development of her power sector based on Hydel, Natural gas, Oil and Coal resources. With a total population of over 2.2 crores and a total geographical area of nearly 80,000 sq. Km, Assam encompasses varying geographical terrain covering number of ethnic groups and culture. With the earlier norm of rural electrification of one light point in a villages terming the village to be electrified, may be somewhat fulfilling the 70% village electrification achievement, but with the present scenario of rural electrification, there are a very large number of villages which stands as 'remote and inaccessible' and cannot be electrified by conventional mode of grid electricity. The state electricity Board has come out with a list of 2800 villages under this category. But there are further more villages in this category. Though Assam has 6 nos of power projects with an installed capacity of 574 MW against the peak demand of 504 MW, there is always a shortfall as the Plant Load factor (PLF) of these power plants are quite low. Considering all these to fulfil the demand for energy in the state, procurement of renewable energy or non-conventional energy is the need of hour. During 1988, the Energy Division of the ASTE Council has made very significant progress in implementation of New and Renewable Sources of Energy (NRSE) as well as Energy Conservation programmes and projects in Assam. This division is now converted to an agency called Assam Energy Development

Agency (AEDA) to act as a State Nodal Agency for implementation of different renewable energy programs as well as to take up energy conservation activity under MNES, Govt. of India.

Solar Photovoltaic Programme

The Energy Division of ASTE Council installed 32 solar home lighting systems in Oct, 1992 the total achievements in installation in solar home lighting systems upto December 2002 had been 2641. Under the Solar Photovoltaic Programme till March- 2003, 76 villages have been electrified with solar home lighting units under projects sponsored by NEC, MNES and the State Govt. Of late i.e. by July 2003, another 1700 houses has been electrified by SPV home lighting systems distributed throughout the state.

Few similar project implemented by ASTEC in Assam

- Solar Electrification of 9 villages in Sonapur Area, in Kamrup district.
- Solar Electrification of 11 villages in Impoi Area, in N.C. Hills district.
- Solar Electrification of 36 villages in Cachar District.
- Solar electrification of 400 rural houses of Bodo tribal women in Gohpur area engaged in weaving. 100 systems have already been installed and 200 are under installation.
- Solar Lighting in Aazan Peer Dargah:-The historic Aazan Peer Dargah at Sivasagar was povided with Solar Lighting with 14 Solar Home Lighting Systems and 6 solar Street Lights.

Solar thermal Programme

During 1998-99 and 1999-2000 Energy division of ASTE Council installed Solar Water Heating Systems of total capacity of 800 LPD in various locations in Assam at a subsidised price @ Rs.4,000/- per 50 LPD capacity. The beneficiaries are NL Nursing Homes, Sanjita Enterprise. Bhergaon Tea Estate and NERIWALM at Tezpur. During the year 2000-2001, a total capacity 2500 LPD system is installed at Indian Institute of Entrepreneurship at Guwahati.

4.2.1 Solar Electrification in Villages of Assam

Table-29

Year	No. of Villages	No. of Families	Total Power Generated (Watt)	Conventional Power Savings (Watt)
1991 - 92	1	6	222	480
1992 - 93	2	28	1036	2240
1993 - 94	3	97	3589	7760
1994 - 95	3	94	3478	7520
1995 - 96	9	367	13579	29360
1996 - 97	3	77	2849	6160
1997 - 98	5	235	8695	18800
1998 - 99	1	450	16650	36000
1999 - 2000	11	357	13209	28560
2000 - 2001	36	950	35150	76000
2001 - 2002	Distributed	400	14800	32000
2002-2003	35	2000	74000	160000
2003 - 2004(P)	250	10000	370000	800000

2004 - 2005 (P)	500	20000	740000	1600000
2005 - 2006 (P)	850	34000	1258000	2720000
2006 - 2007(P)	1050	42000	1554000	3360000
2007 - 2008 (P)	1200	48000	1776000	3840000

Source: The Ministry of Non-conventional Energy Sources

(Assuming one Home Lighting System replaces 80 watt of grid power supply) Total No. of Remote un-electrified Villages in Assam = 2800
P: Provisional Courtesy: Assam Energy Development Agency/Assam Science Technology & Environment Council, Assam

Solar electrification can be an alternative for the conventional energy users or for them who want get connected newly. The system of making power from the sunlight is no doubt getting popularity in some of the countries of the world but in Assam the progress is still very slow. Not only that the per capita cost of producing and distributing the solar energy is not favourable to the people of Assam but also it covers up a large area for using the sunlight. This alternative is working very slowly in the country since a large section of the mass is lying below poverty line. However the solar energy can be useful alternative in saving the conventional energy and making its use in some other productive activities.

4.2.2 Wind Energy

Under the sanctioned by MNES wind masts were installed in 30 sites in Assam. Data collection works under the project have been completed. The data collected is now being used by the Indian Institute of Tropical Meteorology, Bangalore for preparation of Wind Maps for Assam.

Annual Wind Speed in Wind Mapping Station, Assam

Table-30

Sites	Latitude	Longitude	Elevation	Wind speed (KMPH)
Akaya	26.58 N	91.20 E	173 MASL	3.8
Amoni	25.47 N	92.95 E	66 MASL	3.6
Baithalangso	25.97 N	92.62 E	234 MASL	1.7
Bakuliaghat	26.07 N	93.20 E	307 MASL	3.0
Barpeta	26.33 N	91.02 E	140 MASL	5
Bokakhat	26.63 N	93.62 E	390 MASL	3.2
Boko	25.97 N	91.25 E	46 MASL	No data
Chhaygaon	26.05 N	91.40 E	145 MASL	2.3
Chaprakata	26.50 N	90.58 E	244 MASL	3.1
Chariduar	26.87 N	92.77 E	84 MASL	2.1
Chutianala	25.83 N	93.43 E	388 MASL	1.2
Dalgaon	26.55 N	92.20 E	233 MASL	4.1

Dhemaji	27.47 N	94.60 E	326 MASL	No data
Dholla	27.75 N	95.62 E	127 MASL	No data
Dinjan	27.55 N	95.27 E	155 MASL	2.8
Duliajan	27.35 N	95.30 E	510 MASL	3.1
Gazarikandi	25.53 N	89.87 E	272 MASL	4.6
Jonai	27.75 N	95.20 E	421 MASL	2.2
Kheroni	25.88 N	92.90 E	234 MASL	No data
Khowang	27.27 N	94.93 E	256 MASL	2.5
Kochugaon	26.58 N	90.07 E	186 MASL	No data
Majuli	26.97 N	94.17 E	277 MASL	2.6
Margherita	27.28 N	95.70 E	138 MASL	1.7
Marigaon	26.23 N	92.35 E	181 MASL	3.5
Parakhowa	26.05 N	93.08 E	-	No data
Patherkhandi	24.60 N	92.30 E	20 MASL	3.5
Rangjuli	25.97 N	90.95 E	166 MASL	3.5
Sapekhati	27.08 N	95.18 E	470 MASL	No data
Sarihajan	26.03 N	93.78 E	100 MASL	2.4
Umrangso	25.50 N	97.72 E	640 MASL	No data

Source: The Ministry of Non-conventional Energy Sources

The Ministry of Non-conventional Energy Sources (MNES) sanctioned a Wind Monitoring Project during 1995-96. Under this project sophisticated Wind Monitoring equipment were installed by Energy Division of ASTE Council in five sites having good wind potential with an objective of assessing feasibility of putting up big Wind energy generators in these sites. Wind data were collected for three continuous years submitted to Indian Institute of Tropical Meteorology (IITM), Bangalore for scrutiny.

Monthly Mean Wind Speed (MPH) at Project sites

Table-31

Month	Monthly wind Speed (MPH									
	Lela		Singri		Putsari		Umphabeng		Borgaon	
	10M	25M	10M	25M	10M	25M	10M	25M	10M	25M
Mar-97	6.19	6.93	6.97	8.96	-	-	-	-	-	-
Apr-97	6.79	6.36	5.02	6.28	6.46	7.50	-	-	5.63	7.30
May-97	.16	-	5.49	6.78	5.13	-	3.82	4.90	4.69	6.10
Jun-97	6.37	-	3.67	4.87	4.90	-	4.90	6.80	4.01	5.53
Jul-97	5.25	-	3.1S3	4.62	5.10	-	3.74	5.24	4.33	5.9
Aug-97	No Data	No Data	-	-	5.67	-	3.29	4.65	4.30	5.99
Sep-97	7.94	8.78	-	-	4.46	-	3.52	5.14	3.77	5.31
Oct-97	3.87	3.88	-	-	5.74	-	2.64	3.54	2.74	4.15
Nov-97	3.88	3.83	-	-	4.16	-	2.59	3.49	3.33	4.97

Dec-97	3.87	3.79	-	-	4.82	-	-	-	3.28	4.66
Jan-98	4.39	4.63	3.11	4.80	No Data	No Data	3.43	4.68	3.48	4.99
Feb-98	6.11	6.30	3.12	4.53	No Data	No Data	4.47	5.77	4.44	6.14
Mar-98	7.11	-	3.90	5.43	4.57	-	4.87	6.47	5.68	7.42
Apr-98	7.42	-	3.84	5.29	5.98	-	4.85	6.56	4.87	6.47
May-98	6.19	-	3.22	4.74	5.06	-	4.17	5.83	-	-
Jun-98	6.71	2.25	2.95	4.33	-	-	5.98	8.56	-	-
Jul-98	5.34	1.28	2.65	4.48	-	-	-	-	-	-
Aug-98	4.70	0.95	3.08	4.72	-	-	-	-	-	-
Sep-98	4.21	0.79	No Data	No Data	-	-	-	-	-	-
Oct-98	3.82	0.43	-	-	-	-	-	-	-	-

M-Meter

MPH: Miles per hour

The Ministry of Non-Conventional Energy Sources (MNES) sanctioned a Wind Energy Assessment Project during 1998-99. Under this project five 10 meter wind monitoring mast were installed and data was collected continuously for three months and submitted to National Aerospace Laboratory (NAL) for scrutiny.

Monthly Wind Speed at Wind Energy Assessment Project

Table-32

Sites	Monthly Wind Speed (KMPH)
Telecom-tower, Guwahati	12.83
Muldam, N.C.Hills	17.2
Tolpoi, N.C.Hills	11.9
Khalimku, N.C.Hills	16.5
P-Leikul, N.C.Hills	17.1

Monthly Wind speed at Wind Energy Assessment Project sites

Under a different programme, 6 wind generator cum battery chargers of 1 KW capacity has been installed and commissioned at the six APRO Repeater stations viz Jalukbari, Bhubaneswari, Morianka (Kamrup District) Abhayapuri (Goalpara), Kamala Than (Nagaon) and Mahamaya peak (Karbi Anglong district). The Ministry of Non-Conventional Energy Sources (MNES) sanctioned a Wind Monitoring Project at 25M Mast at 3 locations P-Leikul, Kalimkhu, Tolpoi in N. C. Hills district to be undertaken.

4.2.3 Hydel Energy

Micro hydel Development

From the year 1993-94, Energy Division of ASTE Council started preliminary survey in the area of Kalmoni Thiapani, Nazirakhat, Ganapati (Kamrup district), Champabati, Umsing (Nagaon district) Amlong, Majar, Longpai, Umrasii & Umbasso (Karbi Anglong District for Microhydel development. Detailed survey and investigation has been taken up and completed at Kalmoni, Nazirakhat, Amlong and Majar small hydel project sites and Reports were prepared.

Details of Small Hydropower Project sites in Assam

Table-33

Name of the project	Stream	District	Capacity
Kalmoni	Kalmoni	Kamrup	170 KW
Thiapani	Kopili	Kamrup	200 KW
Nazirakhat	Motbhangadong	Kamrup	10 KW
Barkasarang	Barkasarang	Kamrup	10 KW
Amlong	Amlong	Karbi Anglong	100 KW
Majar	Majar	Karbi Anglong	10 KW
Longpai	Longpai	Karbi Anglong	20 KW
Ganapati	Kopili	Kamrup	500KW

Source: The Ministry of Non-Conventional Energy Sources

Kalmoni Microhydel project (50 x 2= 100 KW) has been identified as a project tos be taken up as a demonstration project under UNDP GEF Hilly Hydro project Programme. Civil works including installation is already completed. The project is commissioned in June 2003 and is presently used in full capacity Rani Tea Estate. Work in Nazirakhat Microhydel Project (2 x 5=10 KW) has also been commissioned in June 2003 under ASTE Council is complete.

4.2.4 Bio-Mass

National Biomass Resource Assessment Programme (NBRAP)

Ministry of Non-Conventional Energy Sources Govt. of India had sanctioned this project to undertake the Biomass Assessment Study in different taluka throughout the country. The objective of the project is to prepare a National Level Data Bank on biomass availability so that Biomass based Power Projects can be taken up in prospective talukas of the country. During NBRAP - 1st Phase, ASTEC had conducted this study in three blocks in Assam viz Mayong in Morigaon district, Margherita in Tinsukia district and Lowerpowa in Karimgang district.

During NBRAP - 3rd Phase, ASTEC had conducted this study in five blocks in Assam viz Sarukhetri in Barpeta District, Jugijan in Nagaon District, Pubchaiduar in Sonitpur District, Lahowal in Dibrugarh District and Katigaragh in Cachar District. During NBRAP - 4th phase This study had been conducted in five more blocks in Assam viz Bezera in Kamrup district, Balajana in Goalpara district, Patharkandi in Karimganj district, Dhemaji in Dhemaji District and Lakuwa in Sibsagar District. As a whole, in Assam, a biomass assessment study has already been completed in 13 Blocks and a number of pockets have been identified for remote village electrification.

Centre for Energy Research Application and Development (CERAD)
CERAD has been set up under the Council during the year 1992-93 with the objective of taking up Research & Development activities related to renewable energy and energy conservation. Activities taken up under the centre are solar data collection, performance monitoring of PV systems, designing and fabrication of Solar Water Heaters, Solar Driers and Solar Cookers.

A Solar Bamboo Drier was designed and developed with an objective to meet the demand of the rural population particularly for drying cash-crops like chilli, ginger, turmeric, mushroom, beetle-nut etc. The model was quite successful because of the use of indigenous materials such as bamboo thatch dried beetle-nut fibre for insulation and of its low cost. However it needs further Research & Development for commercialisation.

Technical Backup Support Unit for Improved Chulhas

The Technical Backup Support Unit for Improved Chulhas (TBU) under the Council was set-up during 1990 to provide training, Research & Development and other technical inputs in implementation of Improved Chulhas Programme in 8 North East states including Sikkim. The unit is fully funded by MNES. During the year 1992-93, the Bureau of India Standard (BIS) approved the laboratory of this TBU for Certification of portable Biomass based Metallic Chulhas. TBU has made very significant contribution towards propagation of Improved Chulha programme in the NE states.

Eleven small Energy Parks have been set up at Assam Engineering Institute, Guwahati, Silchar Polytechnic, Silchar, Girls Polytechnic, Guwahati, Cotton College, Guwahati, H.S. Kanoi College, Dibrugarh, College of Home Science, Jorhat, Diphu Govt. College, Diphu, Nalbari College, Nalbari, Assam University, Silchar, Tezpur University, Tezpur, Srimanta Sankardeva Kalakshetra with financial assistance from MNES. Another state level Renewable Energy Park has been sanctioned by MNES at Srimanta Sankardeva Kalakshetra, Panjabari, Guwahati with an estimated cost of around Rs. 91 lakhs. Some civil works has already been computed under this park.

The Energy Division of ASTE Council has taken up energy conservation related activities since the year 1991-92. The Council has taken up the following activities.

- Organised eight workshop on Energy Conservation for different target groups in association with National Productivity Council
- A number of Energy Audits were conducted through consultants
- Industrial Energy Audits - 2 nos through NPC
- Energy Audit in Hospital - 2 nos through NPC
- Energy audit in Tea Estates - 4 nos through NPC
- Conducted 3 nos. of Domestic Energy Audits in different location within Guwahati

Chapter 5

Major Issues of Sustainable Development in Barak Valley Zone of Assam

5.1 An Introduction to Geography and Climate

5.2 Gross Domestic Product of Barak Valley

5.3 Demographic Profile

5.4 Agriculture in Barak Valley

5.5 Human Development Profile

5.6 An Analysis of Agro-Human Development Linkage

5.1 An Introduction to Geography and Climate

The Barak Valley covers an area of 6222 sq. km. and is administratively divided into 27 Blocks, 321 Gaon Panchayats and 1050 Villages. The valley lies between longitude of 92015' and 93015' East and latitude of 2408' and 2508' North and geographically isolated not only from mainstream of India but also from the rest of the state of Assam owing to difficult topography of the adjoining areas. It is surrounded by other states of India viz., Tripura, Mizoram and Manipur and a long vulnerable international border with Bangladesh. The topography of the valley is heterogeneous having hills, low lands and plain areas. The Barak-Surma-Kusiara river system passes through this valley.

It is geographically the (Journal of NEICSSR, Vol.-27 (1), pp. 13-26, 2003.) part of what was known as Surma Valley in pre-partition days consisting of the old districts of Sylhet (now included in Bangladesh) and Cachar. Of the Surma Valley, only Cachar and a part of Karimganj sub-division of Sylhet district forms the present Barak Valley deriving its name from the main river, Barak. The valley is covered with a network of sluggish streams and saucer-like depressions. Numerous hillocks stand all over the valley. The valley is also covered by hill ranges from north, east and south. It has vast tracts of forest land in its southern side. The forest cover of the valley has been on the decline and the forest area decreased from 44.4 percent of the geographical area of the valley in 1951 to 34.9 percent in 1994-95.

Assam in the North Eastern Region consisting of 23 districts can be broadly divided into three zones namely, the Brahmaputra Valley, the area comprising two hill districts of North Cachar Hills and Karbi Anglong, and the Barak Valley consisting of the districts of Cachar, Hailakandi and Karimganj. These three regions of Assam are geographically, historically, socially and economically different from one another in many respects. The Barak Valley in particular, has all the characteristics of a problem region. Stilwell (1972, p.10) has pointed out that there are three main types of problem areas: underdeveloped, depressed and congested. Barak Valley possesses the features of all these three types of problem regions. Firstly, it shares the common features of underdevelopment of the North East. Secondly, it is a depressed region in the sense that within the state of

Assam it has suffered most owing to severance of its link with what is now known as Bangladesh as a result of partition of India. It is a demographically congested region as it has experienced unprecedented inflow of population from the erstwhile East Pakistan (now Bangladesh) and its towns and suburb have absorbed substantial quantum of middle class migration from the rest of the North Eastern Region owing to social tension. In the following sections we have undertaken an exercise of analyzing the features of the Barak Valley in a comparative framework. We have also dealt with certain indicators of development in order to highlight the specific problems of this area.

The hilly terrain in the valley is used for tea plantation and the principal crops produced in the plain areas are rice, jute, sugarcane, potato, rape seed, mustard seed etc. About 90 percent of the gross cropped area is used for cultivation of rice and tea plantation. The climatic condition of the valley is characterized high humidity to the extent of 89 percent. Average rainfall is as high as 2700 mm and the minimum and maximum annual rainfall have been noted to be 1700 mm and 4000 mm respectively. Consequently, the valley often experiences flood havoc. The air during the monsoon remains surcharged with moisture. The minimum and maximum temperature observed in the valley during winter and summer respectively are 80 C and 370 C. The geographical features analysed above endow the valley a distinct regional identity leading to the justification of drawing up special programmes within the integrated development plans for Assam and North East India. The valley's unique geographically location makes it worthy of a nodal point in developing inter-state economic links and cooperation between Assam, Tripura, Meghalaya, Mizoram and Manipur (Goswami, 1994). The valley is also likely to play an important role in Indo-Bangladesh economic cooperation if economic ties are developed between the two countries.

5.2 Gross Domestic Product of Barak Valley (by adding three districts).

Table-34

	GDP at 1993-94 prices (in lakhs)	NDP at 1993-94 prices (in lakhs)	Contribution of sectors to GDP (%)	Contribution of Barak valley to GSDP of Assam (%)
1	2	3	4	5
A. Primary (Total)	63617	61136	38.30	8.86
1. Agriculture	54985	53334	33.10	10.48
2. Forest and logging	2679	2642	1.61	8.08
3. Fishing	5510	4832	3.31	4.59
4. Mining and quarrying	443	328	0.27	0.36
B. Secondary (Total)	28186	34047	16.96	10.20
1. Manufacturing	14506	11758	8.73	9.49
(a) Registered	13691	11114	8.24	11.48
(b) Unregistered	816	643	0.49	2.29
2. Construction	12157	11182	7.32	12.32
3. Electricity and water supply	1523	-650	0.92	6.44
C. Tertiary	74310	66158	44.73	9.44

(Total)				
1. Railway	1045	169	0.63	6.57
2. Storage	-5	-5	-0.003	-3.59
3. Transport by other means	4325	1608	2.60	11.57
4. Communication	3746	2676	2.26	14.28
5. Trade, hotel and restaurant	25465	24461	15.33	10.73
6. Banking and insurance	10442	10114	6.29	12.47
7. Real estate, ownership of dwellings and Business services	2016	1609	1.21	3.22
8. Public administration	10024	8862	6.03	7.61
9. Other services	17247	16664	10.38	8.95
10. Total	166113	161341	100.00	9.32
11. Per capita income	5377	5223		

Source :- Department of Agriculture, Government of Assam.

Statistical Handbook of Assam, Directorate Economics and Statististics.

The above table shows the gross domestic product and net domestic product at 1993-94 prices. The contribution of different sectors in the final output of Barak valley along with the contribution of Barak valleys in the state domestic product of Assam have also been shown. Primary sector contributes 38.30% in the total output of the valley while agriculture makes the lions share of 33.10%. Secondary sector adds 16.96% in the total income with the biggest share of manufacturing sector worth of 8.73% and construction worth of 7.32%. However it is the tertiary sector or the service sector of the economy which makes the biggest contribution worth of 44.73%. Trade and hotel-restaurant comprises of 15.33% and other services 10.38%. Contribution of railway (0.63%), storage (-0.03%), transport by other means (2.26%), communication (2.60%) etc are really insignificant and depict a formidable condition of the economic infrastructure.

On the other hand the contribution of Barak Valley in the GSDP of Assam is not bad at all. The agriculture alone adds 10.48% of the GSDP while secondary and tertiary sector add 10.20% and 9.44% respectively. The total contribution of the valley in the state income is 9.32%. The per capita income of Barak valley is Rs. 5223 thousand.

5.3 Demographic Profile

Decadal growth rate of population in Barak valley, Assam and all India (in percentage) & District-wise scenario in Barak Valley

Table-35

Year 1	Barak valley 2	Assam 3	India 4	Cachar	Karaimganj	Hailakandi
1901-11	13.80	6.90	5.7	12.33	12.94	16.09
1911-21	5.60	20.5	0.3	5.98	3.91	7.59

1921-31	6.30	19.9	11.0	7.60	8.91	7.08
1931-41	11.00	20.4	14.2	13.08	9.52	10.29
1941-51	23.80	19.9	13.3	23.92	29.87	17.48
1951-61	24.30	34.9	21.6	22.60	22.96	27.23
1971-81	24.20	34.9	24.1	23.96	25.13	23.61
1981-91	45.20	53.3	48.5	47.59	42.08	45.94
1991-2001	19.97	18.85	21.34	18.66	21.35	20.92
2001-2011	20.79	16.93	17.64	20.17	20.74	21.44

Source:-Department of Agriculture, Government of Assam, Statistical Handbook of Assam, Directorate Economics and Statistics, Human Development Report- 2003 (Assam)

The demographic change took place in Barak valley and Assam very rapidly within one century. The growth rate was 13.80% in 1901-11, after the opening of rise in population once due to higher birth rate along with inflow of people from eastern part of Bengal. The rate of growth could not be controlled. From 1930s to 1990s, it went upwards like anything and in 1991-2001; the rate was 19.97% while in 2001-2011, the growth rate was 20.79%. The rate of growth has been consistent more or less with the state and India as a whole. This is evident from the above table. The district wise growth rate also shows that the rate of growth has been consistent with the valley, state and nation.(see the above tables).

To have a comparative and clear idea of the growth of population in the Barak Valley, annual average growth rates of (Journal of NEICSSR, Vol.-27 (1), pp. 13-26, 2003.) population for different decades have been estimated along with those of Assam and India. The data reveal that the valley during the five decades witnessed fluctuating growth rates of population. It had the highest demographic growth rate of 2.23 percent per annum during 1941-51. This was marginally reduced to 2.13 percent in the decade, 1951-61. Again it increased to 2.20 percent in 1961-71 and further declined to 1.8 percent during the two decades of 1971-91, where as the Barak Valley witnessed a decrease in the growth rate of population between 1941-51 and 1951-61, Brahmaputra Valley witnessed a substantial increase in population growth during the same span of time. Perhaps this can be explained by greater impact of inter-state migration to Brahmaputra Valley during this period. The trend was reversed in both the valleys between the decades 1951-61 and 1961-71. Assam as whole and Barak and Brahmaputra Valleys in particular, have witnessed higher growth rate of population than India as a whole in the post-partition era.

5.4 Agriculture in Barak Valley

Land utilization in Assam and Barak valley

Table-36

Classification	Area (in hectare)		Percentage of reporting area	
	Assam	Barak valley	Assam	Barak valley
1	2	3	4	5
1. Total geographical area	7843800	692200		
2. Reporting area	7850005	691097	100.0	100.0
3. Forest	1931631	261741	24.61	37.87
4. Notavailable for cultivation	2530925	134445	32.24	19.45
(a)Non agricultural uses	1069891	74671	13.63	10.8

(b) Barren and uncultivable	1461034	59774	18.61	8.65
5. Other uncultivable land (excluding fellow land)	477368	43617	6.08	6.31
(a) Permanent pastures and other grazing land	162968	6242	2.08	0.90
(b) Miscellaneous tree crops and groves	234206	32963	2.98	4.77
(c) Cultivable waste land	80194	4412	1.02	0.64
6. Fellow land	175620	17441	2.24	2.52
(a) Fellow land other than current fellows	65219	9081	0.83	1.31
(b) Current fellows	110401	8360	1.41	1.21
7. Net area sown	2734461	233853	34.83	33.85
8. Gross cropped area	4087341	302272	-	-
Area sown more than once	1352880	68419	-	-
Cropping intensity	149	129		

Source :- Department of Agriculture, Department of Forest, Government of Assam.

Statistical Handbook of Assam, Directorate Economics and Statististics.

The economy of the Barak Valley is pre dominated by agriculture and allied sectors. More than 58 percent of the total working population in the valley is either cultivators or agricultural laborers and 70.7 percent of its workers earn their livelihood from the primary sector activities according to 1991 Census. But agriculture is already overcrowded and it shows that only 30.9 percent of the total geographical area in the valley constitutes its net sown area against 41.6 percent in the State of Assam. This means that the Barak Valley suffers from relative scarcity of cultivable land. In the consequence, Barak Valley is constrained to feed as any as 8277 persons per 1000 hectares of cultivable land. The corresponding figures for the Brahmaputra Valley and the State of Assam are 6445 and 6567 (Journal of NEICSSR, Vol.-27 (1), pp. 13-26, 2003) respectively whereas the all-India figure is 4305. Added to the scarcity of cultivable land in the valley is its inadequate progress in intensive farming.

Gross Cropped area and its percentage share of reporting area in Barak Valley and Assam, 1981-82 and 1999-2000.

Table-37

Year	Barak valley		Assam	
	G.C.A. (In hectare)	Percentage of the reporting area	G.C.A. (In hectare)	Percentage of the reporting area
1981-82	268943	38.9	3460082	44.1
1997-98	299191	43.29	3926143	50.88
1999-2000	302272	43.74	4087341	52.07

Source :- Department of Agriculture, Government of Assam, Statistical Handbook of Assam, Directorate Economics and Statistics.

The above figures show a distinguishing picture of Barak valley and entire state. The gross cropped area in the valley has increased from 38.9% in 1981-82 to 43.74% in 1999-2000 while for Assam it was 44.1% in 1981-82 to 52.07% in 1999-2000. The ratio of gross cropped area to net sown area in the valley works out to 1.25 whereas it is 1.29 in the Brahmaputra Valley and 1.28 in Assam. Low intensity of cropping in the Barak Valley is mainly owing to poor irrigation facilities. Hardly 6.4 percent of the net sown area in the Barak Valley have irrigation facilities compared 18.3 percent in the Brahmaputra Valley,

17.3 percent in Assam and 32.5 percent in India. Irrigation facilities in the Barak Valley are also less assured as these are mainly devised at individual farmers' level.

It goes to the credit of the farmers of the Barak Valley that in spite of serious limitations in irrigation, they have succeeded in bringing about 48 percent of the net sown area under HYV. But introduction of HYV crops can not achieve its full impact on productivity and crop intensity because of lack of irrigation facilities. As chemical fertilizers have complementary relation with irrigation as inputs, the valley's progress in the application of chemical fertilizer is also retarded. Per hectare consumption of fertilizer in the Barak Valley is as low as 16.4 kg in great contrast to India's 69.9 kg. Consequently, average yield of rice per hectare in the valley is as low as 1447 kg as against India's figure of 1745 kg. Significantly enough, the relevant figure of the Brahmaputra Valley the most fertile region of Assam is only 1131 kg. i.e., lower than that of the Barak Valley. The first generation problem of the green revolution has been to induce farmers to adopt the new technology to raise production (Ghatak, 1995).

It seems that the Barak Valley is able to solve this problem but it is still unable reap the benefits of the green revolution because of the serious infrastructural deficiency in the form of irrigation facility. It may be added that average yield of rice in the Barak Valley during the period from 1950-51 to 1973-74 has been higher than that India. It is only after 1973-74 that the valley has been lagging behind the average of India. This only highlights uneven regional impact of the green revolution to the disadvantage of regions like the Barak Valley owing to disparity in infrastructural development. The upshot of the above discussion is that the Barak Valley requires a special pattern of State intervention in agriculture. This is only possible through area specific agricultural planning. Journal of NEICSSR, Vol.-27 (1), pp. 13-26, 2003.

Percentage share of principal crops in total cropped area in the Barak valley region during the period 1971-72 to 2004-05:-

Table-38

CROPS	1971-72	1979-80	1984-85	1990-91	1994-95	2001-02	2004-05
1	2	3	4	5	6	7	8
Autumn rice	16.55	19.36	13.85	16.49	11.20	8.47	8.95
Winter rice	71.32	68.40	72.52	70.95	76.30	73.48	72.11
Summer rice	5.52	4.94	5.27	5.64	5.20	5.59	7.18
Total rice	93.39	92.70	91.64	93.08	92.70	87.54	88.23
Other cereals	0.15	0.20	0.12	0.11	0.06	0.11	0.11
Total cereals	93.54	92.90	91.76	93.18	92.76	87.64	88.34
Pulses	0.80	0.93	1.41	1.32	2.36	2.38	5.69
Total Food grains	94.34	93.83	93.17	94.50	95.12	90.02	94.03
Rape and mustard	0.66	0.80	1.78	1.77	0.93	1.04	1.23
Other oilseed	0.16	0.20	0.20	0.15	0.27	0.13	0.16
Total oilseed	0.82	1.00	1.98	1.92	1.20	1.17	1.39
Total fibre	0.50	0.35	0.29	0.17	0.15	0.14	0.17
Potato	1.13	1.11	1.74	1.42	1.63	1.86	1.96
Sugarcane	2.12	2.76	1.86	1.24	1.17	0.53	0.48
Others	1.09	0.96	0.96	0.75	0.73	6.27	1.97
Total	100.00	100.00	100.00	100.00	100.00	100.00	100.00

Source :- Department of Agriculture, Government of Assam, Statistical Handbook of Assam, Directorate Economics and Statistics.

Percentage share of principal crops shows that autumn rice has declined overtime since 1971-72 from 16.55% to 8.95% in 2004-05. The share of winter rice has been steady and the most important contributor in the rice production in the valley. Perhaps the geographical and climatic problem of flood and the heavy risk that is associated with the production and sale of agricultural produce during the other seasons especially in the time of April to October ; the farmers prefer to produce during winter season. From 1971-72 to 2004-05, it remained more than 71% always. The share of summer rice has shown insignificant growth since 1971-72 with 5.52% to 7.18% in 2004-05. Most of the cropped area remained under paddy as crop diversification is poorer in the zone and paddy has been cultivated in the 93.39% in 1971-72 to 88.23% in 2004-05 of the total area under cropping. Other cereals are insignificant as the share has risen from only 011% in 1971-72 to 0.15% in 2004-05.

Area under pulses production is insignificant yet the share of cultivation has been on the rise overtime since 1970s to this millennium. The area under pulses increased from 0.80% in 1971-72 to 5.69% in 2004-05. However the share of total food grains has remained the principal crop in this valley with 94.03%.the area under oilseeds increased from a meagre 0.82% in 1971-72 to 1.39% in 2004-05. Rape and mustard rose from 0.66% in 1971-72 to 1.23% in 2004-05. Other oilseed production has been less important as remained with share of only 0.16% overtime. Total fibre production covers only 0.17% of the cropped area. Another important vegetable potato covers 1.13% in 1971-72 to 1.96% in 2004-05. Others are mostly insignificant regarding cropping intensity while sugarcane lost its importance as the share has declined from 2.12% in 1971-72 to 0.48% in 2004-05. Cash crops and raw materials depend on industrial demand which is poorer in Barak valley while vegetables and fruits depend on infrastructural improvement.

Distribution of area under different categories of paddy to the total area under paddy in the Barak valley region and Assam:-

Table-39

	Barak valley (percentage to the total area)			Assam (percentage to the total area)		
Year	Autumn	Winter	Summer	Autumn	Winter	Summer
1	2	3	4	5	6	7
1971-72	17.72	76.37	5.91	26.77	71.62	1.61
1974-75	22.44	71.56	6.00	27.38	71.10	1.52
1979-80	20.90	73.80	5.30	25.42	72.84	1.74
1984-85	15.11	79.14	5.75	26.11	71.85	2.04
1989-90	14.97	78.30	6.37	25.44	71.42	3.14
1992-93	13.31	80.67	6.02	24.82	69.40	5.78
1994-95	12.08	82.31	5.61	26.00	68.70	5.30
1999-2000	9.49	85.37	5.14	24.24	66.63	9.13
2004-05	10.14	81.72	8.14			

Source :- Department of Agriculture, Government of Assam.

Statistical Handbook of Assam, Directorate Economics and Statististics.

The above table depicts that since 1971-72, the share of autumn rice in the total paddy production in the valley has gone down regarding distribution of area under the autumn rice. It was 17.72% in 1971-72 while 10.14% in 2004-05 in Barak valley while the percentage share summer rice has increased slowly from 5.91% in 1971-72 to 8.14% in 2004-05. It is the winter crop which plays the most important part in the paddy production of the valley. From 76.37% in 1971-72, it increased to 81.72% in 2004-05. For the state as a whole the share of summer rice and autumn rice are in a little batter position yet the share of winter rice plays the most vital role in the paddy production of the state and the Barak valley together. The share of winter paddy is 66.63% for Assam in 2004-05.

Annual compound growth rate of different crops in the Barak valley region of Assam from 1979-80 to 1999-2000

(In percentage). Figures in brackets provide the data for the state.

Table-40

Crops	Area	Production	Yield
1	2	3	4
1. Autumn	-2.85 (0.34)	-1.71 (1.68)	1.17 (1.34)
2. Winter	0.75 (0.81)	3.52 (2.35)	2.75 (1.54)
3. Summer	1.51 (7.61)	1.34 (10.39)	-0.17 (2.77)
Total	0.15 (0.89)	2.46 (2.51)	2.30 (1.62)
4. Pulses	5.99 (1.93)	7.58 (3.16)	1.50 (1.23)
5. Sugarcane	-6.22 (-0.85)	-4.86 (0.14)	1.46 (1.00)
6. Potato	2.95 (5.22)	2.64 (7.48)	-0.30 (2.26)
7. Rape and mustard	8.07 (4.10)	8.24 (5.52)	0.15 (1.42)

Source :- Department of Agriculture, Government of Assam, Statistical Handbook of Assam, Directorate Economics and Statistics.

The above table enumerates the annual compound growth of major crops of Barak valley from 1979-80 to 1999-2000. The 20 years compound growth rate explains the stagnant condition of agriculture in the Barak valley region of the state. Only winter rice could be able to achieve positive growth rate over 20 years period. The area under production has increased at rate of 0.75% in Barak valley and o.81% in the state. The production rate is better than the state with 3.52% while sate has obtained 2.35%. Regarding yield the performance of the valley has improved with 2.75% and the state with 1.54%.

The performance of the autumn rice and summer has not increased at a rate up to the marks. However the production of total rice and the yield are in line with the performance of Assam as shown in the table. The growth rate of pulses was 7.58% and area under pulses rose at 5.99% which are commendable in relation to the performance of the state as whole. Rape and mustard grew also considerably but at a rate lower than that of the state. The most terrible experience was made by potato and sugarcane as is revealed from the above table. They achieved negative growth rate while states performance was considerably batter.

Irrigated and unirrigated areas of Barak valley,2004-05.

Table-41

	Irrigated area (in hactres)	Unirrigated area(in hactres)	Net area sown (in hactres)
1	2	3	4
Cachar	1809.1 (1.5 %)	121692.39 (98.6%)	123451.5 (100.0)
Karimganj	1945.47 (2.3%)	82848 (97.7%)	84793 (100.0)
Hailakandi	126.26 (0.3 %)	47072.49 (99.7%)	47198.75 (100.0)
Barak valley	3880.83 (1.5%)	251612.88 (98.5%)	255493.7 (100.0)

Source :- Department of Agriculture, Government of Assam. Statistical Handbook of Assam, Directorate Economics and Statistics.

The above two tables show that irrigation potential in the valley is heavily inadequate and a primary obstacle towards rapid improvement of agriculture. The irrigation in the valley is only 1.5% of the total sown area. Hailakandi district with 2.3%, Cachar with 1.5% and karimganj with 0.3% are very poor regarding irrigation facility. The second table shows that irrigation potential available and actually utilized in the valley. Estimated utilization ratio has fallen over the years from 1990-91 to 2000-01.

5.5 Human Development Profile

Economists like Amartya Sen have forcefully argued in favour of judging socioeconomic performance of a country by the achievements in the field of extending capabilities and enhancing functioning4. Taking cue from this approach the United Nations Development Programmes (UNDP) has been publishing Human Development Report since 1990. According to this approach, human development is the end and economic growth is the means.

Human development index in Barak valley

District	HDI value	Income index	Education index	Health index	HDI Rank	Income Rank	Education Rank	Health Rank
Cachar	0.402	0.266	0.634	0.307	8	7	9	12
Hailakandi	0.363	0.234	0.563	0.293	11	9	14	14
Karimganj	0.301	0.078	0.620	0.207	19	19	11	18
Assam	0.407	0.286	0.595	0.343				

Source:- Assam Human Development Report-2003.

According to the ranking of the districts, it can be easily perceived that Barak Valley exists in the medium category of the human development zone. Not only lagging behind in all over HDI value but also in all parameters i.e. income, education and health as well. Jorhat tops in the overall value along with education and health. Kamrup is the first regarding the income. Cachar is 8th in HDI ranking, Hailakandi is 11th and Karimganj is formidably at the 19th position. The income, education and health ranking of Cachar district is at 7th, 9th and 12th while that of Hailakandi district is at 9th, 14th and 14th respectively. The condition of Karimganj district is the most terrible in the valley. It is at the 19th, 11th and 18th position in income, education and health respectively. The districts of lower Assam and hill districts of N.C.Hills and Karbi Anglong are at low human development zone.

Human Development Characteristics of Barak Valley

Educational, Health and Household characteristics (In Percentage)

Table-42

District	Literacy rate (age 7+)			School attendance (age 6-11)		Have Electricity connection	Have Access to toilet facility	Improved source of drinking water	Have a television	Have a mobile phone	Infant Mortality Rate (per 1000)
	Total	Male	Female	Boys	Girls						
Cachar	80.36	85.85	74.62	97.8	97.4	36.7	87.3	48.1	32.4	29.0	57
Hailakandi	75.26	81.61	68.54	98.5	98.8	32.2	96.5	40.9	18.5	26.0	55
Karimganj	79.72	85.70	73.49	97.2	98.2	26.8	85.6	50.5	18.6	23.1	69
Assam	73.18	78.81	67.27	98.3	98.6	37.1	69.9	74.9	29.1	28.7	60

Source: NFHS-3, Vital Statistics Division, Office of the Registrar General,

The educational, health and household characteristics present the socio-economic condition of the valley. Regarding literacy rate the position of Barak Valley is better than the state average. The literacy rate is 80.36% in Cachar District and 79.72% in Karimganj district while 75.26% in Hailakandi district and all three district have achieved better than the state average. In case of male and female literacy rate the condition remains the same. All three districts have better situation than the state average while regarding the male-female differences our valley is a little worse the state position. School attendance (age 6-11) is same for the state position and Hailakandi district while Cachar and Karimganj are little lagging behind, however school attendance has shown much improvement in the entire state including Barak Valley.

Regarding household characteristics the performance of Barak Valley is not much improved along with the entire state. The population having electricity connection is 36.7% in rural areas of Cachar district which is higher than other two districts of the valley. Hailakandi has 32.2% people having electricity connection and Karimganj has only 26.8% but Assam has 37.1% people having electricity connection in the rural area. 87.3% population have access to toilet facility in Cachar district but 96.5% people have toilet facility in Hailakandi district and it is one of the highest in the state. Karimganj district has only 85.6% people having access to toilet facility. However all three districts have achieved much better in this respect than the state average of only 69.9%. Regarding improved source of drinking water, Barak Valley is lagging behind. Cachar district has 48.1% people having access to it while in Hailakandi district only 40.9% and in Karimganj district only 50.5%. But in Assam it is much higher than that of the entire Barak Valley with 74.9%. people having access to a television shows a peculiar picturesque in Assam and Barak Valley. Cachar district has a better position with 32.4% than the entire state with 29.1% but other two districts are much lagging behind the state average with a score of only 18.5%. Similar situation is found in the case of having access to mobile phone. Cachar district has 29.0% people having access which is more than the state average of 28.7% but Hailakandi and Karimganj districts have 26.0% and 23.1% respectively. The infant mortality rate in Assam is the fifth highest in India and is highest among all the North-Eastern states. Cachar and Hailakandi have lower infant mortality than the state average but Karimganj has higher.

Urbanization in Barak Valley:

Table-43

District	Number of towns	Urban population (in %)	Rural population (in %)
Cachar	2	13.94	86.06
Karimganj	3	7.27	92.73
Hailakandi	2	8.29	91.71

Source:- Assam Human Development Report-2003.

Urbanization is regarded as one of the most important factor in the human development of any area. In this category once again upper Assam districts are ahead of others. Barak Valley is lagging behind here too. Cachar has 2 towns and 13.94% population in urban area while Karimganj has 3 towns and 7.27% population. Hailakandi has 2 towns and 8.29% population having access to urban amenities of life. The Kamrup district has the highest position in this regard with 7 towns and 35.79% population having access to urban amenities of life, Ngaon has 7 towns with 12.01% population, Dibrugarh with 6 towns and 18.17% population. Lower Assam districts are also lagging behind and flood affected district of Dhemaji is at the lowest.

5.6 An Analysis of Agro-Human Development Linkage

Per hectare productivity in various districts along with other salient characteristics:-

Table-44

District	Production per hectare (value in RS.)	Production per worker (value in RS.)	Fertiliser-NPK per hectare (NSA)	AFV %	Crop Intensity %	Worker per hectare	Rainfall: mm	NSA: 000 ha	Rural poor %
Cachar	29728	21491	44	14.8	127	1.38	2366.1	115	33.50
Hailakandi	34515	17890	30	11.7	141	1.93	3094.2	46	37.00
Karimganj	29037	16638	60	9.2	140	1.75	4559.9	69	40.90

Source: Statistical Abstract, Directorate of Agriculture/Horticulture, CSO

Fertiliser-NPK per kg per hectare of net sown area in Barak Valley, AFV- Area under fruits and vegetables, Cropping intensity, Worker per hectare, Rainfall in Barak Valley, Net sown area and % of Rural poor have high level causal relationship among them.

Production per hectare of agricultural crop has been turned in to value terms by using state level prices of various agricultural crops. These prices were generated by dividing state level value of output of each crop estimated by CSO by the output of the crop for the year 2003-04 and 2004-05. According to CSO methodology such prices represent farm gate prices. The value of per hectare productivity in Cachar district was Rs.29728 which is lower than Hailakandi district with Rs.34515 and Karimganj district was with Rs.29037. But output per worker is higher in Cachar district i.e. Rs.21491, in Hailakandi district with Rs.17890 and Rs.16638 in Karimganj district.

Data used in Regression Analysis

Table-45

Districts	HDI	HPI	HPI Rank	ADI	PPW-Production per worker (value in RS.)	Rural poor %
Cachar	0.402	39.71	17	0.18	21491	33.50
Hailakandi	0.363	41.02	19	0.17	17890	37.00
Karimganj	0.301	40.22	18	0.14	16638	40.90

A linear regression model has been prepared on the basis of Productivity, Agricultural Development Index, Human Development Index and % of Rural Poor in Assam to study their interrelationship and interlinked role for sustainable development.

The interrelation between Human Development Index and Production Per Worker.

Model Summary-1   **Table-46**

Model	R	R Square	Adjusted R Square	Std. Error of the Estimate	Change Statistics				
					R Square Change	F Change	df1	df2	Sig. F Change
1	.920	.846	.692	1398.114	.846	5.495	1	1	.257

a. Predictors: (Constant), HDI

b. Dependent Variable: PPW

In the Model Summary-1, we see that the coefficient of multiple correlation r(R) is .920, indicating a good positive linear relationship between the predictor HDI and the dependent variable PPW-production per worker. The coefficient of determination r^2 (R Square) of .846 indicates that for the sample, 84% of the variation of PPW can be explained by the variation in human development index. But this may be an overestimate for the population from which the sample is drawn, so we use the Adjusted R Square as a better estimate for the population i.e. .692. Finally, the Standard Error of the Estimate is 1398.114.

The interrelation between Agricultural Development Index and Human Development Index

Model Summary-2   **Table-47**

Model	R	R Square	Adjusted R Square	Std. Error of the Estimate	Change Statistics				
					R Square Change	F Change	df1	df2	Sig. F Change
1	.989	.978	.955	.010786	.978	43.597	1	1	.096

a. Predictors: (Constant), ADI

b. Dependent Variable: HDI

In the Model Summary-2, we see that the coefficient of multiple correlation r(R) is .989, indicating a good positive linear relationship between the predictor ADI-Agricultural Development Index and the dependent variable HDI- human development index. The coefficient of determination r2 (R Square) of .978 indicates that for the sample, 97% of the variation of HDI can be explained by the variation in Agricultural Development Index. It may be an overestimate for the population from which the sample is drawn, so we use the Adjusted R Square as a better estimate for the population i.e. .955.

The interrelation between % of Rural Poor and Production Per Worker

Model Summary-3   Table-48

Model	R	R Square	Adjusted R Square	Std. Error of the Estimate	Change Statistics				
					R Square Change	F Change	df1	df2	Sig. F Change
1	.954	.911	.821	1065.550	.911	10.182	1	1	.193

a. Predictors:(Constant), Rural Poor

b. Dependent Variable: PPW

In the Model Summary-3, we see that the coefficient of multiple correlation r(R) is .954, indicating a strong linear relationship between the predictor % of Rural Poor and the dependent variable PPW-production per worker. The coefficient of determination r2 (R Square) of .911 indicates that for the sample, 91% of the variation of PPW can be explained by the variation in % of Rural Poor. It may be an overestimate for the population from which the sample is drawn, so we use the Adjusted R Square as a better estimate for the population i.e. .821.

CONCLUSION

The profile of Barak Valley shows condition of the valley in different sectors of the economy. The heavy pressure of population along with declining land holding due to increasing fragmentation of land may create a formidable situation. The characteristics of health, education, enrolment, access to basic amenities of life show that our valley is gripped in the hand of vicious circle of poverty. The agricultural productivity and growth rate is low enough to make any solid contribution to the Quality of Life of the people of the valley.

The condition of health, education employment, poverty, and agriculture proves that there is ample scope for the human resource to be applied in the primary sector to raise its level of performance and contribution of agriculture in the development of health, nutrition employment, education and overall rural development. In spite of the special problems faced by the Barak Valley, no specific or separate planning agency or for this region has been created so far. The problem has been left to be dealt by Panchayati Raj Institutions, other local bodies like municipalities and District Rural Development Agencies etc. Thus the necessity of the comprehensive program for human development and agricultural growth is a must.

Chapter 6

Health and Sustainable Development in Assam

6.1 Health Performance in Assam: A Comparison with other North-Eastern states and India

6.1.1 Introduction to Health and Development

6.1.2 Socio-economic and Health profile of North-East States as compared to India

6.1.3 Comparison on the Basis of Major Health Outcomes

6.1.4 Disparity on the basis of nutrition, women and child health

6.2 Women, Child and Reproductive Health: A Comparative Study of Rural-Urban Development in Assam

6.2.1 Introduction to the Issue

6.2.2 Assam - Key Indicators of Rural Development and Health Environment

6.1 Health Performance in Assam: A Comparison with other North-Eastern states and India

North-East region is one of the most marginalised parts of India. In 21st century when India has entered in to the 9% growth trajectory the region of Seven-Sisters plus Sikkim are lagging behind in almost every aspect of development. However the region has shown some good performance regarding achievement in literacy or some health aspects yet there is a long way to go in public health services.

The chapter endeavours to make a comparative analysis of health performance of North-East states with national performance. Moreover an interstate disparity among the states of this region is made and looks in to the status and determinants of health outcomes. Data has been collected from secondary sources mostly from government published reports and various health indicators like birth rate, death rate, IMR, MMR, BMI, women and child nutrition etc have been used to analyse the disparity.

6.1.1 Introduction to Health and Development

The region comprising of the eight states of Arunachal Pradesh, Assam, Manipur, Meghalaya, Mizoram, Nagaland, Sikkim (the last to be included in the region) and Tripura, constitutes a land surface of 262,230 square kilometres where a population of 38.9 million belonging to different ethnic and cultural groups inhabits. Topographically the region is a mixture of hills and plains. While Arunachal Pradesh, Meghalaya, Mizoram, Nagaland and Sikkim are almost entirely hilly, about four fifths of Assam is plain. Manipur and Tripura have both plain areas and hilly tracts. The hills account for about 70 per cent area and accommodate about 30 per cent of population of the region and the plains constituting the remaining 30 per cent of area hold about 70 per cent of its population.

Economic and social developments are complimentary to each other. Empirical evidence suggests that mere emphasis on economic development and neglect of social development results in lopsided development and ultimately slowing down the tempo of economic development. This rapid economic development has not been accompanied by social development particularly in health sector development. Health sector has been accorded very low priority in terms of allocation of resources. Public expenditure on health is only 1.3 per cent of GDP in India. It has further witnessed decline during the post economic liberalization period. The meagre resource allocation to health sector has adversely affected both access and quality of health services. The unequal access to health services is reported across strata, gender and location (i.e. states, region etc). With a view to improve access and quality of health services, government should enhance public spending on health sector in the vicinity of 3 per cent of GDP. India's North-Eastern part, comprising of eight states including Sikkim is a lowly developed, tribal population dominated region in India. The present paper, through a state-wise analysis, makes an attempt to find out the extent of this disparity, especially on health front. It illustrates the situations prevailing in health sector.

The 3rd National Family Health Survey (2007) depicts the vulnerable situation of health across different states. India Human Development Report (2011) reveals the regional disparity that exists in India regarding birth rate, death rate, IMR, MMR, child and reproductive health, health expenditure etc. Debasis Neogi (2010) in International Journal of Human and Social Sciences discussed the internal variety in North-East region in health and socio-economic status. Ghuman and Mehta (2010) discussed problems and prospects of health outcomes and expenditure in India. Apart from them some other literature like State HDRs, NRHM reports have been reviewed.

6.1.2 Socio-economic and Health profile of North-East States as compared to India

Table-49

Name of states	Per capita state income (in Rs)	Household in pucca & semi-pucca houses	Access to electricity	Population below poverty line	Literacy rate	Sex ratio	Child sex ratio (0-6 yrs)	Population served per hospital bed	Access to safe drinking water
Arunachal Pradesh	17018	38.84	54.69	17.6	66.95	920	960	495	77.5
Assam	12529	50.6	24.90	19.7	73.18	954	957	2059	58.8
Manipur	12641	63.52	60.04	17.3	79.85	987	934	905	37
Meghalaya	15932	59.63	42.74	18.5	75.48	986	970	975	39
Mizoram	17245	78.53	69.63	12.6	91.58	975	971	536	36
Nagaland	16540	66.69	63.60	19.0	80.11	931	944	912	46.5
Tripura	16947	55.8	41.84	18.9	87.75	961	953	1165	52.5
Sikkim	9472	60.0	80.0	20.1	82.20	889	944	818	85
All India Average	16762	81.75	55.85	27.5	74.04	940	914	1138	77.9
Highest among states & UTs	40301 Delhi	98.34 Daman & Diu	94.81 Himachal Pradesh	46.4 Orissa	93.91 Kerala	1084 Kerala	971 Mizoram	2165 Orissa	99.8 Chandigarh
Lowest	5972	38.84	10.25	8.4	63.8	618	830	162	4.6

| among states & UTs | Bihar | Arunachal Pradesh | Bihar | Punjab | 2 Bihar | Daman & Diu | Haryana | Pondicherry | Lakshadweep |

Statistical Abstract of India 2003, Basic statistic of NER 2006, (Source: RHS Bulletin, March 2011, M/O Health & F.W., GOI), India Human Development Report (2011).

In terms of various indicators of human development, the region presents us with a mixed picture. Mizoram has the highest position regarding child-sex ratio in the country and sex ratio in the region. Arunachal Pradesh has better position in population served per hospital beds but that is mainly due to the low density of population of the state. All other states including Assam (2059) have worse position while Arunachal Pradesh herself is much behind the best ST/UT i.e. Pondicherry (162).

Per capita state income of Mizoram (Rs. 17245), Arunachal Pradesh (Rs 17018) and Tripura (Rs. 16947) respectively is above the all India average (Rs. 16762) and the remaining states are below it. However, Nagaland is close to national average in respect of per capita state income. Assam has the lowest per capita (Rs 12529) income in NEI.

As far households in pucca and semi-pucca houses are concerned, all the concerned states lag behind all India average. 78.53 (highest among NE states) percent households in Mizoram reside either in pucca or semi-pucca houses followed by Nagaland with 66.69 percent. 61.16 percents of total households in Arunachal Pradesh dwell kuchcha or unclassified houses. Access to electricity recorded among the states shows a mixed picture in relation to national average (55.85). Access to electricity is the highest in Mizoram (69.63), Nagaland (63.60) and Manipur (60. 04) respectively. In Assam, only one-quarter of households have access to electricity which is the lowest in NE region. Meghalaya and Tripura records much lower than all India average. States like Mizoram, Nagaland, Tripura, and Manipur have literacy rates which are higher than national average. Mizoram (91.58 percent) has the 3rd best literate state in the country. Arunachal Pradesh (66.59 percent) has the least achievement in terms of literacy rate among states of NEI and only above Bihar at the national level.

Determinants of the gap between national level and North-East

Low level of human development in north-eastern states of India only reflects the high human deprivation among its populace. Mizoram, of course is an exception with moderate development in human development and health. Two crucial factors responsible for a dismal performance are low per state capita income and paucity of medical facilities revealed through number of population served per hospital bed as well as lower access to safe drinking water. The low level of economic activity and dependence on central grants is responsible for low level of human development in the region even though the state has achieved regarding poverty reduction as India Human Development Report says. Though poverty level is better than the national average but it does not tell the ground deprivation of the common mass. There is tardiness in economic growth. Health care facilities are in a gloomy state. Along with these features, there remains the alarming problem of scarcity of water in the region. This is mostly due to the physical and climatic features of the region - being hilly and tropical in nature and at the same time, failure of government to make provisions for safe drinking water to the average citizens. Baring Arunachal Pradesh and Assam which has its many river tributaries and streams, availability of safe drinking water is in a meagre position with more than half of the population being deprived of this organic need of life. There is also the trace of high incidence of poverty which only speaks about the high volume of shortfalls in human development. However, the single area which shows considerable progress in the region is literacy rate.

6.1.3 Comparison on the Basis of Major Health Outcomes-

Table-50

Indicator	India	Arunachal Pradesh	Assam	Manipur	Meghalaya	Mizoram	Nagaland	Tripura	Sikkim
Birth rate(per 1000)	22.1	20.5	23.2	14.9	24.5	17.1	16.8	14.9	17.8
Death rate(per 1000)	7.2	5.9	8.2	4.2	7.9	4.5	3.6	5.0	5.6
Natural growth rate(per 1000)	14.9	14.6	14.9	10.7	16.6	12.5	13.6	9.9	12.3
Infant mortality rate(per 1000)	47	31	58	14	55	37	23	27	30
Under five mortality rate(per 1000)	74.3	87.7	85.0	41.9	70.5	52.9	64.7	59.2	40.1
Life expectancy	66.9	69.9	62.2	69.9	70.0	70.0	69.9	69.9	69.8
Public expenditure as % of GSDP	1.3	3.46	0.86	1.32	1.75	3.28	2.49	1.32	3.82

Per capita exp. On health by govt.(in Rs.)	383.16	841	162	294	430	867	639	328	1082
Per capita exp. On health by private (in Rs.)	780.83	613	612	379	464	266	180	1158	425

L.E. projected by Ministry of Health and Family Welfare, (Source: RHS Bulletin, March 2011, M/O Health & F.W.,GOI)

Arunachal Pradesh and India

The Total Fertility Rate of the State is NA. The Infant Mortality Rate is 31 and Maternal Mortality Ratio is NA (SRS 2007 - 09). The Sex Ratio in the State is 920 (as compared to 940 for the country). Under-five mortality rate is 87.7 against the all India average of 74.3 and in life expectancy also better than all India position. She is spending 3.46% of her GSDP in health sector far higher than India. Moreover per capita expenditure on health by government is Rs.841 which is higher than India but lags behind per capita private expenditure.

Assam and India

The Total Fertility Rate of the State is 2.5. The Infant Mortality Rate is 58 and Maternal Mortality Ratio is 390 (SRS 2007 - 2009) which are higher than the National average. The Sex Ratio in the State is 954 (as compared to 940 for the country). Under-five mortality rate is 85.0 against the all India average of 74.3 and in life expectancy also lower than all India position. Assam is spending 0.86% of her GSDP in health sector far lower than India. Moreover per capita expenditure on health by government is Rs.162 which is worse than India and also lags behind per capita private expenditure.

Manipur and India

The state is having higher population growth rate but regarding other health indicators she has performed better. The Total Fertility Rate of the State is NA. The Infant Mortality Rate is 14 and Maternal Mortality Ratio is NA (SRS 2007 - 2009). The Sex Ratio in the State is 987 (as compared to 940 for the country). Under-five mortality rate is 41.9 against the all India average of 74.3 which is really a good achievement and in life expectancy also higher than all India position. Manipur is spending 1.3% of her GSDP in health sector far equal to India. On the other hand per capita expenditure on health by government is Rs.294 which is worse than India and also lags behind per capita private expenditure.

Meghalaya and India

This state is one of the highest rainfall zones of the world while she has achieved much lower than national average in respect of growth rate of population as well as in IMR and MMR, the state's performance is not satisfactory. The Total Fertility Rate of the State is NA. The Infant Mortality Rate is 55 and Maternal Mortality Ratio is NA (SRS 2007 - 2009). The Sex Ratio in the State is 986 (as compared to 940 for the country). Her performance in expenditure on health, child mortality and life expectancy is average.

Mizoram and India

She has performed better than other states of the region regarding health indicators. The Total Fertility Rate of the State is NA. The Infant Mortality Rate is 37 and Maternal Mortality Ratio is NA (SRS 2007 - 2009). The Sex Ratio in the State is 975 (as compared to 940 for the country). Per capita government expenditure on health is much higher than national average with Rs.867 against Rs.383.1 and public expenditure as % of GSDP is 3.28 against national average of 1.3%.

Nagaland and India

Nagaland is the only state to achieve negative growth rate of population and has better position in the other health indicator in comparison to India. The Total Fertility Rate of the State is NA. The Infant Mortality Rate is 23 and Maternal Mortality Ratio is NA (SRS 2007 - 2009). The Sex Ratio in the State is 931 (as compared to 940 for the country). Under-five mortality rate is 64.7 against the all India average of 74.3 and in life expectancy also higher than all India position. She is spending 2.49% of her GSDP in health sector far higher than India. Moreover per capita expenditure on health by government is Rs.639 which is better than India but falls behind per capita private expenditure.

Sikkim and India

The Total Fertility Rate of the State is NA. The Infant Mortality Rate is 30 and Maternal Mortality Ratio is NA (SRS 2007 - 2009). The Sex Ratio in the State is 889 (as compared to 940 for the country). Under-five mortality rate is 40.1 against the all India average of 74.3 and in life expectancy also better than all India position. She is spending 3.82% of her GSDP in health sector far higher than India. Moreover per capita expenditure on health by government is Rs.1082 the highest in India and Rs.425 in per capita private expenditure which good for a small state like Sikkim.

Tripura and India

The Total Fertility Rate of the State is NA. The Infant Mortality Rate is 27 and Maternal Mortality Ratio is NA (SRS 2007 - 2009). The Sex Ratio in the State is 961 (as compared to 940 for the country). Under-five mortality rate is 59.2 against the all India average of 74.3 and in life expectancy also she has a position. She is spending 1.32% of her GSDP in health sector that is equal to India. But per capita expenditure on health by government is Rs.328 the 2nd lowest after Assam in NER and Rs.1158 of per capita private expenditure which shows bad condition of public health for a small state like Tripura.

Interstate disparity in North-East

Within North-East region there exists wide variety regarding health status. The infant mortality rate came down well below the country average in all the states of the region barring Assam and Meghalaya. While identifying yawning gap between states, Mizoram had just a single nurse for every 22,000 persons, it was 5353 persons in case of Assam. Per capita expenditure on health by government of Sikkim is Rs.1082, the highest in India and Rs.425 in per capita private expenditure which is good for a small state like Sikkim. But per capita expenditure on health by government of Tripura is Rs.328 the 2nd lowest after Assam in NER and the amount of Rs.1158 per capita private expenditure which shows bad condition of public health for a small state like Tripura.

The north-eastern states, excluding Assam, are generally doing better in all development parameters, despite the high concentration of STs in the population. However, it is important to qualify here that these groups form the majority and the mainstream in the total population, unlike forest dwelling STs in states of central and eastern belt. Thus, north-eastern state governments have ensured that they share every benefit of the development process. Any policy/scheme undertaken by the government is in effect directed towards this majority group and thus they are included in their development achievements (Government of Nagaland 2004). The State Governments have emphasized not only the adequate provision of primary health care, but education and awareness of health issues, dissemination of information on prevention, hygiene and healthy practices, food security and nutrition, safe drinking water and good sanitation, maternal, child health and family welfare. People in these states now live longer than their parents did, and health profiles have improved. Yet, health indicators in the state reveal inequity between districts, between income and other groupings. There is a rural – urban divide, and a gender gap reflected across almost all indicators. Life expectancy at birth (LEB) is below that of the country as a whole, and is one of the lowest amongst major Indian states. In the 1970's men could expect to live longer than women. This has since been reversed; women can now expect to live longer than men. This is a trend that began to take place initially in urban areas, but is now true of rural areas as well. There is still a very significant gap between the LEB for rural and for urban areas. There is rural – urban gap and a gender gap too; males have a better chance of surviving beyond forty years of age. In a word there is a lot of disparity among the states of North-East.

Major heads of differences within the North-East region-

Table-51

Names of states	Decadal Growth of population (%)	Crude Birth Rate	Crude Death Rate	Natural Growth Rate	Infant Mortality Rate	Maternal Mortality Rate	Total Fertility Rate	Sex Ratio
Arunachal Pradesh	25.92	20.5	5.9	14.6	31	NA	NA	920
Assam	16.93	23.2	8.2	14.9	58	390	2.5	954
Manipur	18.65	14.9	4.2	10.7	14	NA	NA	987
Meghalaya	27.82	24.5	7.9	16.6	55	NA	NA	986
Mizoram	28.82	17.1	4.5	12.5	37	NA	NA	975
Nagaland	-0.47	16.8	3.6	13.6	23	NA	NA	931
Tripura	14.75	14.9	5.0	9.9	27	NA	NA	961
Sikkim	12.36	17.8	5.6	12.3	30	NA	NA	889

Source: RHS Bulletin, March 2011

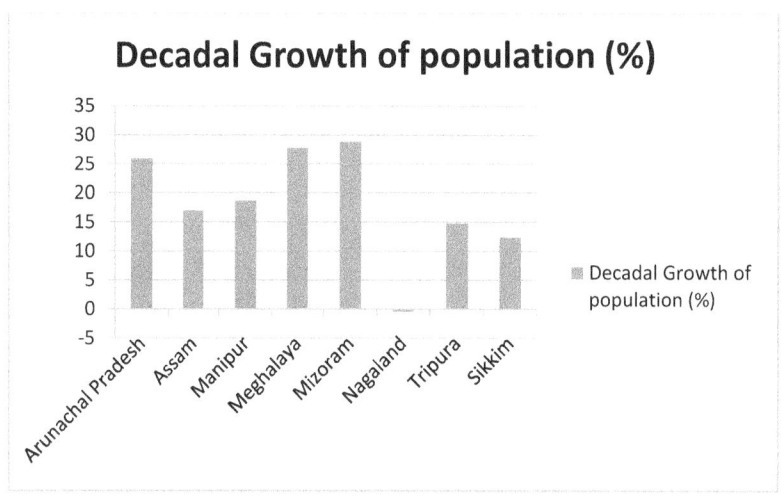

All the states of Northeast have higher growth rate of population with the exception of Nagaland. Arunachal Pradesh is a state with low density of population and high biodiversity. However decadal growth rate of population is 25.92% which is higher than national average of 17.64%. Meghalaya, Mizoram have much higher growth rate than the national average while Sikkim and Tripura have lower than India and Assam and Manipur are at par with all

India figure. Assam is the largest state of North-East with huge diversity in population as well as in development experiences. Assam has achieved lower decadal growth rate of population than India as a whole but regarding IMR and MMR her position is not at all satisfactory.

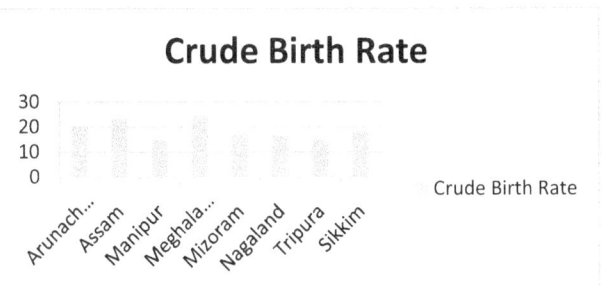

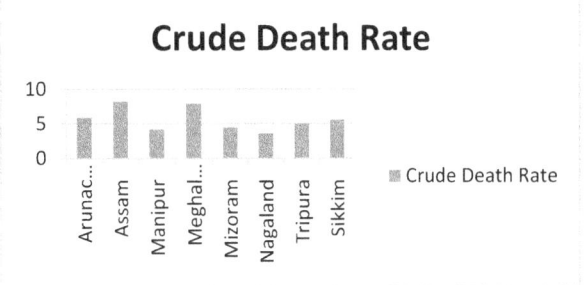

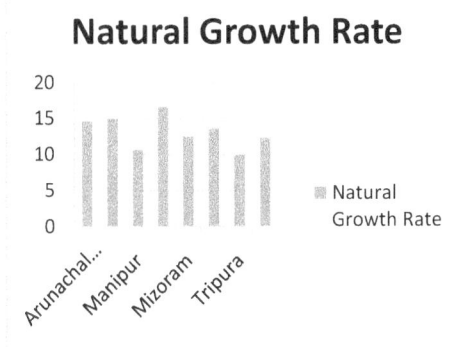

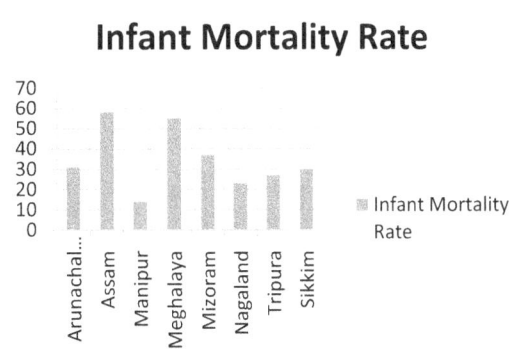

6.1.4 Disparity on the basis of nutrition, women and child health

Percentage of Adult Population with BMI<18.5, 2005–6

Table-52

Name of states	Male	Female
Arunachal Pradesh	15.2	16.4
Assam	35.6	36.5
Manipur	16.3	14.8
Meghalaya	14.1	14.6
Mizoram	9.2	14.4
Nagaland	14.2	17.4
Tripura	41.7	36.9
Sikkim	12.2	11.2
All India	34.2	33

Source: NFHS 2 and 3.

Body mass index shows the lack of body fitness more specifically, malnutrition level of adult population if scored less than 18.5. In this regard all states of the North-East have performed better than the national average except Assam and Tripura. The national achievement is 65.6% population having BMI more than 18.5 i.e. 34.2% below the cut-off level for male and 33% for female. Arunachal Pradesh has 15.2% male below the cut-off level and 16.4% female. Assam and Tripura are the only states in the North-East who have performed worse than the national level with 35.6% male and 36.5% female and 41.7% male and 36.9% female respectively below the deadline. Manipur has got 16.3% male and 14.8% female, Meghalaya with 14.1% male and 14.6% female, Mizoram with 9.2% male and 14.4% female, Nagaland with 14.2% male and 17.4% female, Sikkim with 12.2% male and 11.2% female undernourished.

Nutritional Status of Children (0–5 years), 2005–6

Table-53

Name of states	Height for age	Weight for height	Weight for age
Arunachal Pradesh	43.3	15.3	32.5
Assam	46.5	13.7	36.4
Manipur	35.6	9	22.1
Meghalaya	55.1	30.7	48.8
Mizoram	39.8	9	19.9
Nagaland	38.8	13.3	25.5
Tripura	35.7	24.6	39.6
Sikkim	38.3	9.7	19.7
All India	48	19.8	42.5

Source: NFHS- 3. By the percentage of children below 2-SD.

The nutrition level of children is measured by height for age, weight for height and weight for age. Children are considered malnourished if their z-score of height-for-age, weight for height and weight for age is below minus two standard deviations from the median of the reference population. In this parameter also, North-East states have performed at the tune of national average. In height for age India's condition is not only bad but also formidable as the figure is 48% i.e. almost half of the children could not grow to the desired height according to their age. In Arunachal Pradesh the figure is 43.3% and in Assam 46.5%. Meghalaya has performed the worst with 55.1% children below the deadline. In weight for height all states have performed better than the national average except Tripura and Meghalaya. In weight for age it is once again Meghalaya who has performed the worst. But truly speaking India along with all N-E states must go a long way in respect of children's health.

Percentage of Women with Anaemia, 2005–6

Table-54

Name of states	Any anaemia	Moderate anaemia	Severe anaemia
Arunachal Pradesh	50.6	12.5	1.6
Assam	69.5	21.2	3.4
Manipur	35.7	5.1	0.5
Meghalaya	47.2	12.6	1.8
Mizoram	38.6	8.8	0.7
Nagaland	NA	NA	NA
Tripura	65.1	14.8	1.3
Sikkim	60	16.3	1.7
All India	55.3	15	1.8

Source: NFHS 2 and 3.

Anaemia shows the malnutrition of women especially lack of iron in the blood or decline in the level of haemoglobin. Women's health is the most important from the point of view of children health and future human capital formation. The all India level condition is itself very gloomy as 55% women are malnourished while more than 50% in Arunachal Pradesh and 60% in Sikkim. In Assam the situation is formidable as it is near to 70% thus causing danger for pregnant and children. In Manipur and Mizoram the situation is a little better in Tripura once again it is 65.1% women are anaemic.

Percentage of Children with any Anaemia (0–5 years), 2005–6

Table-55

Name of states	Any anaemia	Moderate anaemia	Severe anaemia
Arunachal Pradesh	56.9	29.1	0.8
Assam	69.6	38.7	2.2
Manipur	41.1	15.2	0.3
Meghalaya	64.4	31.7	1
Mizoram	44.2	20	0.6
Nagaland	NA	NA	NA
Tripura	62.9	34.6	0.7
Sikkim	59.2	29.5	0.8
All India	69.5	40.2	2.9

Source: NFHS 3.

The children born with anaemia also show a dismal condition in India. The horrible picture of children health can be understood from the above table. Once again Assam is the most formidable state with nearly 70% children anaemic and more than the national average of 69.5%. Tripura and Meghalaya are along with all India position while other states have kept the level below the national level.

6.2 Women, Child and Reproductive Health: A Comparative Study of Rural-Urban Development in Assam

6.2.1 Introduction to the Issue

As per Population Census, 2011, the rural population of the State was 86 percent of the total population. This percentage was much higher than that for All-India (69 percent). Four–fifths of households in Assam live in rural areas, and one–fifth is in urban areas. On average, households in Assam are comprised of 4.7 members. People in the state now live longer than their parents did, and health profiles have improved. Yet, health indicators in the state reveal inequity – between districts, between income and other groupings. There is a rural – urban divide, reflected across almost all indicators. Life expectancy at birth (LEB), Infant Mortality Rate is one of the lowest among major Indian states. Health parameters today play a vital role in the determination of development goals. Health environment is highly responsible for rural development. This chapter seeks to study rural-urban gap in women, child and reproductive health, access to electricity, access to toilet facility, access to drinking water, regarding health awareness etc. Delivery care, Child immunization, Child feeding practices, Child diseases and Women health awareness etc shall be studied in relation to socio-economic factors. Data has been used from secondary sources and results have been analysed on the basis of them.

6.2.2 Assam - Key Indicators of Rural Development and Health Environment

Table-56

Indicators	Rural	Urban
Population literate age 7+ years (%)	76.4	89.8
Population below age 15 years (%)	32.6	25.6
Mean household size	5.1	4.6
Have electricity (%)	30.3	85.0
Have access to toilet facility	66.2	95.9
Live in a *Kachcha* house	76.5	34.0
Improved source of drinking water	72.9	88.4
Lowest wealth quintile	15.5	15.5
Highest wealth quintile	7.1	54.1

Aware of DOTS (Tuberculosis) (%)	55.7	77.1
Aware of Leprosy Eradication (%)	31.9	62.4
Aware of Malaria/Dengue/ChikunGuinea (%)	89.8	94.8
Aware of Prevention of Sex Selection (%)	24.5	57.6

(Source: NFHS-3, RHS Bulletin, March 2011, M/O Health & F.W.,GOI)

Education, health, living conditions, awareness, etc are important factors of rural development. The literacy rate in Assam shows huge rural urban disparity. The rural literacy is 76.4% while in urban Assam it is 89.8%. Population below 15 years indicates the population which is dependent on the adults and that is much more in rural area with 32.6% while 25.6% in urban areas. Mean household size is also higher in rural area showing more children or bigger family size. There is formidable gap in access to electricity as we see that in rural Assam only 30% of the household are having access to electricity but in urban area it is 85%. Electricity is an important means to improve the human development of the people as well as reduce the health risks and hazards. Regarding toilet facility, 66.2% rural households have access to improved toilet according to the guideline of the Ministry of Health and Family Welfare but once again urban Assam is advanced with 95.9% household access.

In Assam still 76.5% of the rural household live in *Kachcha* houses while it is only 34% in urban areas. 72.9% of the rural household have access to safe drinking water against the 88.4% urban households. In the income and wealth parameter, 15.5% households are in lowest wealth quintile but in the highest wealth quintile only 7.1% of rural households exist against 54.1% urban households. Regarding health awareness urban people are more aware than the rural population. 55.7% of the rural households are aware of the DOTS (Tuberculosis) against the 77.1% urban households. 31.9% rural families are aware of Leprosy Eradication while 62.4% of the urban households know it. Awareness of Malaria/Dengue/ChikunGuinea is 89.8% in rural area against 94.8% in urban area. Awareness of Prevention of Sex Selection is 57.6% in urban area but only 24.5% households in rural Assam know about it.

6.2.3 Results of Women and Reproductive Health

Fertility

Table-57

Fertility	Rural	Urban
Births to women during age 15-19 out of total births (%)	5.4	3.7
Women age 20-24 reporting birth of order 2 & above (%)	41.0	34.1
Women with two children wanting no more children (%)	77.5	86.7
Mean children ever born to women age 40-44 years.	4.0	2.9
Women had primary or secondary infertility (%)	4.8	4.7
Women had problem of obstetric fistula (%)	4.8	3.2

Source: NFHS-3

According to NFHS-3, "Fertility in rural areas, at 2.7 children per woman, is more than one child higher than in urban areas, where the fertility rate, at 1.4 children per woman, is lower than the replacement level of fertility. Among births in the three years preceding the survey, 26 percent were of birth order four or higher". Births to women during age 15-19 out of total births is 5.4% in rural Assam while 3.7% in urban Assam. Women age 20-24 reporting birth of order 2 & above is 34.1% in urban area against 41% in rural area. Women with two children wanting no more children are 77.5% in rural Assam against 86.7% in urban areas. Mean children ever born to women age 40-44 years, women having primary or secondary infertility and women with obstetric fistula are higher in rural Assam than that of urban area.

Family Planning and Contraception

Table-58

Methods	Rural	Urban
Any method (%)	49.7	58.9
Any modern method (%)	29.8	42.2
Female sterilization (%)	9.9	17.0
Male sterilization (%)	0.1	03

Pill (%)	16.4	17.8
IUD (%)	1.5	1.8
Condom (%)	1.9	5.4
Any traditional method (%)	18.6	16.6
Rhythm/Safe period (%)	10.9	10.1
Couple using spacing method for more than 6 months (%)	16.5	20.9
Ever used Emergency Contraceptive Pills (ECP) (%).	1.3	2.0
Currently married non-user women who ever received counselling by health personnel to adopt family planning (%)	16.4	15.5
Current users ever told about side-effects of family planning methods (%)	10.4	9.9
Users who received follow-up services for IUD/sterilization within 48 hours (%)	51.5	61.5

Source: NFHS-3, NRHM Report- 2010-11

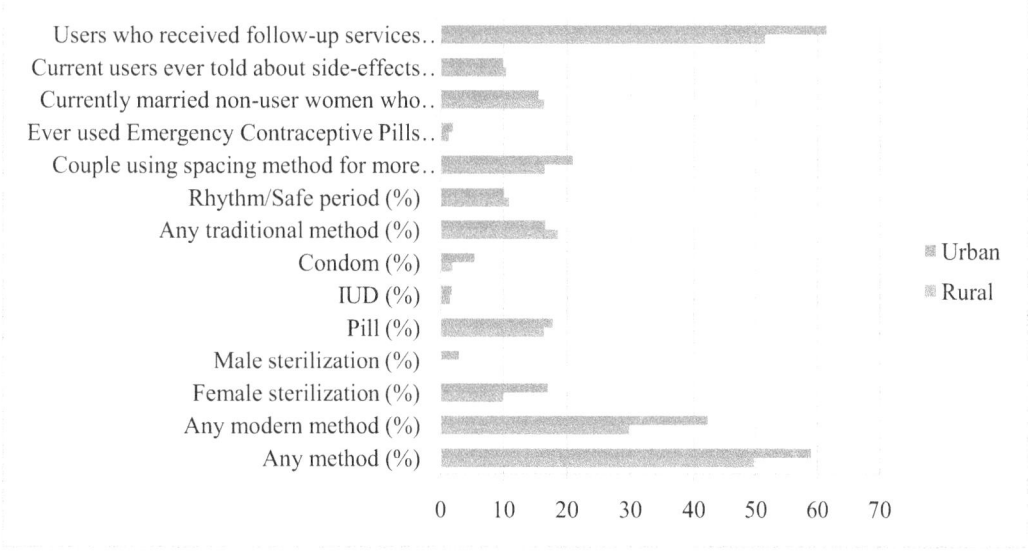

There is wide variety in family planning practices in Assam. Rural-urban divide is vividly seen from the above table. Those who have gone for any method of family planning in the state is 49.7% in rural area while 58.9% in urban area. Modern method appliers are 29.8% in rural area and 42.2% in urban area. Female sterilisation is 9.9% in rural area only against 17%

in urban area. Male sterilisation very low in the state as it is a common perception among the males that sterilisation is completely a matter of women's. However pill takers are 16.4% in rural area while 17.8% in urban area. IUD users are 1.5% in rural area against 1.8% in urban area. Condom users are much higher in urban area with 5.4% in urban area against only 1.9% in rural area. Who have followed any traditional method is 16.6% in urban area against 18.6% in rural area. Rhythm/Safe period is more or less same in the state nearly 10% in both urban and rural area. Couple using spacing method for more than 6 months is 16.5% in rural area while 20.9%in urban area. Ever used Emergency Contraceptive Pills (ECP) is 1.3% in rural area but 2% in urban area. Currently married non-user women who ever received counselling by health personnel to adopt family planning is 16.4% in rural area but 15.5% in urban Assam. Regarding Current users ever told about side-effects of family planning methods and users who received follow-up services for IUD/sterilization within 48 hours are better in urban area than that of rural Assam.

Marriage indicators-

Table-59

Marriage	Rural	Urban
Mean age at marriage for boys (marriages that occurred during the reference period)	26.7	28.5
Mean age at marriage for girls (marriages that occurred during the reference period	20.5	23.2
Boys married below age 21(marriages that occurred during the reference period) (%)	11.8	6.5
Girls married below age 18 (marriages that occurred during the reference period) (%)	22.3	7.7
Currently married women age 20-24 who were married before age 18 (%)	40.5	34.0
Currently married non-literate women (%) (age 15-44)	34.3	14.9
Currently married women with 10 or more years of schooling (%) (age 15-44)	15.1	40.2
Unmarried non-literate women (%).(age 15-24)	7.8	3.6

| Unmarried women with 10 or more years of schooling (%).(age 15-24) | 35.5 | 56.5 |

Source: NFHS-3

We find wide disparity in Assam regarding marriage indicators also. The table and diagram shows that mean age at marriage for boys is 26.7years in rural Assam while 28.5 years in urban areas. Mean age at marriage for girls is 20.5 years against 23.2years in urban area. Marriages occurred below the age of 21 is 11.6% in villages while 6.5% in urban areas. Girls married below age 18 are 22.3% against only 7.7% in urban Assam. Currently married women age 20-24 who was married before age 18 is 40.5% while 34% in towns and cities. Currently married non-literate women (age 15-44) are much higher in rural area with 34.3% but in urban it is only 14.9%. Currently married women with 10 or more years of schooling (age 15-44) are 15.1% in rural Assam against 40.2% in urban area. Unmarried non-literate women (age 15-24) are 3.6% in urban while 7.8% in rural area. Unmarried women with 10 or more years of schooling (age 15-24) are 35.5%in rural area while 56.5% in urban area.

Reproductive and Antenatal care (based on women whose last pregnancy outcome was live/still birth during the reference period)

Table-60

	Rural	Urban
Mothers who received any antenatal check-up (%)	73.3	89.0
Mothers who had antenatal check-up in first trimester (%)	37.2	59.9
Mothers who had three or more ANC (%)	42.2	67.7
Mothers who had at least one tetanus taxied injection (%	67.7	84.9
Mothers whose Blood Pressure (BP) taken (%)	33.3	64.4
Mothers who consumed 100 IFA Tablets (%)	37.3	32.2
Mothers who had full antenatal check-up (%)	7.0	16.1

(Source: NFHS-3, RHS Bulletin, March 2011, M/O Health & F.W.,GOI)

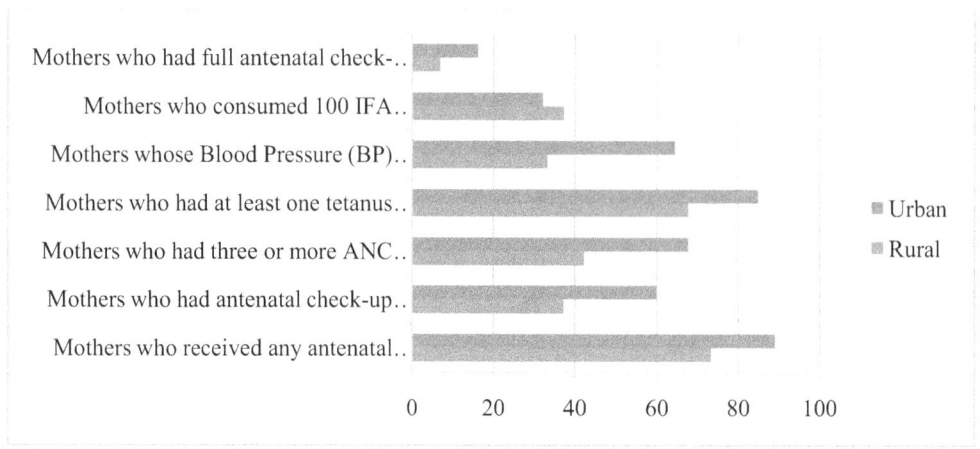

There is wide disparity in the reproductive care in Assam. Reproductive care is very important from the point of view of safe birth and good health of the infant as well as mother. Mothers who received any antenatal check-up are 73.3% in rural area which is much lower than the urban achievement of 89%. Those mothers who have got antenatal check-up in first trimester is 59.9% in urban area while only 37.7% in rural area. Mothers who had three or more ante natal check-up are 42.2% in rural Assam against 67.7% in towns and cities. Mothers who had at least one tetanus taxied injection is 67.7% in villages while 84.9% in town and cities. Urban area has an upper hand in those mothers whose Blood Pressure (BP) is taken with 64.4% against only 33.3% in rural area. However mothers who consumed 100 IFA Tablets is higher in rural area with 37.3% and in urban area it is 32.2%. Mothers who had full antenatal check-up is only 7% in rural Assam against 16.1% in urban area.

Delivery care (based on women whose last pregnancy outcome was live/still birth during reference period)

Table-61

	Rural	Urban
Institutional delivery (%)	32.3	66.8
Delivery at home (%)	66.9	31.3
Delivery at home conducted by skilled health personnel (%)	5.6	6.3
Safe Delivery (%).	37.6	73.1

Mothers who received post-natal care within two weeks of delivery (%)	29.8	62.6
Mothers who received financial assistance for delivery under JSY (%)	25.3	23.9

Source: NFHS-3

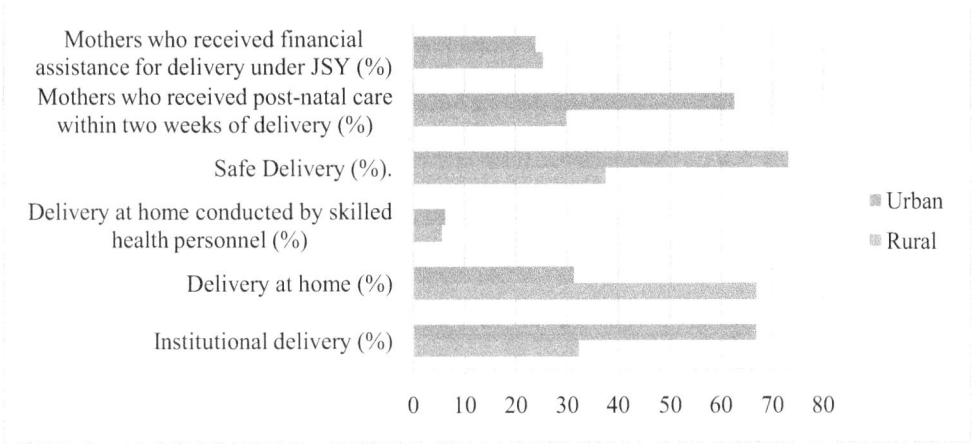

Delivery care is perhaps the most important to ensure safe birth and proper care of the mother and child. Institutional delivery is an important indicator of birth under the supervision of doctor and nurse along with proper care. Institutional delivery is only 32.3% in rural area which indicates a bad picture of delivery care as well as health awareness. In urban area it is 66.8% which indicates sizable number births, more than 30% take place in traditional method. Delivery at home is 66.9% in rural area against 31.3% in urban area. The dangerous picture is that 'Delivery at home' conducted by skilled health personnel is only 5.6% in rural area and 6.3% in urban area. Safe Delivery ensured in the state is 37.6% in rural area while 73.1%in urban area. Mothers who received post-natal care within two weeks of delivery is 29.8% in rural area and 62.6% in urban area. Assam government has started 'Janani Suraksha Yojna' (JSY) for providing incentive and inspiration for 'Institutional delivery'. Mothers who received financial assistance for delivery under JSY is 25.3% in rural Assam while 23.9% in urban area that shows underachievement of the state.

Child health care:-

Table-62

Child Immunization	Rural	Urban
Children 12-23 months fully immunized (%)	50.0	55.3
Children 12-23 months not received any vaccination (%)	11.6	7.2
Children 12-23 months who have received BCG vaccine (%)	83.4	88
Children 12-23 months who have received 3 doses of DPT vaccine (%)	60.0	65.1
Children 12-23 months who have received 3 doses of polio vaccine (%)	64.6	68
Children 12-23 months who have received measles vaccine (%)	63.7	71.2
Children (age 9 months and above) received at least one dose of vitamin A supplement) (%)	46.6	61.2

(Source: NFHS-3, RHS Bulletin, March 2011, M/O Health & F.W., GOI)

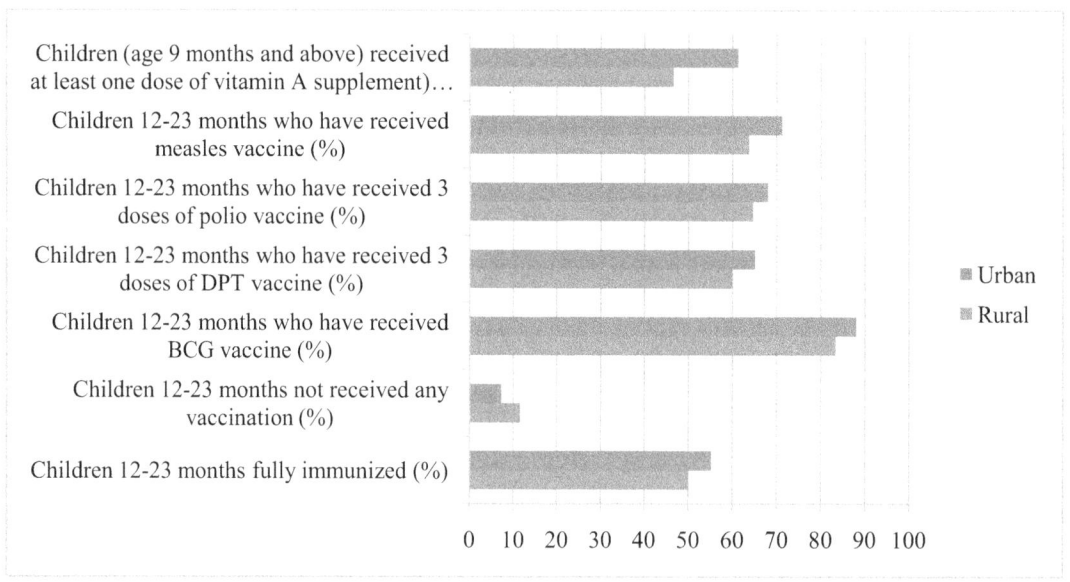

There exists significant distinction between urban and rural area in the achievement regarding child health care. Those children within 2years or 12-23 months who have been fully immunized fully immunized are 50% in rural area but 55.3% in urban area. Actually there is still a long way to go for the state in the immunization of children. Almost half of the children in the state whether rural or urban resident remain deprived of full immunization. Children 12-23 months not received any vaccination are 11.6% in rural area while 7.2% in urban area which shows the vulnerability of the children of our state. Children 12-23 months who have received BCG vaccine is 88% in urban area against 83.4% in rural area. Children 12-23 months who have received 3 doses of DPT vaccine is 60% in rural area while 65.1% in urban area. Children 12-23 months who have received 3 doses of polio vaccine are 64.6% in rural area and 68% in urban area. Children 12-23 months who have received measles vaccine are 63.7% in rural area against 71.2% in urban area. Children (age 9 months and above) received at least one dose of vitamin A supplement) are 46.6% in rural area while 61.2% in urban area.

Child Feeding Practices (based on last-born children) (%)
Table-63

Indicators	Rural	Urban
Children under 3 years breastfed within one hour of birth	66.1	61.0
Children age 0-5 months exclusively breastfed	61.1	70.0
Children age 6-35 months exclusively breastfed for at least 6 months	31.6	37.8
Children age 6-9 months receiving solid/semi-solid food and breast milk	67.4	64.3

Source: NFHS-3

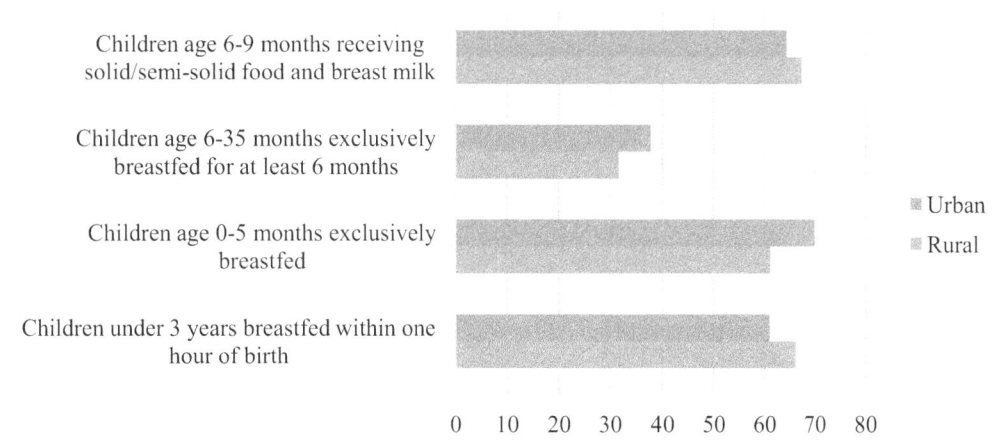

Child feeding practices are also widely skewed in the state. Children under 3 years breastfed within one hour of birth are however better in the rural area with 66.1% and in urban area it is 61%. Children age 0-5 months exclusively breastfed are 61.1% in the rural area while 70% in the urban area. Children age 6-35 months exclusively breastfed for at least 6 months are 31.6% in rural Assam against 37.8%in urban area. This is a formidable situation in our state as 70% of the children of the state are not exclusively breastfed for at least 6 months which affects the children health and growth. Children age 6-9 months receiving solid/semi-solid food and breast milk are 67.4% in rural Assam and 64.3% in urban area.

Treatment of childhood diseases (based on last two surviving children born during the reference period)

Indicators	Rural	Urban
Children with diarrhoea in the last 2 weeks who received ORS (%)	33.3	47.6
Children with diarrhoea in the last 2 weeks who sought advice/treatment (%)	57.8	54.5
Children with acute respiratory infection or fever in last 2 weeks who sought advice/treatment (%)	65.5	75.5

Source: NFHS-3

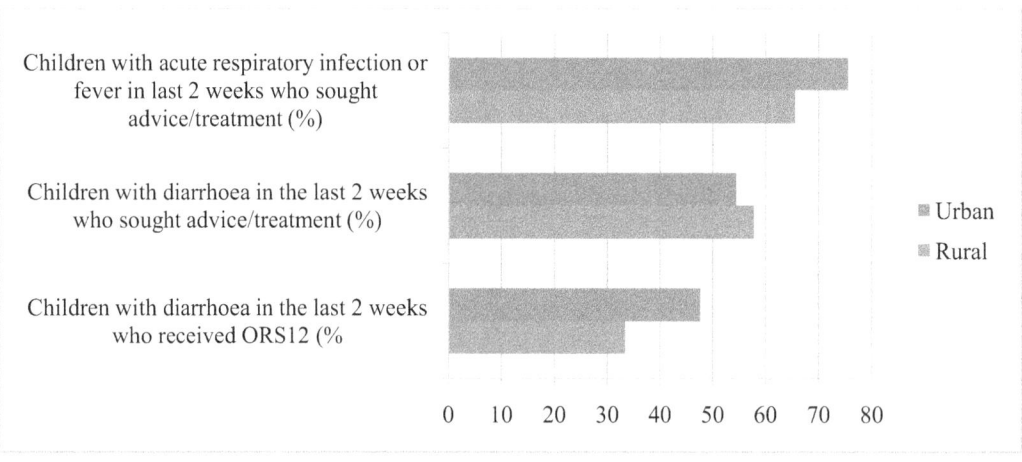

Highly skewed picture is seen between the rural-urban indicators of treatment of childhood diseases. Children with diarrhoea in the last 2 weeks who received ORS are 33.3% in rural area while 47.6 in the urban area. Children with diarrhoea in the last 2 weeks who sought advice/treatment are however more in rural area with 57.8% against urban achievement of 54.5%. Children with acute respiratory infection or fever in last 2 weeks who sought advice/treatment is 65.5% in rural area while 75.5% in urban area. In the state 7% of children under age five had symptoms of an acute respiratory infection (cough and short, rapid breathing that was chest related and not due to a blocked or runny nose). Of these children, 34 percent were taken to a health facility or health provider and 9 percent received antibiotic drugs. Overall, 8 percent of children had diarrhoea, 14% of children under age five years were reported to have had fever in the two weeks preceding the survey.

Health Awareness among women

Table-64

Awareness about Diarrhoea and ARI, RTI/STI and HIV/AIDS

Awareness	Rural	Urban
Women aware about danger signs of ARI	38.1	49.8
Women who have heard of RTI/STI (%)	16.0	23.1
Women who have heard of HIV/AIDS (%)	51.3	82.1
Women who have any symptoms of RTI/STI (%)	28.3	20.0
Women who know the place to go for testing of HIV/AIDS	34.0	47.9
Women underwent test for detecting HIV/AIDS	0.9	1.6

Source: NFHS-3

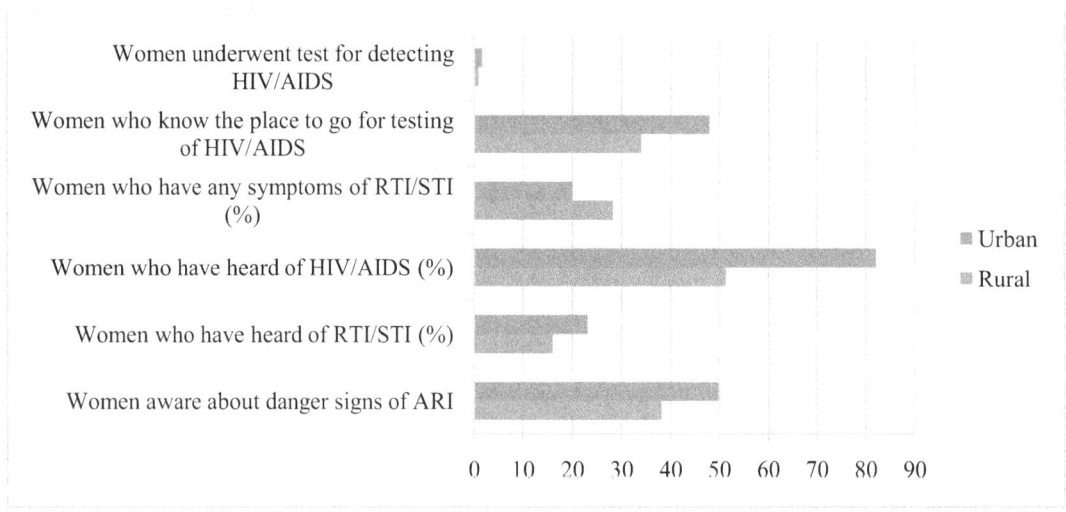

Health awareness shows the possibility of better and quicker treatment as people get more conscious of their health. Women aware about danger signs of ARI are 38.1% in rural area and 49.8% in urban area. Those Women who have heard of RTI/STI are 16% in rural area and 23.1% in urban area. Women who have heard of HIV/AIDS are 82.1% in urban area while much lower in rural area with only 51.3%. Those women who have any symptoms of RTI/STI are 28.3% in rural area against 20% in urban area. Women who know the place to go for testing of HIV/AIDS are 34% in rural area while 47.9% in urban area. Women underwent test for detecting HIV/AIDS are very low in the state.

Chapter 7

A Cross Sectional Data Analysis on Sustainability of Rural Development

-A Study in Barak Valley

7.1 Agriculture and Human Development Performance

7.2 Study of Inter-linkage among Variables

7.3 ADO Circle Wise Performance

7.4 Agriculture and Poverty Interface

7.1 Agriculture and Human Development Performance

Agricultural performance is defined as results/achievements in the field of agriculture. Agricultural production performance has been measured in terms of productivity of the factors of production – land, labour and capital. The level of agricultural productivity that is achieved by producers, however, depends on the effectiveness and efficiency in the operation of markets for both inputs and outputs, and the adequacy of infrastructure, research, technical and financial services. Agricultural Performance Index (API) would comprise the weighted measure of: i) Physical potential – as measured by levels of land fertility, ii) Availability and accessibility of markets, as measured by commercial sale levels of key agricultural commodities; iii) Level of technological achievements (innovations) as measured by use of improved seeds and other modernizing agricultural technologies; and iv) Level of human effort (output per worker), returns to factors of production (land, labour); etc. API is a composite index of all four dimension index having equal weights.

Performance in human development has been measured by achievement in quality of life/standard of living. A composite index has been formed to measure the progress in quality of life by 28 indicators of household- housing characteristics, quality of sanitation, electricity, drinking water, cooking fuel, a bunch of electronic goods, essential goods, vehicles etc. Moreover education index made of literacy level and enrolment, health index made of BMI- Body Mass Index and child mortality have been prepared. Quality of life index is a composite measure of all three dimension indices having equal weights.

Classification of Farm Families (Agriculture Census, 2005-06) in Assam

Table-65

Class	Size of land holdings	Percentage of total farm families
Marginal	Below 1.0 hectare (7.5 bigha)	63.7
Small	1.0 – 2.0 hectare (7.5-15 bigha)	21.5
Semi medium	2.0 – 4.0 hectare (15-30 bigha)	11.6
Medium	4.0 – 10.0 hectare (30-75 bigha)	3.0
Large	10.0 hectare & above (75 bigha & above)	0.2

My study area Barak valley consists of three districts- Cachar, Karimganj and Hailakandi. Primary data has been collected from all the three districts. Multistage sampling has been followed. In the Barak Valley region there are six agricultural subdivisions—(1) Cachar district (3 subdivisions), (2) Karimganj district (2 subdivisions) (3) Hailakandi (1 subdivisions). From each subdivision one ADO circle has been selected subject to the condition that the selected circle represents the entire subdivision. From each ADO circle two villages (one agriculturally developed having at least some marketing network and other agriculturally underdeveloped) has been selected in consultation with Agricultural Development Officer. From the selected villages total sample of 450 farming households (determined on the basis of population size) has been selected for the study.

Land distribution in ADOs (Number of farmers according to land holdings) [1 hectare= 7.5 bigha]

Table-66

ADO	Marginal (Below 1.0 hectare i.e.7.5 Bigha)	Small (1.0 – 2.0 hectare i.e.7.5-15 Bigha)	Semi medium (2.0 – 4.0 hectare i.e.15-30 Bigha)	Medium (4.0 – 10.0 hectare i.e.30-75 Bigha)	Large (10.0 hectare & above i.e.75 Bigha & above)	Total
Dullabcherra	4	34	21	15	1	75
Sadarashi	4	26	27	17	1	75
Arunachal	7	17	29	21	1	75
Sonai	4	25	32	13	1	75
Motinagar	9	29	25	10	2	75
Hailakandi	14	25	27	8	1	75
Total	42	156	161	84	7	450
Percentage of farm families	9.34%	34.67%	35.78%	18.66%	1.55%	100

Source: Calculated by scholar from 450 samples.

The above table depicts the land holdings of the farmers in my study area. Out of 450 samples from 6 ADOs in 3 districts, most of the farmers are small, semi-medium and marginal farmers. The land size has been categorised according to the classification of the government. Land holding below 1 hectare or 7.5 Bigha constitute 9.34% of the total samples while a total of 42 are marginal farmers. Small farmers are those who have land holdings 1-2 hectare or 7.5-15 Bigha of land. They are 20-30 in each ADO and a total of 156 or 34.67%, which indicates that large section of farmers are small farmers. Semi medium farmers are the most in the study as 161 or 35.78% of samples belong to them. They hold 2-4 hectare or 15-30 Bigha of land and 20/ 30 farmers in each ADO. 84 are Medium farmers i.e.18.66% of the total and they hold sizable farm land in Barak Valley. The large scale farmers according to the survey are only 7; as in Barak Valley only a few large scale farmers are there and practise commercial agriculture.

Agricultural Performance Index (API) in Barak Valley

Agriculture constitutes the most significant (and usually also the most important) component of the rural sector in the developing countries, Barak Valley inclusive. The performance of the agricultural sector, therefore, directly impacts on the rural sector as a whole because it employs a large population and utilizes considerable rural resources especially land and labour. However, the concept of rural development is much wider, and includes agricultural and non-agricultural activities. Agricultural production performance has to be measured in terms of productivity of the factors of production – land, labour, capital, raw materials like seed, fertiliser, machines etc. The level of agricultural productivity that is achieved by producers, however, depends on the effectiveness and efficiency in the operation of markets for both inputs and outputs, and the adequacy of infrastructure, research, technical and financial services. These constitute the cornerstone for analysing agricultural performance, and its link to rural and human development.

Agricultural Performance Index (API) would comprise the weighted measure of: i) Physical potential – as measured by levels of land fertility, ii) Availability and accessibility of markets, as measured by commercial sale levels of key agricultural commodities; iii) Level of technological achievements (innovations) as measured by use of improved seeds and other modernizing agricultural technologies; and iv)

Level of human effort (output per worker). API is a composite index of all four dimension indices having equal weights.

7.1.1 Land fertility index

Land fertility denotes the level of output in relation to the size of land. Barak Valley is a land on basin of river Barak and it's tributaries which carry alluvial and sedimentary soil that provides the natural fertility to the agrarian land. Moreover the hardworking farmers make it possible to produce higher output even with the problem of floods and infrastructral bottlenecks.

Land fertility is measured by the output per Bigha. In Assam 7.5 Bigha is equal to 1 hectare of land while output is measured in quintals. Output per Bigha has been calculated by deviding total production of a farmer by the total land under cultivation. Thus production per Bigha of land has been calculated for all 450 samples. Then dimension index for 450 farmers i.e. Land Fertility Index has been calculated by using the formula mentioned in methodology chapter.

Table-67

			Statistic	Std. Error
LFI	Mean		.51419	.007156
	95% Confidence	Lower Bound	.50012	
	Interval for Mean	Upper Bound	.52825	
	5% Trimmed Mean		.51757	
	Median		.52389	
	Variance		.023	
	Std. Deviation		.151807	
	Minimum		-.012	
	Maximum		.978	
	Range		.990	
	Interquartile Range		.191	
	Skewness		-.382	.115
	Kurtosis		.479	.230

Source: Calculated by scholar from 450 samples.

- ❖ The mean Land Fertility Index in Barak Valley is 0.514 which is not bad at all. The Standard Error of the Mean is a measure of how much the value of the mean may vary from repeated samples of the same size taken from the same distribution and the value is 0.007156 in Barak Valley. The 95% Confidence Interval for Mean are two numbers that we would expect 95% of the means from repeated samples of the same size to fall between.
- ❖ The 5% Trimmed Mean is the mean after the highest and lowest 2.5% of the values have been removed and this is 0.517 in Barak Valley.
- ❖ Skewness measures the degree and direction of asymmetry. A symmetric distribution such as a normal distribution has a skewness of 0, a distribution that is skewed to the left, when the mean is less than the median, has a negative skewness, and a distribution that is skewed to the right, when the mean is greater than the median, has a positive skewness. Here the skewness is negative as the value of median is greater than mean and the value is -.382.
- ❖ Kurtosis is a measure of the heaviness of the tails of a distribution. A normal distribution has kurtosis 0. Extremely abnormal distributions may have high positive or negative kurtosis values, while nearly normal distributions will have kurtosis values close to 0. Kurtosis is positive if the tails are "heavier" than for a normal distribution and negative if the tails are "lighter" than for a normal distribution.

Distribution of farmers according to performance in land fertility

Table-68

Indicator	Land fertility index	Indicator	Number of farmers	% of farmers
Mean observation	0.514	Excellent (0.8 & above)	9	2%
Max. observation	0.978	Very good (0.6- 0.8)	127	28%
Min. observation	0.011	Good (0.5- 0.6)	116	26%
		Average (0.4-0.5)	100	22%
		Poor/ Less than average (0.2- 0.4)	85	19%
		Very Poor/Negligible (Below 0.2)	13	3%
		Total	450	100

Source: Calculated by scholar from 450 samples.

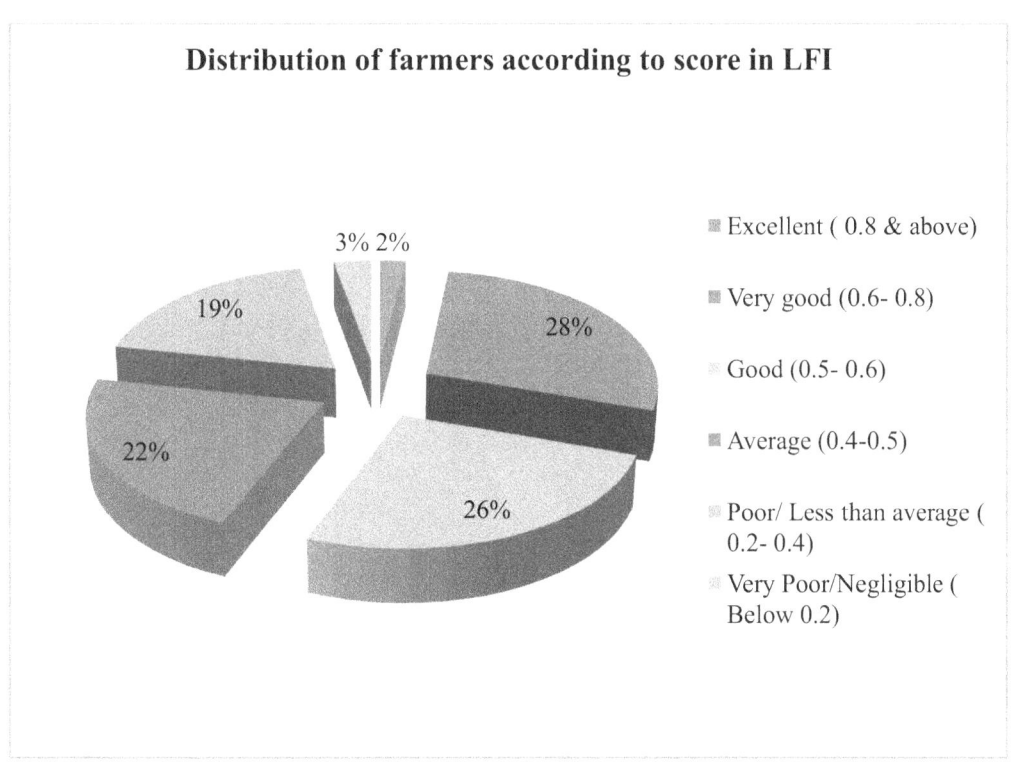

Land fertility index is of huge importance in Barak Valley since the natural fertility of the soil contributes largely for the crop production in right time and in required amount in the midst of infrastructural bottlenecks. Land fertility index has been made to analyse properly the land's contribution in output. The mean observation is 0.514 in Barak Valley which shows moderate performance in this regard.

Now out of 450 sample farmers it has been found that only 9 samples have performed excellent i.e. more than 0.800 value of index. Most of them undoubtedly belong to the big farmers with better irrigation and technology. However the most eyecatching finding is that 127 i.e. the 28% of the farmers have performed in 'very good' club. Most of them are medium, semi-medium farmers having land holding either 15-30 Bigha or 30-75 Bigha. The land fertility from 0.500 to 0.600 has been named as 'good'and out of 450 farmers, 26% i.e. 116 farmers have performed in this group.

From 0.400 to 0.500 is regarded as average performance and in Barak Valley 22% belongs to that group or 100 samples have performed average. 19% samples are regarded as poor because they have scored below 0.400 index value. Total 85 farmers are found to be poor in land fertility index while 13 have performed worst or 3% have index value below 0.200 which is low enough to make any impact on the mean performance of the Valley.

7.1.2 Market index

A market index is calculated to observe the level of commercialisation of agriculture. In Barak Valley, out of 450 samples I have taken their amount of produce that they have sold. The percentage of output sold has been calculated for 450 farmers and dimension index has been found out or market index for 450 samples.

Table-69

			Statistic	Std. Error
MI	Mean		.5266	.01441
	95% Confidence Interval for Mean	Lower Bound	.4983	
		Upper Bound	.5549	
	5% Trimmed Mean		.5318	
	Median		.6100	
	Variance		.093	
	Std. Deviation		.30564	
	Minimum		.00	
	Maximum		1.00	
	Range		1.00	
	Interquartile Range		.52	
	Skewness		-.442	.115
	Kurtosis		-1.089	.230

- The mean Market index is .526 in Barak Valley which is moderate. The Standard Error of the Mean indicates how much the value of the mean may vary from repeated samples of the same size taken from the same distribution and the value is .01441.
- The 95% Confidence Interval for Mean are two numbers that we would expect 95% of the means from repeated samples of the same size to fall between. The 5% Trimmed Mean is .531 in Barak Valley i.e. the mean after the highest and lowest 2.5% of the values have been removed.
- The vriance is .093 and the standard deviation of Market index is .30564.

- ♣ Skewness measures the degree and direction of asymmetry which is -.442 in Barak Valley as the value of median (.610) is is higher than the mean.
- ♣ Kurtosis is a measure of the heaviness of the tails of a distribution while the kurtosis is -1.089. Kurtosis is positive if the tails are "heavier" than for a normal distribution and negative if the tails are "lighter" than for a normal distribution.

Distribution of farmers according to performance in marketing

Tabler-70

Indicator	Market index	Indicator	Number of farmers	% of farmers
Mean observation	0.526	Excellent (0.8 & above)	104	23%
Max. observation	1.00	Very good (0.6- 0.8)	127	28%
Min. observation	0.0	Good (0.5- 0.6)	35	8%
		Average (0.4-0.5)	36	8%
		Poor/ Less than average (0.2- 0.4)	57	13%
		Very Poor/near subsistence (0.1- 0.2)	32	7%
		Scored zero(subsistence farmer)	59	13%
		Total	450	100

Source: Calculated by scholar from 450 samples.

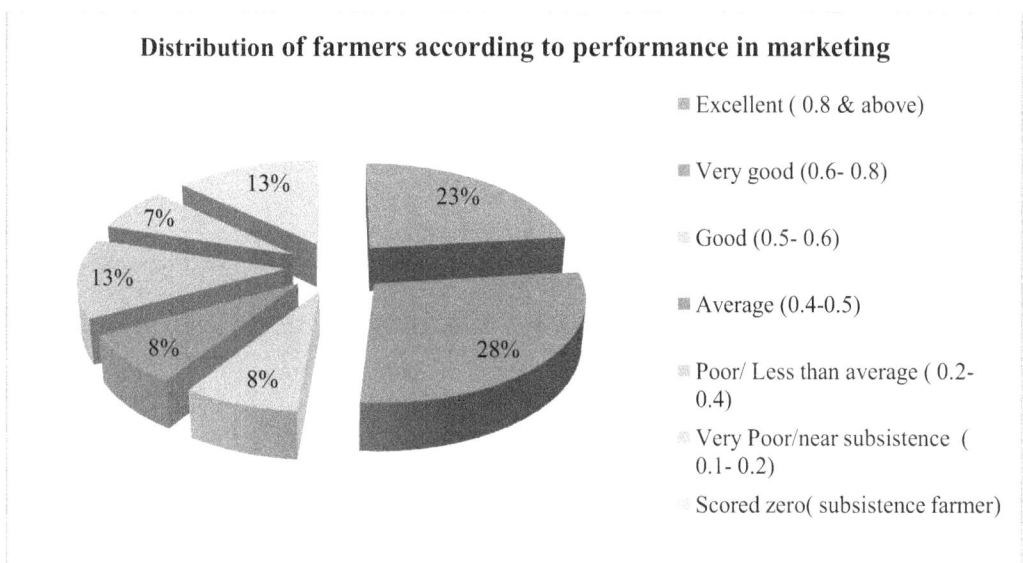

The distribution of farmers according to score in Market index shows that 23% of them have performed in the excellent group i.e. a total of 104 farmers have sold out their 75-95% of the produce in market. Most of these samples belong to medium, semi-medium and large farmers; but some small farmers have also been found during the data collection that they have been able to sell most of their produce. The index value above 0.800 is excellent group and 0.600-0.800 is the very good group. 23% and 28% i.e. a total of 51% farmers are able to market their produce successfully even after so much of infrastructural problems. However the group in the medium level has been found to be low as 8% samples in each of 0.500-0.600 and 0.400-0.500 index value i.e. a total of 35+36=71 samples have perfomed either good or average. 57 samples or 13% have performed badly or less than average with index value 0.200-0.400. another group has been made within 0.100-0.200 as very poor which is 7% of the total. Most of these farmers are marginal and small farmers who face a lot of troubles to sell their output. Most of the part is kept for self while small portion is left for market. 13% of the farmers i.e. 59 have been found to be totally subsistence farmers who sell nothing.

7.1.3 Technology achievement index

Technology Achievement Index is a composite measure of use of improved seeds i.e. HYVseeds and other modernising tools. Adoption of modern technology by the farmers in Barak Valley has been calculated by percentage of output by HYVseeds, use of tractor/powertiller, use of pumpset, use of sprayer, use of harvester/thresher and application of fertiliser & pesticides. All these six dimensions have been given weightage as- 50% for % of output by HYVseeds and 10% weightage for each of the other five dimensions. Thus Technology achievement index for 450 samples have been found out.

Table-71

			Statistic	Std. Error
TAI	Mean		.5428	.01127
	95% Confidence Interval for Mean	Lower Bound	.5206	
		Upper Bound	.5649	
	5% Trimmed Mean		.5428	
	Median		.6000	
	Variance		.057	
	Std. Deviation		.23907	
	Minimum		.10	
	Maximum		1.00	
	Range		.90	
	Interquartile Range		.27	
	Skewness		-.282	.115
	Kurtosis		-.419	.230

♣ The mean Technology Achievement index is .542 in Barak Valley which is moderate. The Standard Error of the Mean indicates how much the value of the mean may vary from repeated samples of the same size taken from the same distribution and the value is .01127.

♣ The 95% Confidence Interval for Mean are two numbers that we would expect 95% of the means from repeated samples of the same size to fall between. The 5% Trimmed

Mean is .542 in Barak Valley i.e. the mean after the highest and lowest 2.5% of the values have been removed.

♣ The vriance is .057 and the standard deviation of Technology Achievement index is .239.

♣ Skewness measures the degree and direction of asymmetry which is -.282 in Barak Valley as the value of median (.60) is higher than the mean.

♣ Kurtosis is a measure of the heaviness of the tails of a distribution while the kurtosis is -.419. Kurtosis is positive if the tails are "heavier" than for a normal distribution and negative if the tails are "lighter" than for a normal distribution.

Distribution of farmers according to performance in technology adoption
Table-72

Indicator	Technology achievement index	Indicator	Number of farmers	% of farmers
Mean observation	0.542	Excellent (0.9 & above)	41	9%
Max. observation	1.00	Very good (0.8- 0.9)	43	9.01%
Min. observation	0.0	Good (0.6-0.8)	143	32%
		Average (0.5-0.6)	63	14%
		Poor/ Less than average (0.4- 0.5)	66	15%
		Very poor/ bad performance	94	21%
		Total	450	100

Source: Calculated by scholar from 450 samples.

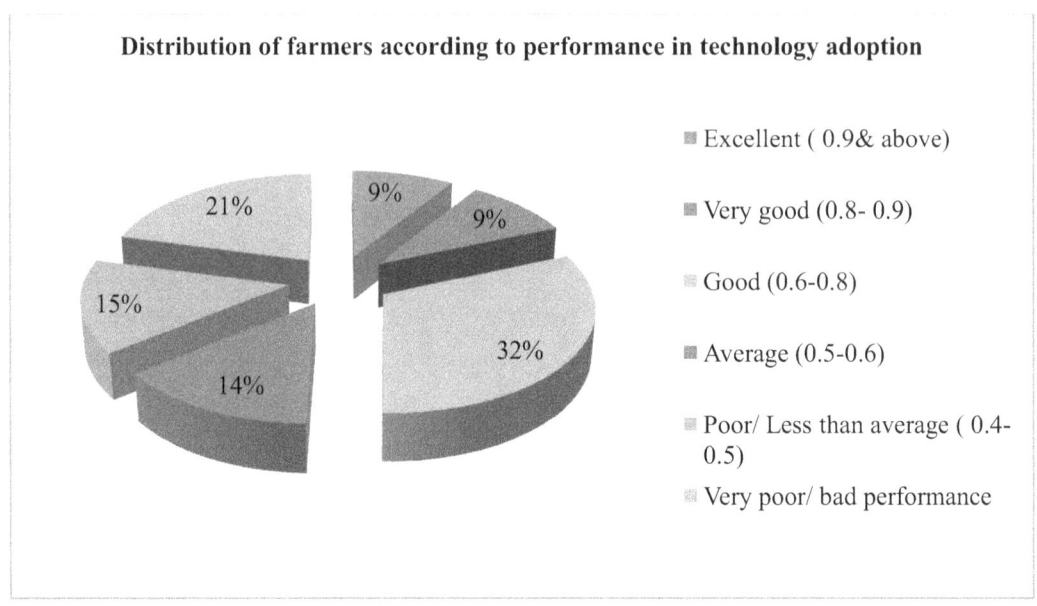

The technology achievement index is 0.542 which is good in the circumstances of Barak Valley. The distribution of farmers shows that those who have performed moe than index value of 0.900 is regarded as excellent and 41 farmers have been found to belong to this group. The cryteria of excellent has changed a little because of the differenceof definition of the index. 50% weightage has been given to HYVseeds and 10% to each of the use of tractor/powertiller, use of pumpset, use of sprayer, use of harvester/thresher and application of fertiliser & pesticides. The index value with 0.800-0.900 is regarde as very good and 9% belongs to this group. 146 or 32% belongs to 'good' category while 14% are average performer. Poor performance came from 15% or 66 farmers. Very poor or bad performers are 21% or 94 in number. This group has very poor access to modern technology.

Technology adoption in Barak Valley

Table-73

% of output by HYV seeds	Number of farmers	% of farmers
100% or entire output by HYV seeds	136	30%
90% output	12	3%
85% output	12	3%
80% output	41	9%
75% output	11	2%
70% output	64	14%
65% output	32	7%
60% output	26	6%
50% output	23	5%
45% output	8	2%
40% output	14	3%
30% output	7	2%
0% or entire output by Traditional seed	64	14%
Total	450	100

Source: Calculated by scholar from 450 samples.

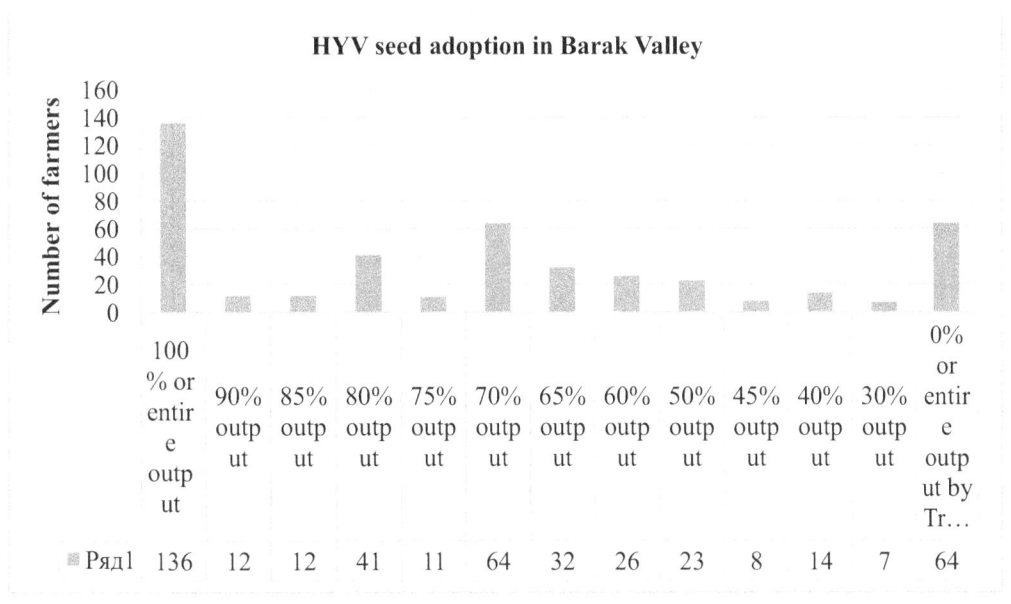

Technology adoption or access to modern technology is a major leap forward anywhere in the world for agricultural development. Green revolution in India took place only after successful implementation of technical change in agrarian practices though may be in a few states or in few areas. In Barak Valley technology adoption has been undergoing a slow progress mainly due to lack of proper government steps in developing the infrastructure like transport and communication mainly with the other parts of the country, warehousing facilities for the better crops so that farmers can be able to market their output at due prices. Even after that farmers have been showing interest in adoption of modern technology for higher output.

Table summary

- ❖ The above table depicts the percentage of sample farmers about their crop production and % of the crop covered by HYV seeds. A total of 136 farmers or 30% of the farmers are there who have transferred completely to the new seeds i.e. entire output has been covered by HYV seeds. This adoption level is significant remembering the precondtions of agriculture in Barak Valley.
- ❖ 12 or 3% of the farmers have produced 90% of their output by new seeds. 12 or 3% are there who produced 85% of their output by new seeds. 80% of the crop is coverd by 41 farmers or 9% of them.
- ❖ 2% or 11 have produced 75% of their output by HYVseeds. A total of 64 farmers or 14% of them covered 70% of the crop by HYVseeds. It makes the 2nd highest peak/column in the diagram. 32 farmers or 7% have produced 65% of theiroutput by new seeds. 26 or 6% samples have covered 60% of the crop by new seeds.
- ❖ 5% or 23 have covered 50% or half of the output by HYV seeds. 2% or 8 have gone covering 45% of their crop by new seeds. 14 farmers have produced 40% of the output by HYV seed. 7 have produced 30% of the crop by new seeds.
- ❖ While the non-adopters have matched with the 2nd peak in the diagram i.e. the traditional seed users are still 14% of the total farmers in Barak Valley.

Access to modern tools and techniques begins with High Yeilding Variety (HYV) of seeds. HYV seed has the advantage of quicker matuirity along with higher quantity than that of traditional seed. Among the HYV seeds the species or types popular among the farmers of Barak Valley are-

HYV seed features observed during the survey

Table-74

Major HYV seeds of Barak Valley	Duration of maturity
Pankaj (Winter Rice-Sali)	145-150 days
Ranjit (Winter Rice-Sali)	150-155 days
Lakhimi (Winter Rice-Sali)	140-150 days
Bahadur (Winter Rice-Sali)	150-155 days
Kushal (Winter Rice-Sali)	150-155 days
KMJ 10-2-2 (Winter Rice-Sali)	150-155 days
TTB 101-15 (Winter Rice-Sali)	150-155 days
Satya (Winter Rice-Sali)	130-135 days
Monohar Sali (Winter Rice-Sali)	155-160 days
Swarnaprova (Winter Rice-Sali)	115-120 days
IR-50 (Summer Rice-Auose)	105-110 days
Govind (Summer Rice-Auose)	100-105 days
Rasi (Summer Rice-Auose)	120-125 days
IR-36 (Summer Rice-Auose)	130-140 days
Kalang Barak (Sugarcane)	60-80 days

Apart from them many other HYV varieties are their in Barak Valley which are extensively used by the farmers to produce different vegetables and other horticultural crops in summer and winter season. HYV seeds are in the need of better irrigation facilities which is very poor in Barak Valley, even then they are not lagging behind in adopting HYVseeds. The output will definitely grow more if the irrigation facility is improved.

Adoption of machines, tools etc.

Table-75

Indicator	Adopted	% of adoption	Not adopted
Tractor/powertiller	222	49.33%	228
Pumpset	101	22.44%	349
Sprayer	126	28%	324
Harvester /thresher	30	6.66%	410
Fertiliser/pesticide	450	100%	0

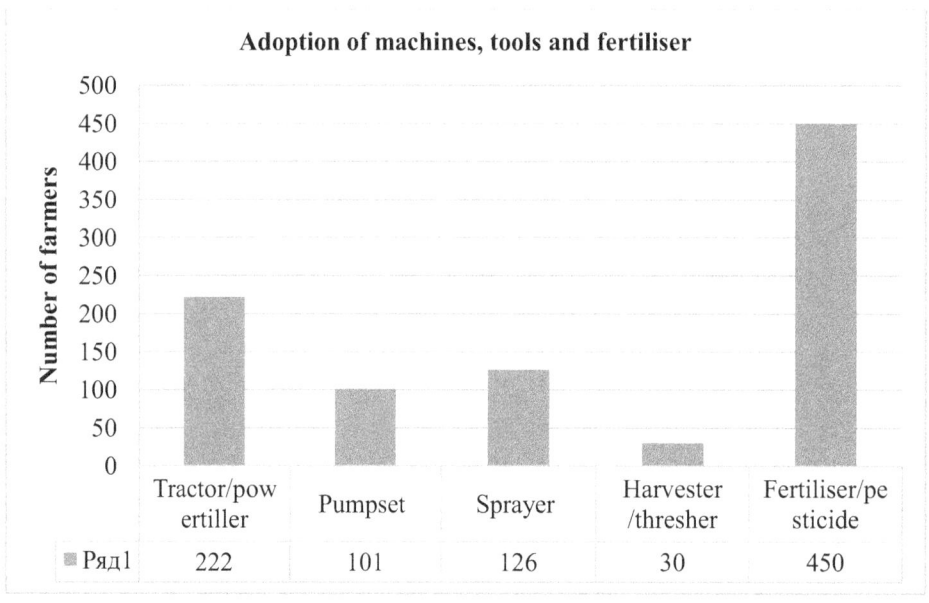

Table summary

- ❖ The above table shows some interesting results about the technology addption in Barak Valley, more specifically about the trend of farm mechanisation. 49.33% of the farmers in Barak Valley have gone for utilizing tractor or powertiller for tiiling of the land. Most of the farmers who have tractors for tilling the land are big farmers having land holding more than 75 Bigha or the medium level farmers having land holding 30-

75 Bigha. Certainly all of them do not own tractors rather most of them hire for tilling the land. However most of the 222 farmers own powertiller while semi-medium and small farmers hire powertiller to till the farm land.

- ❖ The pumpset is an important item for watering the land in Barak Valley. The pumpset users are 22.44% of the total or 101 out of 450 samples. Since there is shortage or absence of major or medium irrigation projects, most of the land in this Valley are not covered by irrgation. As a result pumpset is a major equipment to provide water in the land with the help of electricity from nearby source, mostly nearby pond or river. Howevevr most of the farmers in Barak valley still depend on the nature or monsoon for water. If there is much rain, farm land is flooded or in case of less rain it suffers from drought.
- ❖ 28% of the total or 126 farmers have reported to own and apply sprayer for spraying pesticides. Harvester or thresher users are only 6.66% while almost every farmer or 100% have started using chemical manures and pesticides.

7.1.4 Labour Productivity Index

Labour Productivity Index is prepared to measure the efficacy of human labour. LPI is calculated as output per worker of each sample. From the data of total output and total number of workers, output per worker has been claculated while on the basis of output per worker, dimension index has been found out for 450 samples by using the formula mentioned in methodology chapter.

Table-76

			Statistic	Std. Error
LPI	Mean		.29098	.005969
	95% Confidence	Lower Bound	.27925	
	Interval for Mean	Upper Bound	.30271	
	5% Trimmed Mean		.28510	
	Median		.28006	
	Variance		.016	
	Std. Deviation		.126626	
	Minimum		.000	
	Maximum		1.000	
	Range		1.000	
	Interquartile Range		.158	
	Skewness		1.016	.115
	Kurtosis		2.903	.230

- ♣ The mean Labour Productivity index is .290 in Barak Valley which is less than the average. The Standard Error of the Mean indicates how much the value of the mean may vary from repeated samples of the same size taken from the same distribution and the value is .005969.
- ♣ The 95% Confidence Interval for Mean are two numbers that we would expect 95% of the means from repeated samples of the same size to fall between. The 5% Trimmed

Mean is .285 in Barak Valley i.e. the mean after the highest and lowest 2.5% of the values have been removed.

♣ The vriance is .016 and the standard deviation of Labour Productivity index is .126.

♣ Skewness measures the degree and direction of asymmetry which is positive with 1.016 in Barak Valley as the value of median (.28) is lower than the mean.

♣ Kurtosis is a measure of the heaviness of the tails of a distribution while the kurtosis is 2.903. Kurtosis is positive if the tails are "heavier" than for a normal distribution and negative if the tails are "lighter" than for a normal distribution.

Distribution of farmers according to performance in labour productivity

Table-77

Indicator	Labour productivity index	Indicator	Number of farmers	% of farmers
Mean observation	0.290	Excellent (0.8 & above)	2	0.44%
Max. observation	1.00	Very good (0.6-0.8)	5	1%
Min. observation	0.024	Good (0.5-0.6)	22	5%
		Average (0.4-0.5)	45	10%
		Poor/ Less than average (0.2-0.4)	265	59%
		Very poor/ bad performance (<0.2)	111	25%
		Total	450	100

Source: Calculated by scholar from 450 samples.

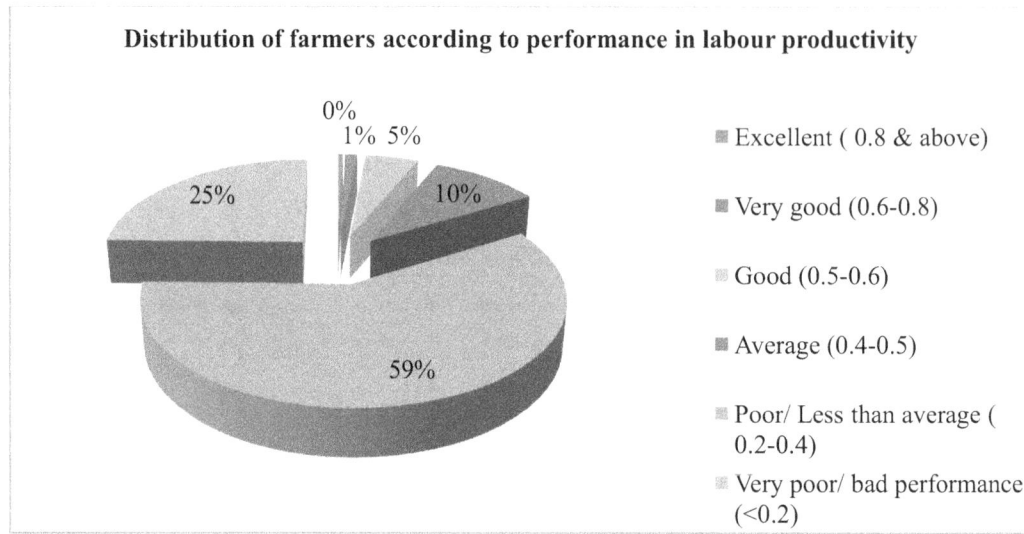

- The labour productivity index in Barak Valley is 0.290 which looks less than average. The farmers more than index value of 0.800 are regarded excellent category are only 0.44%% of the samples or only 2 out of 450 farmers. However the very good farmers are those who have scored 0.600-0.800 index value. They are 5 in total and only 1% of the total sample households. The productivity of these two group of farmers are obviously very high and they belong to wealthy class.

- The good performers are those who have scored in between 0.500-0.600 and average performers are those with value 0.400-0.500. There are 5% or 22 farmers in 'good' and 10% or 45 farmers in average category respectively. Their index values are moderate through out the study area which means the productivity is of medium class.

- The most important finding is that 59% of the farmers do belong to poor performance club. The index score of 0.200-0.400 are the highest in the study area. The productivity of the labour depends however on many other factors like mechnisation, size of the land etc but the poor productivity of the labour is of serious concern in Barak Valley. The higher dependence on agriculture along with excess pressure of population also determines the low level of labour productivity.

- The very poor or negligible performers belong to the last category as they have performed below 0.200 index value. Threre are 111 or 25% farmers who have given bad performance.

7.1.5 Agricultural Performance Index in Barak Valley

Agricultural performance is a measure of the changes (positive or negative) in the principal variables that constitute the agricultural sector. The study has considered all aspects related to farm practices to include in performance so that an agricultural index can be able to present the entire scenario of agriculture and rural development. Agricultural Performance Index is a composite index of all four dimension index-Land Fertility Index, Market Index, Technology Achievement Index and Labour Productivity Index having equal weights.

Table-78

			Statistic	Std. Error
API	Mean		.46847	.007556
	95% Confidence Interval for Mean	Lower Bound	.45362	
		Upper Bound	.48332	
	5% Trimmed Mean		.46915	
	Median		.48011	
	Variance		.026	
	Std. Deviation		.160287	
	Minimum		.071	
	Maximum		.854	
	Range		.783	
	Interquartile Range		.245	
	Skewness		-.102	.115
	Kurtosis		-.659	.230

- The mean Agricultural Performance index is .468 in Barak Valley which is moderate. The Standard Error of the Mean indicates how much the value of the mean may vary from repeated samples of the same size taken from the same distribution and the value is .007556.

- The 95% Confidence Interval for Mean are two numbers that we would expect 95% of the means from repeated samples of the same size to fall between. The 5% Trimmed Mean is .469 in Barak Valley i.e. the mean after the highest and lowest 2.5% of the values have been removed.
- The vriance is .026 and the standard deviation of Agricultural Performance index is .160.
- Skewness measures the degree and direction of asymmetry which is negative with -.102 in Barak Valley as the value of median (.480) is higher than the mean.
- Kurtosis is a measure of the heaviness of the tails of a distribution while the kurtosis is -.659. Kurtosis is positive if the tails are "heavier" than for a normal distribution and negative if the tails are "lighter" than for a normal distribution.

Distribution of farmers according to score in API

Table-79

Indicator	Agricultural Performance index	Indicator	Number of farmers	% of farmers
Mean observation	0.468	Excellent (0.8& above)	2	1%
Max. observation	0.854	Very good (0.6-0.8)	101	22%
Min. observation	0.071	Good (0.5-0.6)	102	23%
		Average (0.4-0.5)	87	19%
		Poor/ Less than average (0.2-0.4)	132	29%
		Very poor/ bad performance (<0.2)	26	6%
		Total	450	100

Source: Calculated by scholar from 450 samples.

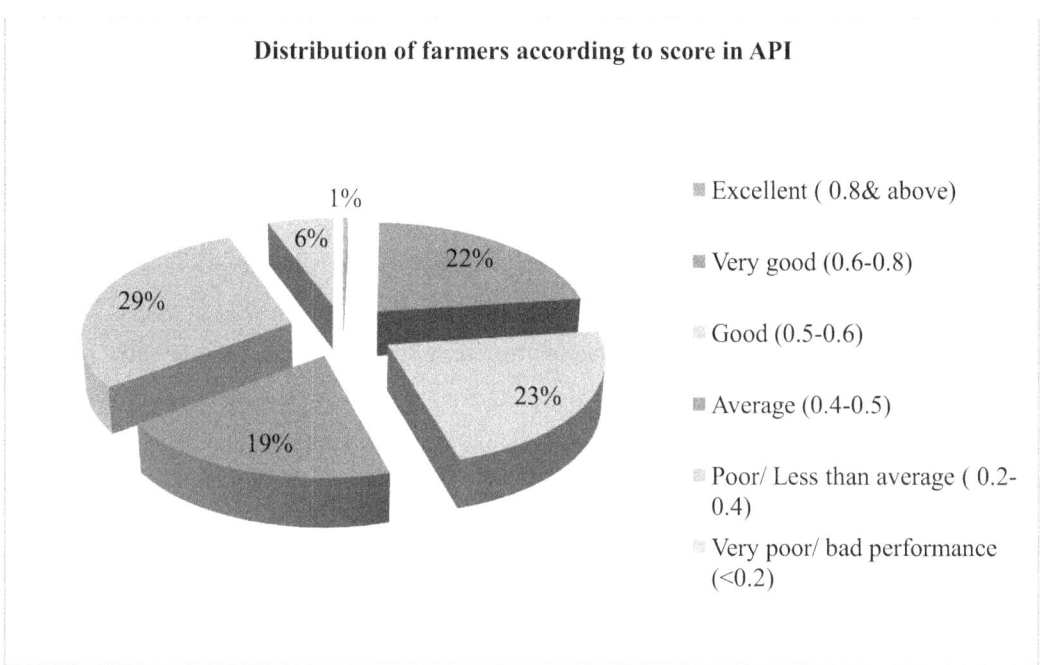

Table summary

- The mean value of Agricultural Performance Index is 0.468 in Barak Valley which shows moderate achievement regading entire agrarian system. The maximum or the best perfomer scored 0.854 who is sample-56 belonging to Dullabcherra ADO circle. The minimum one is the 0.071 or sample-302 in Motinagar ADO and 0.072 i.e. sample-83 in Sadarashi ADO. Those who have scored more than 0.800 index value belongs to the excellent group and they are only 6 in the study area i.e. only 1% of the total households. Agricultural performance is indicative of all aspects of agricultural development land fertility or lbour efficacy or technology or marketing. Thus the API in Barak Valley shows the medium or moderate performance.
- 101 farmers or 22% farmers in Barak Valley denote that they belong to good performer's club. Most of them have performed well in technology achievement or marketing of the crop. Their performance lies in between 0.600 to 0.800 index value.
- 23% farmers or a total of 102 samples performed 0.500 to 0.600 group known as good. Moreover the average performers with index value in between 0.400 to 0.500 are 19% of the farmers or a total of 87 in number. They form a sizable section of farmers in Barak Valley who produce and market the largest amount of crop in Barak

Valley. Those producers with high index value of 0.700 or 0.750 or more than 0.800 are very few in number. On the other hand those who performed at lower index value can not contribute much to the total crop or maketable surplus. Thus farmers with average or medium index value are more in number and contribute the most to the agrcultural output of the Valley.

- However the farmers with index value of 0.200 to 0.400 are not less in nuber. They form 29% of the farming community of the Valley and a total of 132 in my study area. They are regarded as poor performers or unable to utilise the resource properly. Their farm land is overcrowded and output per worker is low. Not only labour productivity the performance in technology adoption or marketing of crops have been low. The lower index indicates that there is misuse and nonutilization of resource properly, moreover the steps to remove their inability is also very poor.
- 6% performers are there whose index result is below 0.200 which is low enough to be included in the efficiency analysis. They performed badly and are mostly marginal farmers who struggle everyday to earn two square meals for their family.

Human Development Performance in Barak Valley

It is measured by three dimension indices- wealth index, educaion index and health index. The human dvelopment is denoted by QLI or Quality of Life Index which is calculated by the three indices having equal weightage. Let us analyse them one by one.

7.1.6 Wealth index

Wealth index does not mean that it has been calculated by only property and income of the farmers, rather wealth index is a composite measure of 28 all such indicators which include every facets of human life and his/her different choices. They are 1) House type 2)Separate room for cooking/Kitchen 3) Ownership of house 4) Flooring 5) Toilet facility 6) Source of Electricity/Lighting 7) Main fuel for cooking 8) Source of Drinking Water 5) Car or Tractor 9) Moped or Scooter 10) Telephone 11) Refrigerator 12) Colour TV 13) Black and white TV 14) Bicycle 15) Electric fan 16) Radio 17) Sewing machine 18) Mattress 20) Pressure cooker 21) Chair 22) Cot or bed 23) Table 24) Clock or watch 25) Ownership of livestock 26) Water pump 27) Bullock cart 28) Thresher. These indicators have been given weights and scores. On the basis of individual scores of 450 samples, dimension index or wealth index has been made.

Table-80

			Statistic	Std. Error
WI	Mean		.56067	.007160
	95% Confidence Interval for Mean	Lower Bound	.54659	
		Upper Bound	.57474	
	5% Trimmed Mean		.55849	
	Median		.56000	
	Variance		.023	
	Std. Deviation		.151895	
	Minimum		.260	
	Maximum		.980	
	Range		.720	
	Interquartile Range		.200	
	Skewness		.217	.115
	Kurtosis		-.549	.230

- The mean of Wealth Index is .560 in Barak Valley which is moderate. The Standard Error of the Mean indicates how much the value of the mean may vary from repeated samples of the same size taken from the same distribution and the value is .007160.
- The 95% Confidence Interval for Mean are two numbers that we would expect 95% of the means from repeated samples of the same size to fall between. The 5% Trimmed Mean is .558 in Barak Valley i.e. the mean after the highest and lowest 2.5% of the values have been removed.
- The vriance is .023 and the standard deviation of Wealth Index is .151.
- Skewness measures the degree and direction of asymmetry which is positive with .217 in Barak Valley as the value of median (.560) is close to equality with the mean.
- Kurtosis is a measure of the heaviness of the tails of a distribution while the kurtosis is -.549. Kurtosis is positive if the tails are "heavier" than for a normal distribution and negative if the tails are "lighter" than for a normal distribution.

Distrbution of farmers according to Wealth Index

Table-81

Indicator	Wealth index	Indicator	Number of farmers	% of farmers
Mean observation	0.560	Rich (0.9 & above)	5	1%
Max. observation	0.980	Upper middle class (0.8-0.9)	29	6%
Min. observation	0.260	Middle class(0.6-0.8)	152	34%
		Lower middle class (0.5-0.6)	111	25%
		Poor (0.5-0.3)	144	32%
		Very poor (<0.3)	9	2%
		Total	450	100

Source: Calculated by scholar from 450 samples.

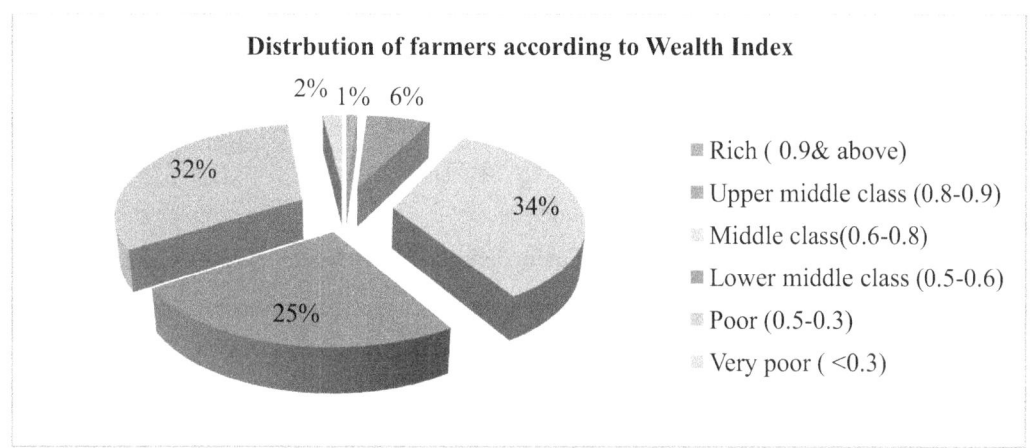

Table summary

- Wealth index is a composite measure of economic and social parameter of life of a man. It includes different facets of human life comprising essential household commodities, utility services or basic civil amenities, electronic gadgets, vehicles etc. The parameter is not only indicative of economic richness rather social and environmental aspects of human life. On the basis of above mentioned 28 indicators the index value of more than 0.900 is regarded as rich man's club. In Barak Valley only 1% of the farmers are big landlords who belong to this group while only 5 in my study area who have performed more than 0.900. The richest sample in the study area is of the index value of 0.980 almost having everything of all 28 indicators and it is the sample-245 and the poorest one is the sample-417 with 0.260 index value.

- The samples close to the rich but below the rich are known as upper middle class who form 6% of the farmers in Barak Valley or a total of 29. The middle class farmers make sizable distinction in my study area, they constitute 34% or 152 of the total. The index value of 0.800 to 0.900 makes the upper section and 0.600 to 0.800 makes moderate section. They are the farmers who contribute the most in Barak Valley's agricultural production. They not only produce surplus above the family consumption but also are able to sell it in the market. Their level of living is at par with the middle class population of the valley or the state or the country even. They can be called middle class rural people who keep the rural market active for not only agro consumption but also cosumption of manufacturing goods including homecare,

- processed food, electronic goods, sometimes conspicuous consumption also like car/truck/computer & internet.
- Lower middle class farmers are no less in Barak Valley but they make the level of living which is just above the poor people. They constitute 25% or 111 of the farming community. They can not maintain the living standard of the middle class but always try to follow that. They scored in between 0.500-0.600. They can consume the essential goods of life but it is difficult for them to purchase conspicuous items.
- A sizable section of our farmers are poor, they form the 2nd largest portion of the distribution in the pie diagram with 32% of the farmers belonging to them while they scored in between 0.300 to 0.500. most of them are small and marginal farmers whose standard of living is hard and fast. They struggle to earn even the essential needs of their life. Those who form the poorest club maintain a formidable living style which constitute 2% of the total farmers in Barak Valley.

One thing has to be noted here. There are farmers making almost 40% of the samples scoring 0.600 or above. But it does not mean that they maintain a much easier life than the other 60% samples. Farmers in Barak Valley can not maintain or purchase gadgets with only agricultural income except those rich and upper middle class farmers. In my study area one interesting feature is that most of the middle class and lower middle class farmers who form 25%+32%=59% i.e. almost 60% of the samples earn non-agricultural income more/less which help a lot to maintain a better life.

7.1.7 Education in Barak Valley

Education is one of the most important aspect of human development. Education index is prepared to analyse the level of improvement in social development parameter. In Barak Valley education has played an important role in fostering human development. Education index is measured by two dimensions- literacy level and child enrolment. Literacy rate can not give any variation in household level indices, moreover it has some limitations to exhibit the education level properly. That is why level of schooling/litercy level is a better parameter along with child enrolment. Level of schooling of farmers in Barak Valley and child enrolment have been given equal weights and dimension index/education index has been prepared at household level for 450 farmers of the Valley.

Here the Literacy Index or Schooling Index of farmers is dicussed below-

Table-82

			Statistic	Std. Error
LI	Mean		.50047	.010132
	95% Confidence Interval for Mean	Lower Bound	.48056	
		Upper Bound	.52039	
	5% Trimmed Mean		.50357	
	Median		.53300	
	Variance		.046	
	Std. Deviation		.214941	
	Minimum		.000	
	Maximum		1.000	
	Range		1.000	
	Interquartile Range		.334	
	Skewness		-.370	.115
	Kurtosis		-.091	.230

- The mean of Literacy Index is .500 in Barak Valley which is moderate. The Standard Error of the Mean indicates how much the value of the mean may vary from repeated samples of the same size taken from the same distribution and the value is .010132.
- The 95% Confidence Interval for Mean are two numbers that we would expect 95% of the means from repeated samples of the same size to fall between. The 5% Trimmed Mean is .503 in Barak Valley i.e. the mean after the highest and lowest 2.5% of the values have been removed.
- The vriance is .046 and the standard deviation of Literacy Index is .214.
- Skewness measures the degree and direction of asymmetry which is negative with -.370 in Barak Valley as the value of median (.533) is higher than the mean.
- Kurtosis is a measure of the heaviness of the tails of a distribution while the kurtosis is -.91. Kurtosis is positive if the tails are "heavier" than for a normal distribution and negative if the tails are "lighter" than for a normal distribution.

Distribution of farmers according to score in Literacy index

Table-83

Indicator	Education index	Indicator	Number of farmers	% of farmers
Mean observation	0.500	Excellent (0.8 & above)	32	7%
Max. observation	1.00	Very good (0.6-0.8)	157	35%
Min. observation	0.00	Good (0.5-0.6)	76	17%
		Average (0.4-0.5)	68	15%
		Poor/ Less than average (0.2-0.4)	74	16%
		Very poor/ bad performance (<0.2)	44	10%
		Total	450	100

Source: Calculated by scholar from 450 samples.

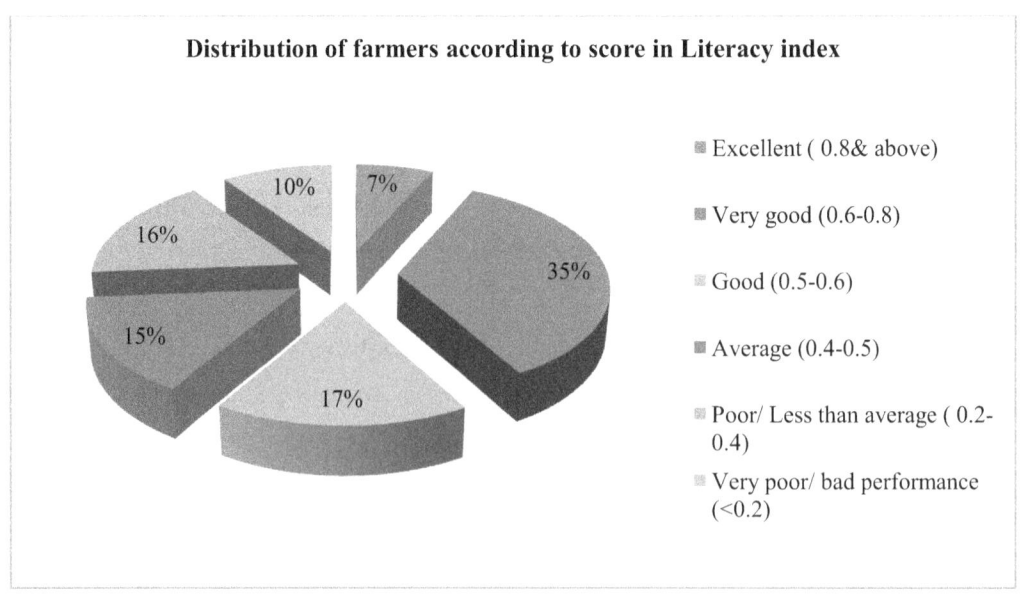

Table interpretation

- Literacy index shows moderate performance in Barak Valley by the farmers. The mean index is 0.500. The highest performers are sample-1,16,20,103,107,206,210,242,246,293,297,395,435 with index value of 1.00 which means they completed graduation. The lowest value is 0.00 which means illiteracy of the farmers. The excellent performers are 32 or 7% of the total in Barak Valley as they have scored more than 0.800 index. These farmers are mostly college educated. This higher education index is however very few.

- The 2nd group of samples make a sizable part of the study area. They are 'very good' group who have achieved index 0.600 to 0.800. They constitute 35% of the total samples. These group has mostly achieved school education. One important feature or change has been noticed during the survey that their attitude towards education has improved a lot. They can understand the importance of education in life and very much eager to send their children to schools. Now they have statrted to believe that education can change the life of people and has the potentiality to improve their honour and esteem.

- The third group of farmers are those who scored in between 0.500 to 0.600 and form 17% of the total samples. One important feature is that almost all of them have gone to the schools but could not continue miuch after 4 /5 /6 /7 years of schooling. They are no doubt literate and belong to the 'good' category of farmers in Literacy index.

- The next group constitutes average performers who scored in between 0.400 to 0.500. They are also literate but could achieve very low level of schooling and one interesting feature is that the number of school dropout children are the highest among them. They form 15% of the total samples or 68 in number.

- Another group of farmers are there who scored in between 0.200 to 0.400 and constitute 16% of the total samples of the study area or 74 in number. They are the farmers who are regarded to perform poorly in Literacy index. They have shown ignorance about the importance of education.

- A sizable section of the farmers in Barak Valley are still illiterate or literate just in name. They are ignorant of their own education as well as education of their children. They constitute 10% of the farmers in Barak Valley who scored below 0.200 index value.

A separate table has been presented below which shows level of schooling of the farmers in Barak Valley. The achievement in schooling denotes that they are getting conscious day by day about the need of education in life to promote the living standard or human dvelopment.

Level of schooling of the farmers in Barak Valley

Table-84

Class standard	Number of farmers	Percentage
0/ illiterate	13	3%
1st	6	1%
2nd	25	6%
3rd	15	3%
4th	38	8%
5th	21	5%
6th	12	3%
7th	56	12%
8th	76	17%
9th	52	12%
10th	83	18%
11th	22	5%
12th	19	4%
15th	12	3%
Total	450	100

Source: Calculated by scholar from 450 samples.

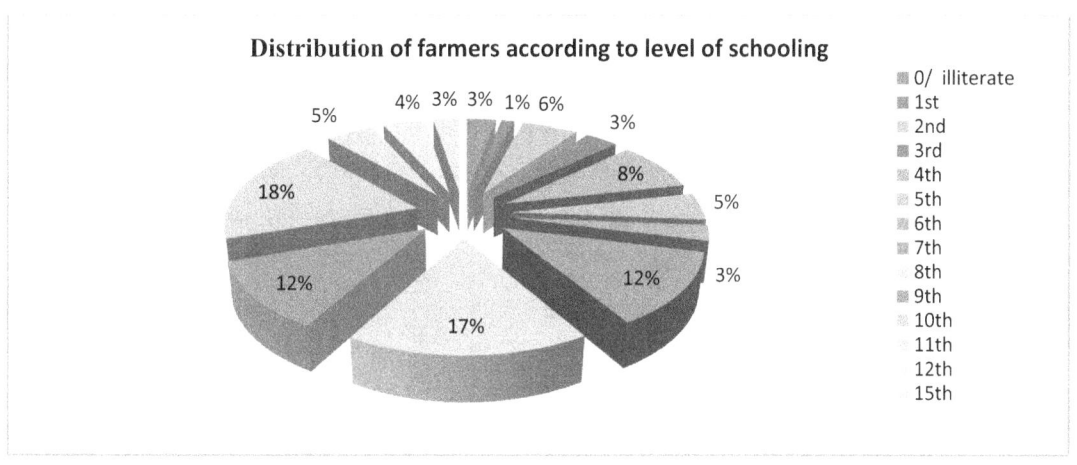

Education Index in Barak Valley

Table-85

			Statistic	Std. Error
EI	Mean		.61686	.012050
	95% Confidence Interval for Mean	Lower Bound	.59318	
		Upper Bound	.64054	
	5% Trimmed Mean		.63058	
	Median		.73300	
	Variance		.065	
	Std. Deviation		.255629	
	Minimum		.000	
	Maximum		1.000	
	Range		1.000	
	Interquartile Range		.433	
	Skewness		-.882	.115
	Kurtosis		-.486	.230

♣ The mean of Education Index is .616 in Barak Valley which is moderate. The Standard Error of the Mean indicates how much the value of the mean may vary from repeated samples of the same size taken from the same distribution and the value is .012050.

♣ The 95% Confidence Interval for Mean are two numbers that we would expect 95% of the means from repeated samples of the same size to fall between. The 5% Trimmed Mean is .630 in Barak Valley i.e. the mean after the highest and lowest 2.5% of the values have been removed.

♣ The vriance is .065 and the standard deviation of Education Index is .255.

♣ Skewness measures the degree and direction of asymmetry which is negative with -.882 in Barak Valley as the value of median (.733) is higher than the mean.

♣ Kurtosis is a measure of the heaviness of the tails of a distribution while the kurtosis is -.486. Kurtosis is positive if the tails are "heavier" than for a normal distribution and negative if the tails are "lighter" than for a normal distribution.

Distribution of farmers according to score in Education index

Table-86

Indicator	Education index	Indicator	Number of farmers	% of farmers
Mean observation	0.616	Excellent (0.9 & above)	24	5%
Max. observation	1.00	Very good (0.8-0.9)	122	27%
Min. observation	0.00	Good/ Average (0.7-0.8)	106	24%
		Poor/ Less than average (0.5-0.7)	82	18%
		Very poor/ bad performance (<0.5)	116	26%
		Total	450	100

Source: Calculated by scholar from 450 samples.

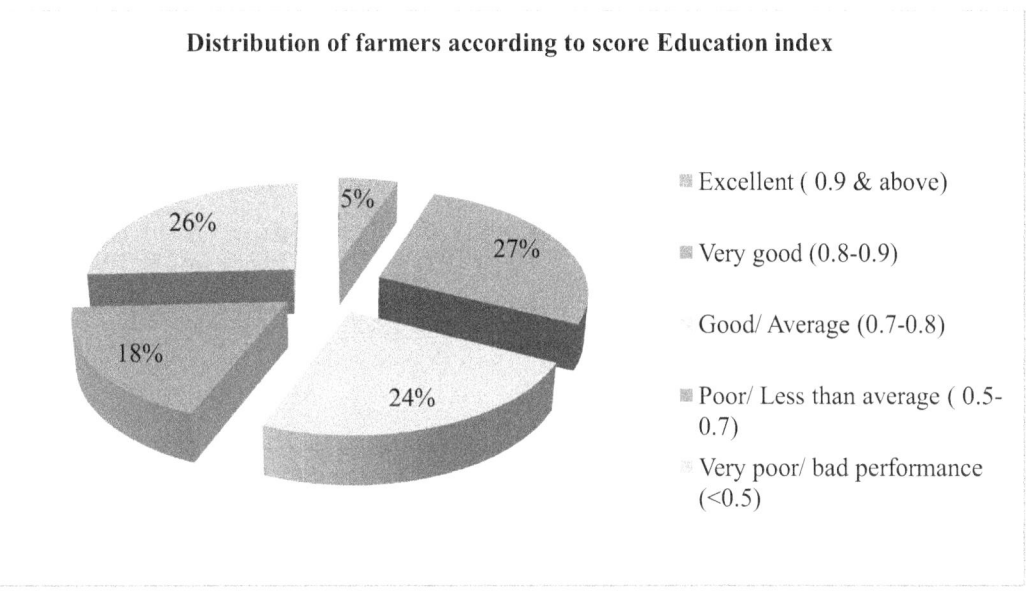

- The above table depicts the peformance in Education Index of Barak Valley. The cryterion of studying their results have changes here as excellent are those above 0.900, very good are with index value of 0.800-0.900, average with 0.700-0.800, poor/less than average with 0.500-0.700 and very poor are those with index less than 0.500. The clssification has been made like this because the enrolment is given 50% weights and those who have got enrolment correct has receieved 0.5. Thus anyone below 0.5 means performed badly in both the indicators.
- The excellent group are those who have got higher literacy level as well as child enrolment right. The index value of 0.900 and above includes 5% of the farmers or 24 in total. The very good group means index of 0.800-0.900 and there are 122 farmers or 27% of the samples. They perfomed well in both the indicators.
- The average group with index of 0.700-0.800 are 18% or 82 in total. Their schooling is of low level but they have enrolled their children in school. The poor or less than average are with 0.500-0.700 index and they have performed badly in any one of the two indicators. Those with index less than 0.500 have performed badly in both the indicators while they constitute 26% or 116 of the total samples which is a sizable proportion.

7.1.8 Health Index in Barak Valley

Health is also one of the most important aspect of quality of life or human development. Health index in Barak Valley has been prepared with the help of two dimensios- Body Mass Index and Child Mortality. Child mortality is measure of mortality and BMI indicates nutrional achievement or the level of body fitness. Both the dimensions have been given equal weights and household level health index has been made for 450 sample households in Barak Valley.

Table-87

			Statistic	Std. Error
HI	Mean		.61600	.006435
	95% Confidence Interval for Mean	Lower Bound	.60336	
		Upper Bound	.62865	
	5% Trimmed Mean		.62346	
	Median		.62100	
	Variance		.019	
	Std. Deviation		.136504	
	Minimum		.000	
	Maximum		.991	
	Range		.991	
	Interquartile Range		.091	
	Skewness		-1.588	.115
	Kurtosis		6.953	.230

- ♣ The mean of Health Index is .616 in Barak Valley which is moderate. The Standard Error of the Mean indicates how much the value of the mean may vary from repeated samples of the same size taken from the same distribution and the value is .010132.
- ♣ The 95% Confidence Interval for Mean are two numbers that we would expect 95% of the means from repeated samples of the same size to fall between. The 5% Trimmed Mean is .623 in Barak Valley i.e. the mean after the highest and lowest 2.5% of the values have been removed.
- ♣ The vriance is .019 and the standard deviation of Health Index is .136.

- ♣ Skewness measures the degree and direction of asymmetry which is negative with -1.588 in Barak Valley as the value of median (.621) is higher than the mean.
- ♣ Kurtosis is a measure of the heaviness of the tails of a distribution while the kurtosis is 6.95. Kurtosis is positive if the tails are "heavier" than for a normal distribution and negative if the tails are "lighter" than for a normal distribution.

Distribution of farmers according to score in health index

Table-88

Indicator	Health index	Indicator	Number of farmers	% of farmers
Mean observation	0.616	Safe (> 0.70)	94	21%
Max. observation	0.991	Moderate (0.6-0.7)	172	38%
Min. observation	0.000	Vulnerable (0.6-0.5)	166	37%
		High risk (<0.5)	18	4%
		Total	450	100

Source: Calculated by scholar from 450 samples.

Vulnerable- Deprived in one prarameter   High risk- Deprived in both.

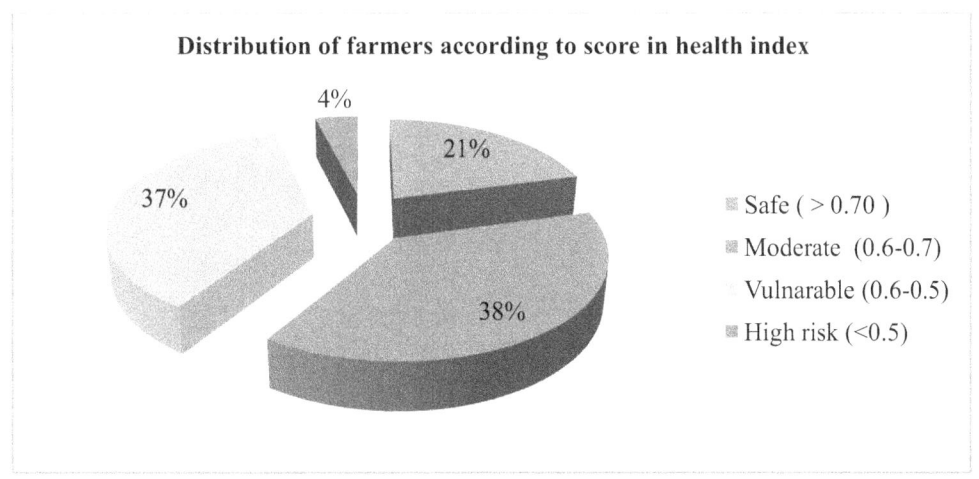

Table interpretation

- The mean performance of 0.616 index denotes moderate achievement in health. The distribution of farmers in Barak valley shows that 21% farmers are there in safe zone which is indicative of better Body Mass Index and no Child Mortality. These group of samples are health conscious and scored more than 0.700 index value.
- The moderate performance means they belong to better health status but that is below the safe zone. They constitute 38% of the farmers in Barak Valley which is 172 out of 450 and the largest group in the pie diagram.
- The vulnerable section are those who have scored in between 0.500-0.600 and constitute 37% of the samples which is a sizable section. They are deprived at least in one of the parameter.
- The section belonging to high risk zone are deprived in both the indicators and scored below 0.500 index value.

Nutritional status in Barak Valley

Nutrition is an important parameter of human development as without proper nutrition work efficiency will decline. In Barak Valley the nutrional status of the farmers have been taken in body mass index which is measured with their hight and weight. Adults are considered malnourished if their BMI is below 18.5 kg/m^2. Whereas BMI = weight (kg) / height (m)².

Table-89

			Statistic	Std. Error
BMI	Mean		21.053	.2139
	95% Confidence Interval for Mean	Lower Bound	20.633	
		Upper Bound	21.474	
	5% Trimmed Mean		20.702	
	Median		20.542	
	Variance		20.598	
	Std. Deviation		4.5385	
	Minimum		14.4	
	Maximum		38.4	
	Range		24.0	
	Interquartile Range		4.9	
	Skewness		1.196	.115
	Kurtosis		1.980	.230

- The mean of Body Mass Index is 21.05 in Barak Valley which is normal. The Standard Error of the Mean indicates how much the value of the mean may vary from repeated samples of the same size taken from the same distribution and the value is .2139.
- The 95% Confidence Interval for Mean are two numbers that we would expect 95% of the means from repeated samples of the same size to fall between. The 5% Trimmed Mean is 20.07 in Barak Valley i.e. the mean after the highest and lowest 2.5% of the values have been removed.
- The vriance is 20.59 and the standard deviation of Body Mass Index is 4.53.

- ♣ Skewness measures the degree and direction of asymmetry which is positive with 1.196 in Barak Valley as the value of median (.621) is higher than the mean.
- ♣ Kurtosis is a measure of the heaviness of the tails of a distribution while the kurtosis is 1.980. Kurtosis is positive if the tails are "heavier" than for a normal distribution and negative if the tails are "lighter" than for a normal distribution.

Distribution of farmers according to BMI score

Table-90

Indicator	BMI	Indicator	Number of farmers	% of farmers
Mean observation	21.053	Properly Nourished (18.5 kg/m^2 -25.5 kg/m^2)	277	62%
Max. observation	38.42	Mal Nourished (< 18.5 kg/m^2)	132	29%
Min. observation	14.39	Over weight (>25.5 kg/m^2))	41	9%
		Total	450	100

Source: Calculated by scholar from 450 samples.

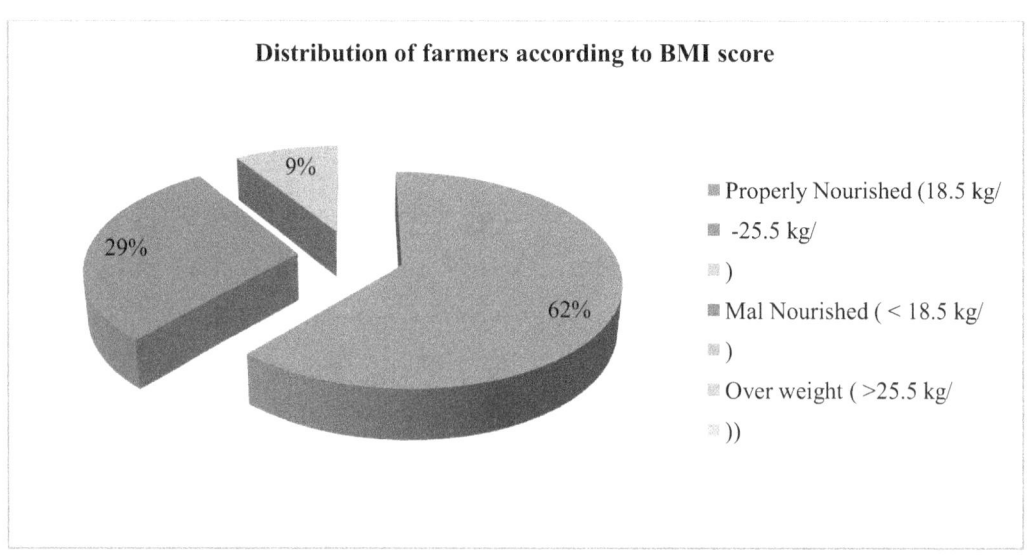

Table summary

- The mean of Body Mass Index is 21.05 in Barak Valley which is normal. The maximum value shows the one who is highly overwight with BMI of 38 and the lowest or the most underweight is 14.39. The achievement in nutritional status of Barak Valley shows that Body Mass Index of 62% of the sampes are in proper zone. They have achieved the safe level of BMI of 18.5 kg/m^2 -25.5 kg/m^2. This zone is referred as normal BMI zone.
- The mal nourished portion constitutes 29% of the samples or 132 in number. Their BMI is below 18.5 kg/m^2. The lack of nutrition affects the work capacity of the farmers, especially those who work in the field.
- The number of overweight people is 41 or 9% of the total in my study area. Their BMI is more than that of the normal range of 18.5 kg/m^2 -25.5 kg/m^2.

7.1.9 Quality of Life Index in Barak Valley

Performance in human development has been measured by achievement in quality of life/standard of living. A composite index has been formed to measure the progress in quality of life by 28 indicators of household- housing characteristics, quality of sanitation, electricity, drinking water, cooking fuel, a bunch of electronic goods, essential goods, vehicles etc. Moreover education index made of literacy level and enrolment, health index made of BMI- Body Mass Index and child mortality have been prepared. Quality of life index is a composite measure of all three dimension indices having equal weights.

Table-91

			Statistic	Std. Error
QLI	Mean		.59186	.005858
	95% Confidence Interval for Mean	Lower Bound	.58035	
		Upper Bound	.60338	
	5% Trimmed Mean		.59704	
	Median		.61145	
	Variance		.015	
	Std. Deviation		.124258	
	Minimum		.132	
	Maximum		.843	
	Range		.711	
	Interquartile Range		.162	
	Skewness		-.699	.115
	Kurtosis		.389	.230

♣ The mean of Quality of Life Index is .591 in Barak Valley which is moderate. The Standard Error of the Mean indicates how much the value of the mean may vary from repeated samples of the same size taken from the same distribution and the value is .005858.

- ♣ The 95% Confidence Interval for Mean are two numbers that we would expect 95% of the means from repeated samples of the same size to fall between. The 5% Trimmed Mean is .597 in Barak Valley i.e. the mean after the highest and lowest 2.5% of the values have been removed.
- ♣ The vriance is .015 and the standard deviation of Quality of Life Index is .124.
- ♣ Skewness measures the degree and direction of asymmetry which is negative with -.699 in Barak Valley as the value of median (.557) is slightly higher than the mean.
- ♣ Kurtosis is a measure of the heaviness of the tails of a distribution while the kurtosis is .389. Kurtosis is positive if the tails are "heavier" than for a normal distribution and negative if the tails are "lighter" than for a normal distribution.

Distribution of farmers according to score in Quality of Life Index

Table-92

Indicator	Quality of Life Index	Indicator	Number of farmers	% of farmers
Mean observation	0.591	Excellent (0.8 & above)	8	2%
Max. observation	0.843	Very good (0.7-0.8)	77	17%
Min. observation	0.132	Good (0.6-0.7)	163	36%
		Moderate/Average (0.5-0.6)	100	22%
		Poor/ Less than average (0.3-0.5)	94	21%
		Very poor/ Negligible (<0.3)	8	2%
		Total	450	100

Source: Calculated by scholar from 450 samples.

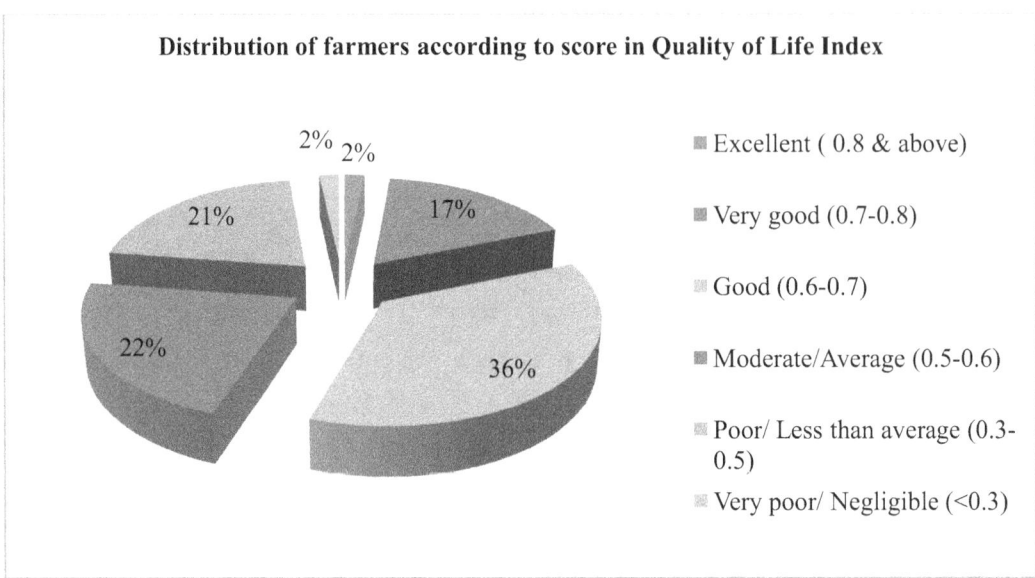

Table interpretation

- India Human Development-2011 Report says, 'The *raison d'être* of development is to improve the quality of people's lives by creating an environment for them to engage in a wider range of activities, to be healthy and well nourished, to be knowledgeable, and to be able to participate in community life'. Sen (1985) calls these 'basic functionings'. Quality of life of the farmers on the basis of wealth, education and health endeavours to fulfill these precondtions.

- The quality of life in Barak Valley or human development is 0.553 which is moderate. The highest one is the sample-435 with 0.843 of index value, the 2nd highest is the s-24 with 0.835 and the lowest one is the sample-60 with index 0.132. The quality of life for the best group of farmers belongs to the index value above 0.800 but only 8 have qualified in this group which makes only 2% of the total.

- Those who have scored in between 0.700 to 0.800 makes the 2nd group and a sizable number of farmers belongs to it. It constitutes 17% of the total or 77 in number while they definitely perfomed better in case of wealth index or BMI or mortality. In this group not only mortality is absent but also illiteracy has not been found. They have performed better in taking care of their children to go to the schools. Their higher quality of life has been promoted from all dimension indices.

- The 3rd group of farmers have scored in between 0.600 to 0.700, they are the good performers who constitute the most important club in the quality of life performance. They form 36% of the total sample farmers or 136 in number, thus making the biggest part of the pie diagram. Most of the farmers in this group perfomed good in at least two dimensions and deprived in the other. To put it other way there are total 4 sub indices of education and health. On the other hand wealth index is made of 28 indicators but dimension indices have been equally weighted to avoid the possibility of wrong assessment.
- The fourth group constitutes also large in Barak Valley as 22% or 100 farmes belong to this club, they are very much average performers while they performed better in half of the indicators.
- The fifth group of farmers also form a sizable part of the farming community but they are regaded as poor performers in quality of life index. They scored in between 0.300 to 0.500. This group makes 21% of the total or 94 in number in the study area. Their performance is below average and they are struggling in maintaining good score in at least two of the dimension indices.
- The last group is the one maintaining a life that can be called less than a human life. It is 2% of the total or 8 out of 450 farmers in Barak Vallley.

7.2 Study of Inter-linkage among Variables

Agricultural Performance Index and Human Development/ Quality of Life Index

Both agricultural performance and human development performance in Barak Valley have been studied along with thier component variables or dimension indices. Now the linkage or interrelationship between the two is studied followingly-

Model Summary-1

Table-93

	R	R Square	Adjusted R Square	Std. Error of the Estimate
1	.568[a]	.322	.321	.090249

a. Predictors: (Constant), API-Agricultural Performance Index

b. Dependent Variable: QLI- Quality of Life Index

In the Model Summary-1, a simple linear regression model, we see that the coefficient of multiple correlations(R) is .568, indicating a good positive linear relationship between the predictor -Agricultural Performance Index and the dependent variable- Quality of Life Index in Barak Valley. The coefficient of determination r2 (R Square) of .322 indicates that for the sample, 32% of the variation in quality of life can be explained by the variation in agricultural performance index. But this may be an overestimate for the population from which the sample is drawn, so we use the Adjusted R Square as a better estimate for the population i.e .321. Finally the Std. Error of the Estimate is 0.090249.

Multiple Linear Regression Analysis

Model Summary
Table-94

Model	R	R Square	Adjusted R Square	Std. Error of the Estimate
1	.578[a]	.335	.329	.089724

a. Predictors: (Constant), LPI-Labour Productivity Index, LFI- Land Fertility Index, TAI-Technology Achievement Index, MI- Market Index
b. Dependent Variable: QLI-Quality of Life Index

We have used our data sets for multiple linear regressions. In this data set, required LFI, MI, TAI and LPI, are used to predict human development or quality of life index-QLI which is a composite measure of wealth, education and health. From left to right, we use the variables y, $x1$, $x2$, $x3$ and $x4$. In the Model Summary, we see that the coefficient of multiple correlation r (R) is .578, indicating a good positive linear relationship between the predictors and the dependent variable. The coefficient of determination $r2$ (R Square) of .335 indicates that, for the sample, 33% of the variation of QLI can be explained by the variation in LPI, LFI, TAI, MI. But this may be an overestimate for the population from which the sample is drawn, so we use the Adjusted R Square .329 as a better estimate for the population. Finally, the Standard Error of the Estimate is .089724.

ANOVA
Table-95

Model		Sum of Squares	df	Mean Square	F	Sig.
1	Regression	1.801	4	.450	55.942	.000[a]
	Residual	3.582	445	.008		
	Total	5.384	449			

a. Predictors: (Constant), LPI, LFI, TAI, MI
b. Dependent Variable: QLI

Preferably, we use the ANOVA table for testing the null hypothesis $\beta_1=\beta_2=\beta_3=\beta_4=0$ with an alternative hypothesis of not all $\beta_i=0$. In the ANOVA table, the Regression Sum of Squares (SSR) is the variation explained by regression, and the Residual Sum of Squares (SSE) is the variation not explained by regression (the "E" stands for error). The Mean Square Regression and the Mean Square Residual are MSR and MSE respectively, with the F value of 55.942 being their quotient. Since the p-value (Sig. = .000) is less than .001, inferring indeed that there is a regression effect.

Coefficients
Table-96

Model		Un standardized Coefficients		Standardized Coefficients	t	Sig.	95% Confidence Interval for B	
		B	Std. Error	Beta			Lower Bound	Upper Bound
1	(Constant)	.338	.018		18.490	.000	.302	.374
	LFI	.159	.030	.225	5.382	.000	.101	.217
	MI	.053	.021	.149	2.565	.011	.012	.094
	TAI	.128	.022	.280	5.762	.000	.085	.172
	LPI	.095	.037	.128	2.556	.011	.022	.168

a. Dependent Variable: QLI

Let y=Quality of Life Index-QLI, x_1=Land Fertility Index-LFI, x_2= Market Index-MI, and x_3= Technology Achievement Index-TAI and x_4= Labour Productivity Index-LPI. We use the regression (least squares) equation $\hat{y}=a+b_1x_1+b_2x_2+b_3x_3+b_4x_4$ to approximate the population regression equation $\mu y|(x_1, x_2, x_3, x_4)=\alpha+\beta_1x_1+\beta_2x_2+\beta_3x_3$.

From the Coefficients table above, a=.338, b1=.159, b2=.053, b3=.128, b4=.095 from the first column of numbers (rows and columns transposed from the output), so the sample regression equation is $\hat{y}$=.338+.159x1+.053x2+.128x3+.095x4. From the last two columns of numbers in the table, one gets that 95% confidence intervals are (.302 & .374) for α, (.101 & .217) for β_1, (.012 & .094) for β_2, (.085 & .172) for β_3 and (.022 & .168) for β_4.

The t test is used for testing the various null hypotheses $\beta_i=0$. It can be used similarly to test the null hypothesis $\alpha=0$, but this is of much less interest. In this case, we read from the above table that, as an example, for $H0:\beta_1=0$, $Ha:\beta_1\neq 0$, we have $t=5.382$. Since the p-value (Sig. = .000) for that t test is less than .001, we can reject the null hypothesis of $\beta_1=0$. Notice that at the $\alpha=.05$ level, we would accept the null hypothesis $\beta_2=0$ since $p=.05$. Also, notice that 0 is in the 95% confidence interval for β_2 (barely). But if using these t tests, keep in mind the dangers of using multiple hypothesis tests and/or finding multiple confidence intervals on the same set of data.

Residuals Statistics
Table-97

	Minimum	Maximum	Mean	Std. Deviation	N
Predicted Value	.37708	.69851	.55344	.063341	450
Std. Predicted Value	-2.784	2.290	.000	1.000	450
Standard Error of Predicted Value	.005	.026	.009	.002	450
Adjusted Predicted Value	.37458	.69819	.55336	.063349	450
Residual	-.420803	.192540	.000000	.089323	450
Std. Residual	-4.690	2.146	.000	.996	450
Stud. Residual	-4.708	2.159	.000	1.001	450
Deleted Residual	-.424122	.196320	.000080	.090352	450
Stud. Deleted Residual	-4.825	2.168	.000	1.005	450
Mahal. Distance	.368	35.651	3.991	3.101	450
Cook's Distance	.000	.048	.002	.005	450
Centered Leverage Value	.001	.079	.009	.007	450

a. Dependent Variable: QLI

Table-98

Model Summary-2 and Parameter Estimates

Dependent Variable: QLI

Equation	Model Summary					Parameter Estimates	
	R Square	F	df1	df2	Sig.	Constant	b1
Linear	.322	213.006	1	448	.000	.368	.379

The independent variable is API.

The relationship between two variables is explained with the help of R square 0.322 i.e. 32% of the variation in human dvelopment is explained by variation in agricultural performance in Barak Valley. The value of F 213.006 is the quotient of Mean Square Regression and the Mean Square Residual -MSR and MSE respectively.

The following diagram shows the positive linear relation between agricultural performance index and quality of life index.

Curve Estimation

Explaining the positive relation between Human Development/ Quality of life (QLI) and Agricultural performance index (API)

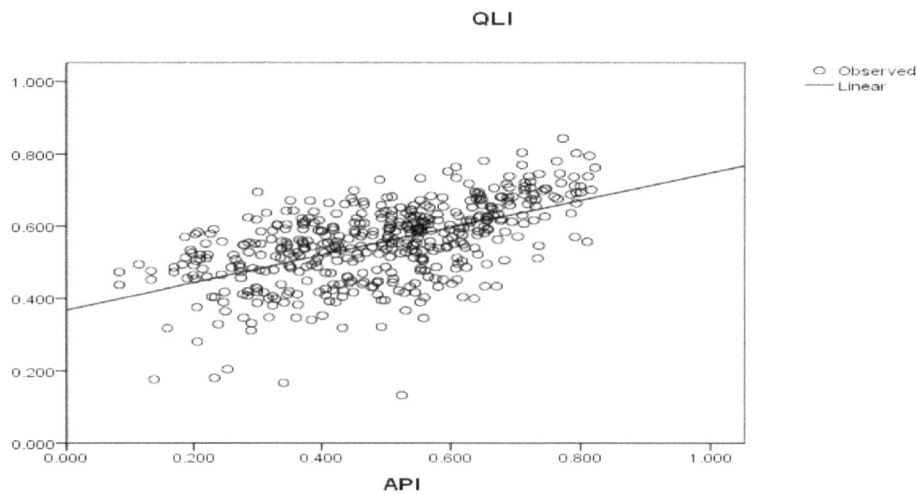

Land Fertility and Agricultural Performance

Model Summary-3

Table-99

Model	R	R Square	Adjusted R Square	Std. Error of the Estimate
1	.521[a]	.271	.269	.140027

a. Predictors: (Constant), LFI

Dependent Variable: API

In the Model Summary-3, a linear regression model, we find that the coefficient of multiple correlations(R) is .521, indicating a good positive linear relationship between the predictor Land Fertility Index and the dependent variable- Agricultural Performance Index in Barak Valley. The coefficient of determination r2 (R Square) of .271 indicates that for the sample, 27% of the variation in Agricultural Performance can be explained by the variation in Land Fertility Index. But this may be an overestimate for the population from which the sample is drawn, so we use the Adjusted R Square as a better estimate for the population i.e .269. Finally the Std. Error of the Estimate is 0.140027.

Table-100

Dependent Variable: API

Equation	Model Summary					Parameter Estimates	
	R Square	F	df1	df2	Sig.	Constant	b1
Linear	.271	166.506	1	448	.000	.195	.550

The independent variable is LFI.

The relationship between two variables is explained with the help of R square 0.271 i.e. 27% of the variation in agricultural performance is explained by variation in land fertility in Barak Valley. The value of F 166.506 is the quotient of Mean Square Regression and the Mean Square Residual -MSR and MSE respectively.

The following diagram shows the positive linear relation between land fertility index and agricultural performance index.

Curve Estimation

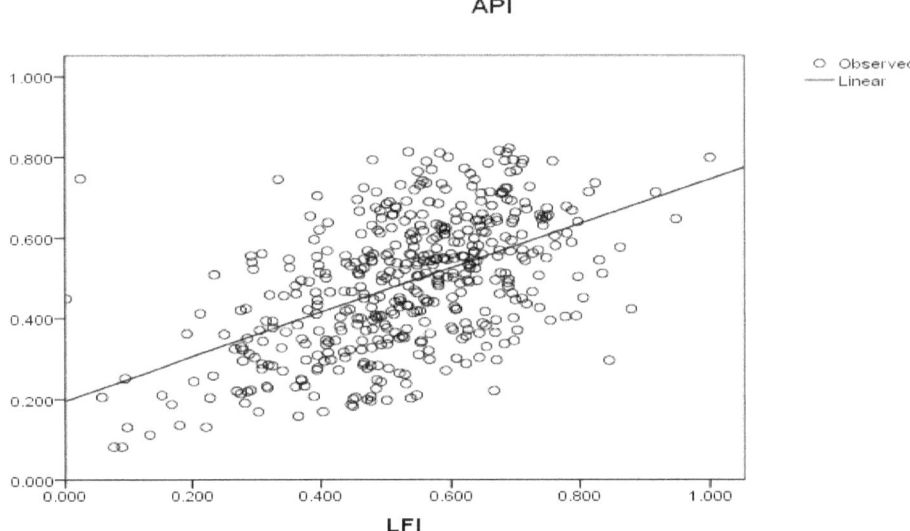

Market and Agricultural Performance

Table-101

Model Summary-5

Model	R	R Square	Adjusted R Square	Std. Error of the Estimate
1	.910^a	.828	.828	.067951

a. Predictors: (Constant), MI

Dependent Variable: API

In the Model Summary-5, a linear regression model, we find that the coefficient of multiple correlations(R) is .910, indicating a strong positive linear relationship between the predictor Market Index and the dependent variable- Agricultural Performance Index in Barak Valley. The coefficient of determination r2 (R Square) of .828 indicates that for the sample, 82% of the variation in Agricultural Performance can be explained by the variation in Market Index. But this may be an overestimate for the population from which the sample is drawn, so we use the Adjusted R Square as a better estimate for the population i.e .828. Finally the Std. Error of the Estimate is 0.067951.

Model Summary-6 and Parameter Estimates

Table-102

Dependent Variable: API

Equation	Model Summary					Parameter Estimates	
	R Square	F	df1	df2	Sig.	Constant	b1
Linear	.828	2.1613	1	448	.000	.231	.488

The independent variable is MI.

The relationship between two variables is explained with the help of R square 0.828 i.e. 82% of the variation in agricultural performance is explained by variation marketing of crops in Barak Valley. The value of F 2.1613 is the quotient of Mean Square Regression and the Mean Square Residual -MSR and MSE respectively.

The following diagram shows the positive linear relation between market index and agricultural performance index.

Curve Estimation

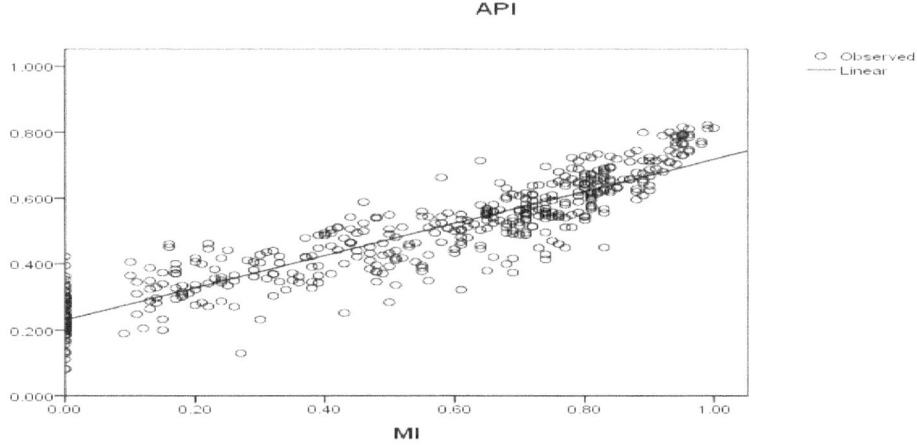

Technology Achievement and Agricultural Performance

Model Summary-7

Table-103

Model	R	R Square	Adjusted R Square	Std. Error of the Estimate
1	.799^a	.638	.637	.098701

a. Predictors: (Constant), TAI

Dependent Variable: API

In the Model Summary-7, a linear regression model, we find that the coefficient of multiple correlations(R) is .799, indicating a strong positive linear relationship between the predictor Technology Achievement Index and the dependent variable- Agricultural Performance Index in Barak Valley. The coefficient of determination r2 (R Square) of .638 indicates that for the sample, 63% of the variation in Agricultural Performance can be explained by the variation in Technology Achievement Index. But this may be an overestimate for the population from which the sample is drawn, so we use the Adjusted R Square as a better estimate for the population i.e .637. Finally the Std. Error of the Estimate is 0.098701.

Model Summary-8 and Parameter Estimates

Table-104

Dependent Variable: API

Equation	Model Summary					Parameter Estimates	
	R Square	F	df1	df2	Sig.	Constant	b1
Linear	.638	788.809	1	448	.000	.190	.547

The independent variable is TAI.

The relationship between two variables is explained with the help of R square 0.638 i.e. 63% of the variation in agricultural performance is explained by variation technology achievement in Barak Valley. The value of F 788.809 is the quotient of Mean Square Regression and the Mean Square Residual -MSR and MSE respectively.

The following diagram shows the positive linear relation between technology achievement index and agricultural performance index.

Curve Estimation

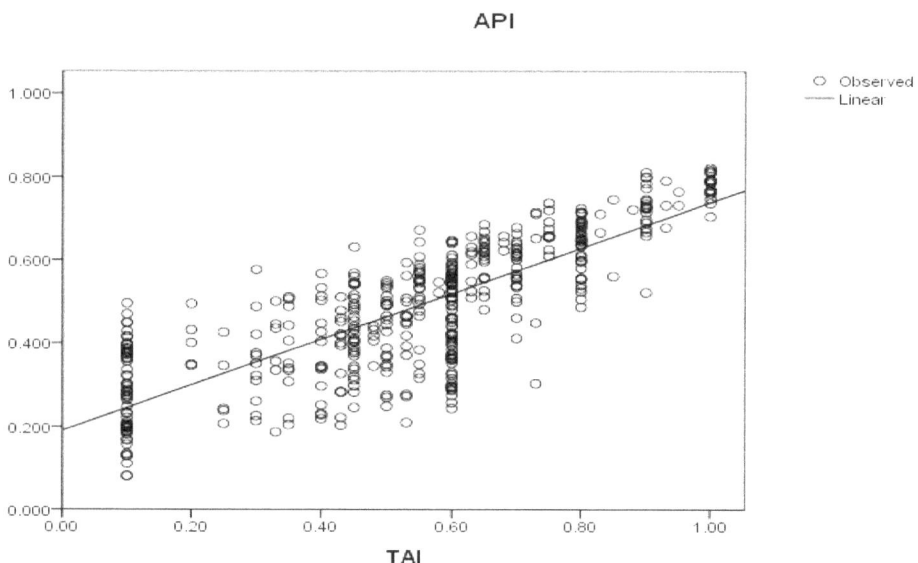

Labour Productivity and Agricultural Performance

Table-105

Model Summary-9

Model	R	R Square	Adjusted R Square	Std. Error of the Estimate
1	.713[a]	.509	.508	.114936

a. Predictors: (Constant), LPI

Dependent Variable: API

In the Model Summary-9, a linear regression model, we find that the coefficient of multiple correlations(R) is .713, indicating a strong positive linear relationship between the predictor Labour Productivity Index and the dependent variable- Agricultural Performance Index in Barak Valley. The coefficient of determination r2 (R Square) of .509 indicates that for the sample, 50% of the variation in Agricultural Performance can be explained by the variation in Labour Productivity Index. But this may be an overestimate for the population from which the sample is drawn, so we use the Adjusted R Square as a better estimate for the population i.e .508. Finally the Std. Error of the Estimate is 0.114936.

Model Summary-10 and Parameter Estimate

Table-106

Dependent Variable: API

Equation	Model Summary					Parameter Estimates	
	R Square	F	df1	df2	Sig.	Constant	b1
Linear	.509	464.086	1	448	.000	.210	.792

The independent variable is LPI.

The relationship between two variables is explained with the help of R square 0.509 i.e. 50% of the variation in agricultural performance is explained by variation labour productivity in Barak Valley. The value of F 464.086 is the quotient of Mean Square Regression and the Mean Square Residual -MSR and MSE respectively.

The following diagram shows the positive linear relation between labour productivity index and agricultural performance index.

Curve Estimation

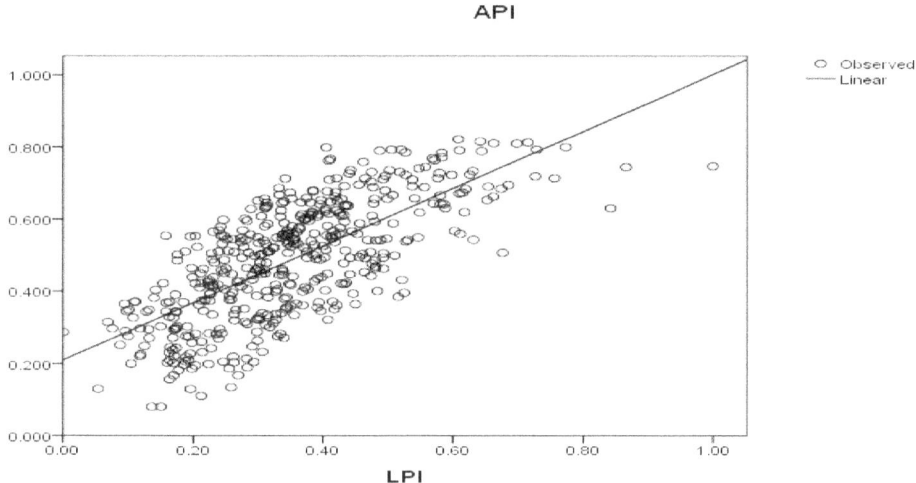

Human Development and Wealth

Model Summary-11

Table-107

Model	R	R Square	Adjusted R Square	Std. Error of the Estimate
1	.647[a]	.419	.418	.083569

a. Predictors: (Constant), WI

Dependent Variable: QLI

In the Model Summary-11, a linear regression model, we find that the coefficient of multiple correlations(R) is .647, indicating a strong positive linear relationship between the predictor Wealth Index and the dependent variable- Quality of Life Index in Barak Valley. The coefficient of determination r2 (R Square) of .419 indicates that for the sample, 41% of the variation in Human Development can be explained by the variation in Wealth Index. But this may be an overestimate for the population from which the sample is drawn, so we use the Adjusted R Square as a better estimate for the population i.e .418. Finally the Std. Error of the Estimate is 0.083569.

Model Summary-12 and Parameter Estimates

Table-108

Dependent Variable: QLI

Equation	Model Summary					Parameter Estimates	
	R Square	F	df1	df2	Sig.	Constant	b1
Linear	.419	322.913	1	448	.000	.292	.467

The independent variable is WI.

The relationship between two variables is explained with the help of R square 0.419 i.e. 41% of the variation in Human Development is explained by variation Wealth Index in Barak Valley. The value of F 322.913 is the quotient of Mean Square Regression and the Mean Square Residual -MSR and MSE respectively.

The following diagram shows the positive linear relation between wealth index and quality of life index.

Curve Estimation

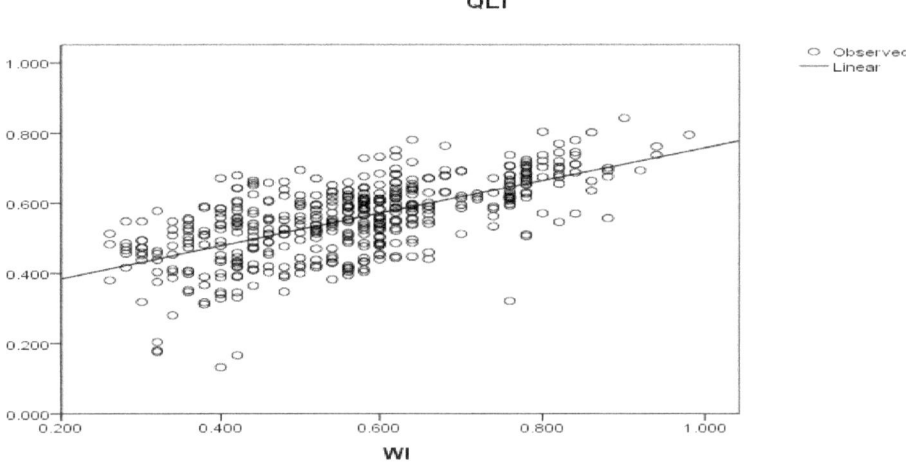

Human Development and Education

Table-109

Model Summary-13

Model	R	R Square	Adjusted R Square	Std. Error of the Estimate
1	.833[a]	.695	.694	.068742

a. Predictors: (Constant), EI

b. Dependent Variable: QLI

In the Model Summary-13, a linear regression model, we find that the coefficient of multiple correlations(R) is .833, indicating a strong positive linear relationship between the predictor Education Index and the dependent variable- Quality of Life Index in Barak Valley. The coefficient of determination r^2 (R Square) of .695 indicates that for the sample, 69% of the variation in Human Development can be explained by the variation in Education Index. But this may be an overestimate for the population from which the sample is drawn, so we use the Adjusted R Square as a better estimate for the population i.e. .694. Finally the Std. Error of the Estimate is 0.068742.

Model Summary-14 and Parameter Estimates

Table-110

Dependent Variable: QLI

Equation	Model Summary					Parameter Estimates	
	R Square	F	df1	df2	Sig.	Constant	b1
Linear	.695	1.0193	1	448	.000	.342	.405

The independent variable is EI.

The relationship between two variables is explained with the help of R square 0.695 i.e. 69% of the variation in Human Development is explained by variation Education Index in Barak Valley. The value of F 1.0193 is the quotient of Mean Square Regression and the Mean Square Residual -MSR and MSE respectively.

The following diagram shows the positive linear relation between education index and quality of life index.

Curve Estimation

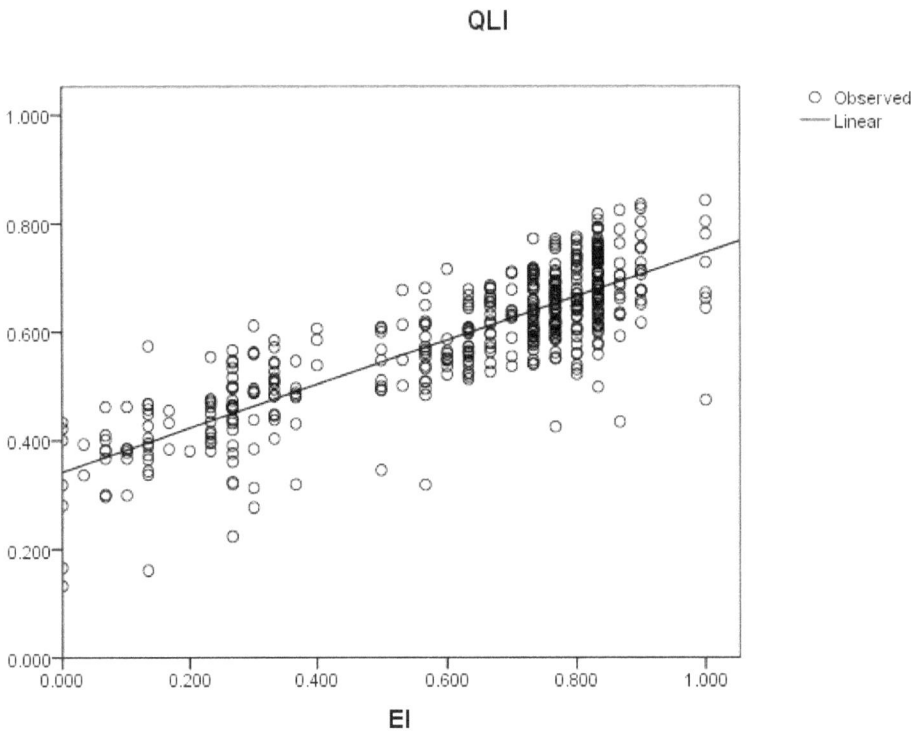

Human Development and Health

Model Summary-15

Table-111

Model	R	R Square	Adjusted R Square	Std. Error of the Estimate
1	.501[a]	.251	.249	.094892

a. Predictors: (Constant), HI

Dependent Variable: QLI

In the Model Summary-15, a linear regression model, we find that the coefficient of multiple correlations(R) is .501, indicating a good positive linear relationship between the predictor Health Index and the dependent variable- Quality of Life Index in Barak Valley. The coefficient of determination r2 (R Square) of .251 indicates that for the sample, 25% of the variation in Human Development can be explained by the variation in Health Index. But this may be an overestimate for the population from which the sample is drawn, so we use the Adjusted R Square as a better estimate for the population i.e .249. Finally the Std. Error of the Estimate is 0.094892.

Model Summary-16 and Parameter Estimates

Table-112

Dependent Variable: QLI

Equation	Model Summary					Parameter Estimates	
	R Square	F	df1	df2	Sig.	Constant	b1
Linear	.251	149.909	1	448	.000	.306	.402

The independent variable is HI.

The relationship between two variables is explained with the help of R square 0.251 i.e. 25% of the variation in Human Development is explained by variation Health Index in Barak

Valley. The value of F 149.909 is the quotient of Mean Square Regression and the Mean Square Residual -MSR and MSE respectively.

The following diagram shows the positive linear relation between health index and quality of life index.

Curve Estimation

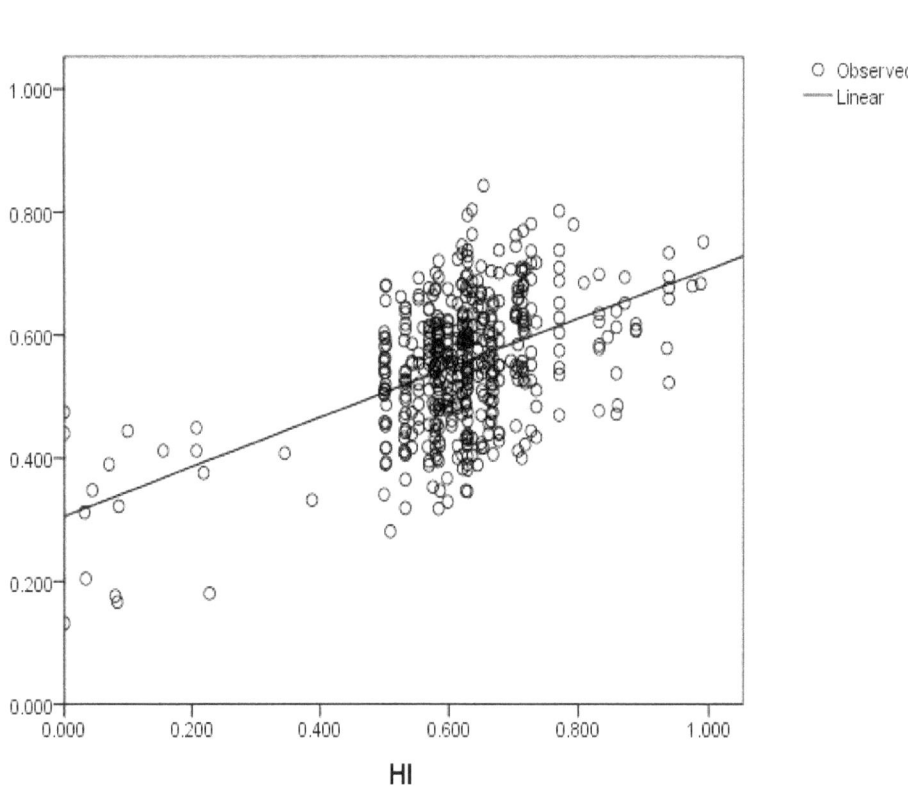

7.3 ADO Circle Wise Performance

Dullabcherra ADO: Villages- Fanairbond & Wangirbond [Dist.- Karimganj]

Production performance is analysed with help of crop production, productivity etc. Output of different agricultural crops in Barak Valley show that though many types of paddy i.e. the staple crop of the Valley is produced yet the Sali paddy occupies the most important position. Aouse is also produced but the gap between Sali and Aouse is huge while Buro paddy is also produced in the Valley but exclusively in low lands or water logged areas called Bil or Haoor. Since my sample Villages do not belong to water logged areas I remained confined to Sali and Aouse paddy, moreover the production of Buro rice is only 6%-6.5% of the total paddy production which is insignificant enough to be included in data collection. Among vegetables, potato is produced by almost every farmer but it is not sufficient to fulfill the local demand. Sugarcane is an important cash crop for the farmers and they make money income out of that; almost all farmers are engaged in producing sugarcane. Summer vegetables is produced by most of the farmers but on subsistence scale and a few of them produce for commercial purposes. Winter vegetables is more appreciable to the farmers as many of them produce commercially, however it remained in subsistence level for a large section.

Table-113

Indicator	Sali	Auose	Potato	Sugarcane	Summer veg.	Winter veg.
Mean	49.9227	14.0000	6.5067	15.8492	1.2977	4.8813
Minimum	4.00	.00	.00	3.50	.00	.70
Maximum	175.00	75.00	60.00	82.50	14.00	31.50
Sum	3744.20	1050.00	488.00	1188.69	97.32	366.10

Source: Calculated by the scholar from 75 samples.

> Fanairbond and wangirbond are two villages under Dullabcherra ADO circle in Ramkrishnanagar subdivision of Karimganj district. 38 samples from Fanairbond and 37 samples from Wangirbond have been collected. Most of the farmers are small and medium farmers, some of them are marginal farmers and very few are large farmers.

A common feature is that Sali paddy is the major crop produced by all farmers. The average production of Sali paddy is 48.2 quintals in Dullabcherra ADO circle. 8 farmers have produced more than 100 quintals. The largest prducer is s-24 with 175 quintals of Sali paddy where as 155 quintals has been produced by s-23, 145 quintals by s-52 etc. The lowest production was from s-11 worth of only 4 quintals; while 5 quintals by s-6, 8.2 quintals by s-5 etc.

- Mean production of auose is 14q indicating much lower proportion in the total paddy cultivation of the ADO circle. The highest producer is the s-56 who is a large farmer and produces 75q of auose; there are a few farmers producing more than 30q. However most of the farmers sell their auose produce in the market. The farmers prducing very low amt.like 3q-4q-5q are subsistence farmers.
- The mean output of potato is 6.5q showing deficiency and therefore dependence on outside supply. The highest producer is with 60q while most of them sell it in village market or through traders. Those who produce more than 2q-3q can sell. 55 farmers out of 75 samples can sell.
- The sugarcane is an important source of earning for the farmers. Since there was a sugar industry earlier in Chorgaola (a near by village) farmers are inetrested in producing sugarcane. Unfortunately the industry was closed yet they did not stop producing cane. Now they sell it in village market and district haedquarter for molases. Sugarcane is a cash crop and thus an important source for the farmers to earn some extra money. In Dullabcherra ADO Circle almost all farmers produce sugarcane to some extent. The highest producer is with 50q of sugarcane and the lowest is with 3.5q. The mean prduction is 15.4q which is good as it is sold entirely by the farmers. Sugarcane comprises 16.75% of the total output of 75 farmers.
- However the condition of summer and winter vegetables is not at all satisfactory. Most of the farmers are subsistence farmers. Only a few large farmers produce vegetables commercially. The mean produce of the summer vegetables is 1.3q while the highest output is 14q. the condition of winter vegetables is little better as the mean produce is 4.9q and maximum is 31.5q while the minimum is 0.7q.

Productivity in Dullabcherra:-

Table-114

Indicator	Total	Area under production	Workers applied	Output per Bigha	Output per worker
Mean	92.4580	22.800	1.96	3.971	45.156
Minimum	13.90	4.5	1	3.1	8.9
Maximum	438.00	105.0	5	4.8	120.6
Sum	6934.35	1710.0	147		

Source : Calculated by the scholar from 75 samples.

- Total crop is calculated by taking in to account output of all products. The mean volume is 92.4q is not at all bad. The highest producer is the s-56 who is the only large scale farmer taken from Dullabcherra ADO. The most poor one produces only 13.9q. The mean area under cultivation in Dullabcherra ADO is 22.8 Bigha. From earlier table we know that most of the farmers belong to the class of small, marginal and semi medium farmers while medium and large farmers are a few. The workers applied in the production varies in between 1/2/3 for the small farmers and 3/4/5 for the medium and large farmers. The mean observation is 2 and a maximum of 5 has been used in the land.

- The most important parameter to understand the productivity are output per worker and output per bigha i.e. labour productivity and fertility of the land. The output per bigha varies in between 3/4/5q paddy per bigha . The mean value is 4.0q and the maximum one is 4.8q while the minimum one is 3.1q per bigha. The labour productivity varies largely from 8.9q to 101q. As the table depicts the mean productivity is 44.5q per worker. Actually it is largely determined by the size of land.

Performance in marketing (Based on % of output sold)

Table-115

Indicator	Amt sold	% of output sold	Indicator	Number of farmers	Percentage of farmers
Mean observation	59.7q	49.8	Excellent (80% & above)	12	16%
Max. observation	275q	89.6	Very good (60%- 80%)	18	24%
Min. observation	0q	0.0	Good/ medium/average (40%- 60%)	15	20%
			Poor/ Less than average (20%- 40%)	16	21.33%
			Very Poor/Negligible (Below 20%)	14	18.66%
			Total	75	100

Source : Calculated by the scholar from 75 samples.

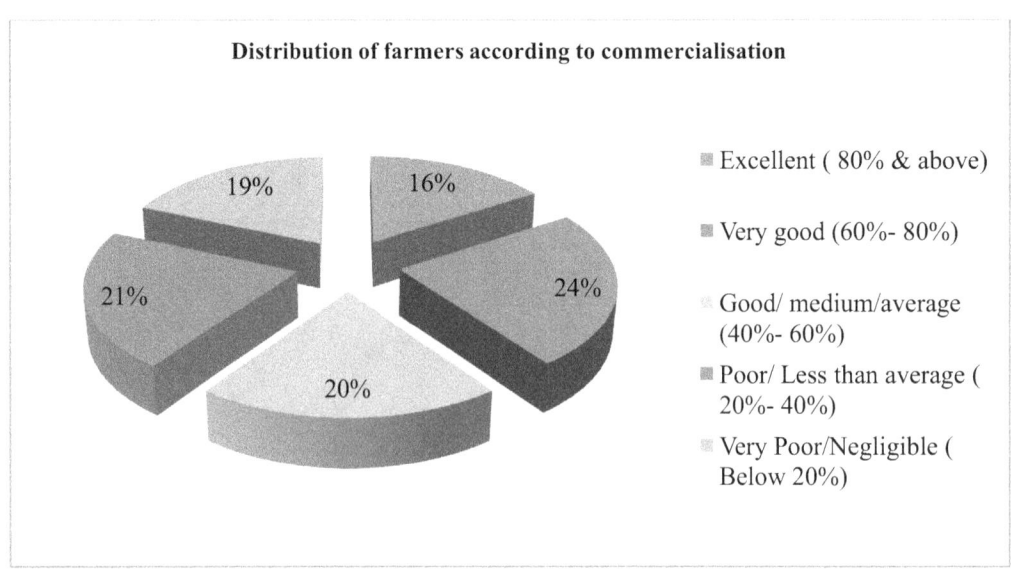

- The marketing performance in Dullabcherra ADO circle is of mixed one. The mean sale of crop is 59.7 quintals and the mean % of output sold is 49.8% thus showing moderate level of performance in selling the output. The highest producer is selling 275q of output or 89% of the total, he is the only one large scale farmer in the Dullabcherra ADO. The minimum or the worst performer is the one sold nothing or they are the subsistence farmers.
- The farmers who have sold more than 80% of their output are 12 in number or 16% of the study samples. They are the best performer in commercialisation of agriculture. Very good farmers are those who have sold 60% to 80% of their crop. They constitute 24% of the ADO or 18 in number. The medium or average farmers contribute the most to the marketable surplus. The good or average farmers constitute 20% of the ADO and they sell 40% to 60% of their output.
- The poor or less than average farmers are also large in Dullabcherra. They form 21.33% of the total samples. If they could utilize their resource properly the performance wouldcertainly increase. They are poor performers and that is mainly caused by deficiency in capacity to use the existing resources. Very poor or bad performers are those who could sell only below 20% of the crop. They are mainly subsistence farmers and their land holding is mostly marginal and small.

Statistical Evaluation of Dullabcherra ADO

Table-116

Major variables		Intra-QLI		Intra-API	
Indicator	Dullabcherra	Indicator	Dullabcherra	Indicator	Dullabcherra
Mean API	0.478	Mean WI	0.593	Mean LFI	0.465
Max API	0.854	Max WI	0.920	Max LFI	0.810
Min API	0.124	Min WI	0.280	Min LFI	0.079
Mean QLI	0.555	Mean EI	0.515	Mean MI	0.531
Max QLI	0.835	Max EI	1.00	Max MI	0.96
Min QLI	0.132	Min EI	0.00	Min MI	0.00
Mean MPI	0.339	Mean HI	0.573	Mean TAI	0.593
Max MPI	0.776	Max HI	0.938	Max TAI	1.00
Min MPI	0	Min HI	0.00	Min TAI	0.10
Correlation between API & QLI	0.636	Mean BMI	21.2	Mean LPI	0.325
Correlation between API & MPI	-0.634	Max BMI	35.8	Max LPI	1.00
		Min BMI	14.3	Min LPI	0.00
		Correlation between QLI & WI	0.680	Correlation between API & LFI	0.588
		Correlation between QLI & EI	0.802	Correlation between API & MI	0.908
		Correlation between QLI & HI	0.623	Correlation between API & TAI	0.811
				Correlation between API & LPI	0.793

Source : Calculated by the scholar from 75 samples.

- In Dullabcherra ADO circle the Agricultural Performance Index is found moderate with index value of 0.478. The maximum value is 0.854 and the minimum one is 0.124. The average performance in API shows the condition of agriculture in this ADO. The productivity and marketing along with technology has been reflected in this performance.

- The Quality of Life Index is a little higher than the average level with index value of 0.555 which shows the level of human development in this ADO circle. It has been constructed with the wealth, education and health performance of the farmers of the ADO. It ranges in between the maximum of 0.835 to the minimum of 0.132.

- The ADO has performed in Multidimensional Poverty Index with a value of 0.339 thus showing the ADO circle as a poor one. The maximum one is 0.776 who is severly poor and the minimum one is 0.0 meaning no deprivation.

- The linkage between human development and agriculture or between API and QLI has been really significant with correlation coefficient of 0.636 showing good positive relationship between these two. On the other hand there has been significant negative relationship between Multidimensional poverty and agriculture. The correlation coefficient is -0.634 thus showing inverse linkge i.e. when API increases, MPI decreases and vice-versa.

- Quality of Life Index is composed of three dimension indices. The Wealth index in Dullabcherra ADO is 0.593 indicating moderate value. The maximum one is 0.920 and the poorest one is 0.280 showing large variation in wealth. The Education index is 0.515; moderate value and the maximum one is 1.00 who is educated as well as taking care of his children's enrolment while the lowest one is 0.00 who is illiterate and also not sending his child to the school. The Health index of this ADO is 0.573 which is good as well as denoting a little more than average performance. The maximum is 0.938 and the lowest is 0.00. the Body Mass Index is 21.8 which is normal and the highest value is 35.8 and the minimum score is 14.3.

- The correlation coefficient between Wealth index and Quality of Life index is quiet postive. It indicates strong positive linkage with the value of 0.680. The correlation coefficient between QLI and Education index is also quiet strong with 0.802 thus showing direct relation between education and human development. The correlation

coefficient between Health index and QLI is also quiet strong with the value of 0.623, it shows the importance of good health for human development.

♣ Agricultural Performance Index is prepared with four dimensional index. The Land Fertility index in this ADO is 0.465 showing close to the moderate. It ranges in between 0.810, the highest to 0.079, the lowest. The Market index is 0.531 and it ranges between 0.96, the highest seller to the subsistence one of index 0.00. The Technology Achievement index is 0.593 and ranges between 1.00 to 0.10. the Labour Productivity index is 0.325 and ranges in the maximum of 1.00 to the minimum of 0.00. The correlation coefficient between LFI and API is 0.588 denoting moderate value, but showing strong correlation between MI and API with 0.908, between TAI and API with 0.811 and between LPI and API with 0.793.

Sadarashi ADO: Villages- Kishorekapan & Lakshmi Bazar [Dist.- Karimganj]

Output Statistics

Table-117

Indicator	Sali	Auose	Potato	Sugarcane	Summer veg.	Winter veg.
Mean	52.0800	15.2733	4.9573	17.1746	1.0145	5.4927
Minimum	11.00	3.50	.00	4.50	.00	.70
Maximum	145.00	60.00	25.00	61.20	6.00	24.00
Sum	3906.00	1145.50	371.80	1288.10	76.09	411.95

Source : Calculated by the scholar from 75 samples.

- Kishorekapan & Lakshmi Bazar are two villages under Sadarashi ADO circle in Karimganj subdivision of Karimganj district. 38 samples from Kishorekapan and 37 samples from Lakshmi Bazar have been collected. Most of the farmers are small and medium farmers, some of them are marginal farmers and very few are large farmers. A common feature is that Sali paddy is the major crop produced by all farmers. The average production of Sali paddy is 52.08 quintals in Sadarashi ADO circle. The largest one has produced 145q of paddy who is the only large farmer and the poorest one produced 11q.

- Mean production of auose is 15.2q indicating much lower proportion in the total paddy cultivation of the ADO circle. The highest producer is the one who is a large farmer and produces 60q of auose; there are a few farmers producing more than 30q. However most of the farmers sell their auose produce in the market. The farmers producing very low amt.like 3q-4q-5q are subsistence farmers.

- The mean output of potato is 4.9q showing deficiency and therefore dependence on outside supply. The highest producer is with 25q while most of them sell it in village market or through traders. Those who produce more than 2q-3q can sell.

- The sugarcane is an important source of earning for the farmers. They sell it in village market and district haedquarter for molases. Sugarcane is a cash crop and thus an important source for the farmers to earn some extra money. Most of the farmers produce sugarcane to some extent. The highest producer is with 61q of sugarcane and the lowest is with 4.5q. The mean prduction is 17.1q which is good as it is sold entirely by the farmers.

➢ However the condition of summer and winter vegetables is not at all satisfactory. Most of the farmers are subsistence farmers. Only a few large farmers produce vegetables commercially. The mean produce of the summer vegetables is 1.01q while the highest output is 6q, the condition of winter vegetables is little better as the mean produce is 5.4q and maximum is 24q while the minimum is 0.7q.

Productivity in Sadarashi ADO

Table-118

	TOTAL	AREA UNDER PRODUCTION	WORKERS APPLIED	OUTPUT PER BIGHA	OUTPUT PER WORKER
Mean	95.9929	23.560	2.01	4.004	44.889
Minimum	21.50	6.5	1	3.0	21.5
Maximum	305.20	77.0	5	5.2	76.3
Sum	7199.47	1767.0	151		

Source : Calculated by the scholar from 75 samples.

➢ Total crop is calculated by taking in to account output of all products. The mean volume is 95.9q is not at all bad. The highest producer produces 305.2 who is the only large scale farmer taken from Sadarashi ADO. The most poor one produces only 21.5q. The mean area under cultivation in Sadarashi ADO is 23.5 Bigha. From land holding table we know that most of the farmers belong to the class of small, marginal and semi medium farmers while medium and large farmers are a few. The workers applied in the production varies in between 1/2/3 for the small farmers and 3/4/5 for the medium and large farmers. The mean observation is 2 and a maximum of 5 has been used in the land.

➢ The most important parameter to understand the productivity are output per worker and output per bigha i.e. labour productivity and fertility of the land. The output per bigha varies in between 3/4/5q paddy per bigha . The mean value is 4.0q and the maximum one is 5.2q while the minimum one is 3q per bigha. The labour productivity varies largely from 21.5q to 76.3q. As the table depicts the mean productivity is 44.8q per worker. Actually it is largely determined by the size of land.

Performance in marketing (Based on % of output sold)

Table-119

Indicator	Amt sold	% of output sold	Indicator	Number of farmers	Percentage of farmers
Mean observation	64q	51.11	Excellent (80% & above)	10	13%
Max. observation	273q	89.52	Very good (60%- 80%)	26	35%
Min. observation	0q	0.0	Good/medium/average (40%- 60%)	17	23%
			Poor/ Less than average (20%- 40%)	7	9%
			Very Poor/Negligible (Below 20%)	15	20%
			Total	75	100

Source : Calculated by the scholar from 75 samples.

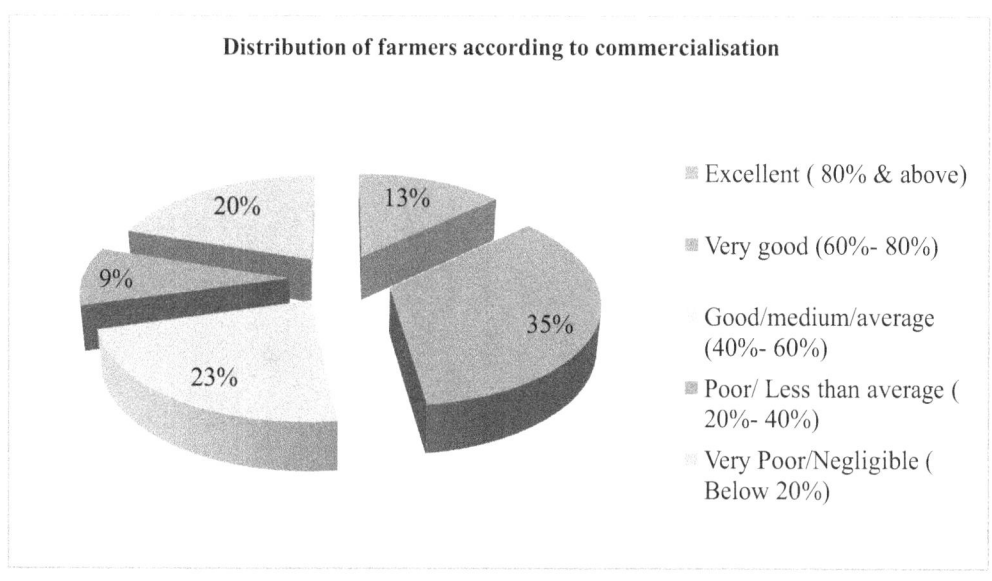

Distribution of farmers according to commercialisation

- The marketing performance in Sadarashi ADO circle is of mixed one. The mean sale of crop is 64 quintals and the mean % of output sold is 51.11% thus showing moderate level of performance in selling the output. The highest producer is selling 273q of output or 89% of the total, he is the only one large scale farmer in the Sdarashi ADO. The minimum or the worst performer is the one sold nothing or they are the subsistence farmers.
- The farmers who have sold more than 80% of their output are 10 in number or 13% of the study samples. They are the best performer in commercialisation of agriculture. Very good farmers are those who have sold 60% to 80% of their crop. They constitute 35% of the ADO or 18 in number. The medium or average farmers contribute largely to the marketable surplus. The good or average farmers constitute 23% of the ADO and they sell 40% to 60% of their output.
- The poor or less than average farmers are also large in Sdarashi. They form 9% of the total samples. If they could utilize their resource properly the performance would certainly increase. They are poor performers and that is mainly caused by deficiency in capacity to use the existing resources. Very poor or bad performers are those who could sell only below 20% of the crop. They are mainly subsistence farmers and their land holding is mostly marginal and small. They constitute 20% of the samples.

Statistical Evaluation of Sadarashi ADO

Table-120

Major variables		Intra-QLI		Intra-API	
Indicator	Sadarashi	Indicator	Sadarashi	Indicator	Sadarashi
Mean API	0.481	Mean WI	0.572	Mean LFI	0.476
Max API	0.776	Max WI	0.880	Max LFI	0.978
Min API	0.072	Min WI	0.260	Min LFI	0.043
Mean QLI	0.583	Mean EI	0.586	Mean MI	0.549
Max QLI	0.792	Max EI	0.900	Max MI	0.96
Min QLI	0.277	Min EI	0.000	Min MI	0.00
Mean MPI	0.267	Mean HI	0.609	Mean TAI	0.579
Max MPI	0.776	Max HI	0.859	Max TAI	1.00
Min MPI	0	Min HI	0.207	Min TAI	0.10
Correlation between API & QLI	0.581	Mean BMI	20.72	Mean LPI	0.322
Correlation between API & MPI	-0.394	Max BMI	33.3	Max LPI	0.604
		Min BMI	14.4	Min LPI	0.113
		Correlation between QLI & WI	0.656	Correlation between API & LFI	0.652
		Correlation between QLI & EI	0.856	Correlation between API & MI	0.939
		Correlation between QLI & HI	0.481	Correlation between API & TAI	0.902
				Correlation between API & LPI	0.760

Source : Calculated by the scholar from 75 samples.

- In Sadarashi ADO circle the Agricultural Performance Index is found moderate with index value of 0.481. The maximum value is 0.776 and the minimum one is 0.072. The average performance in API shows the condition of agriculture in this ADO. The productivity and marketing along with technology has been reflected in this performance.

- The Quality of Life Index is a little higher than the average level with index value of 0.583 which shows the level of human development in this ADO circle. It has been constructed with the wealth, education and health performance of the farmers of the ADO. It ranges in between the maximum of 0.792 to the minimum of 0.277.

- The ADO has performed in Multidimensional Poverty Index with a value of 0.267 thus showing the ADO circle as above the poverty level. The maximum one is 0.776 who is severly poor and the minimum one is 0.0 meaning no deprivation.

- The linkage between human development and agriculture or between API and QLI has been significant with correlation coefficient of 0.581 showing good positive relationship between these two. On the other hand there has been significant negative relationship between Multidimensional poverty and agriculture. The correlation coefficient is -0.394 thus showing inverse linkge i.e. when API increases, MPI decreases and vice-versa.

- Quality of Life Index is composed of three dimension indices. The Wealth index in Sadarashi ADO is 0.572 indicating moderate value. The maximum one is 0.880 and the poorest one is 0.260 showing large variation in wealth. The Education index is 0.586, the moderate value and the maximum one is 0.900 who is educated as well as taking care of his children's enrolment while the lowest one is 0.00 who is illiterate and also not sending his child to the school. The Health index of this ADO is 0.609 which is good as well as denoting a little more than average performance. The maximum is 0.859 and the lowest is 0.207. the Body Mass Index is 20.72 which is normal and the highest value is 33.3 and the minimum score is 14.4.

- The correlation coefficient between Wealth index and Quality of Life index is quiet postive. It indicates strong positive linkage with the value of 0.656. The correlation coefficient between QLI and Education index is also quiet strong with 0.856 thus showing direct relation between education and human development. The correlation coefficient between Health index and QLI is also quiet strong with the value of 0.481, it shows the importance of good health for human development.

♣ Agricultural Performance Index is prepared with four dimensional index. The Land Fertility index in this ADO is 0.476 showing close to the moderate. It ranges in between 0.978, the highest to 0.043, the lowest. The Market index is 0.549 and it ranges between 0.96, the highest seller to the subsistence one of index 0.00. The Technology Achievement index is 0.579 and ranges between 1.00 to 0.10. the Labour Productivity index is 0.322 and ranges in the maximum of 0.604 to the minimum of 0.113. The correlation coefficient between LFI and API is 0.647 denoting moderate value, but showing strong correlation between MI and API with 0.939, between TAI and API with 0.902 and between LPI and API with 0.760.

Arunachal ADO: Villages-Doodhpatil & Kashipur [Dist.- Cachar]

Output Statistics
Table-121

Indicator	Sali	Auose	Potato	Sugarcane	Summer veg.	Winter veg.	Total
Mean	57.4533	17.1933	5.6867	18.3279	1.0960	5.5627	1.05322
Minimum	11.00	4.00	1.00	3.88	.00	.70	24.01
Maximum	160.00	75.00	25.00	78.15	6.00	28.50	371.15
Sum	4309.00	1289.50	426.50	1374.60	82.20	417.20	7899.04

Source : Calculated by the scholar from 75 samples.

- Doodhpatil & Kashipur are two villages under Arunachal ADO circle in Silchar subdivision of Cachar district. 38 samples from Doodhpatil and 37 samples from Kashipur have been collected. Most of the farmers are small and medium farmers, some of them are marginal farmers and very few are large farmers. A common feature is that Sali paddy is the major crop produced by all farmers. The average production of Sali paddy is 57.4 quintals in Arunachal ADO circle. The largest one has produced 160q of paddy who is the only large farmer and the poorest one produced 11q.

- Mean production of auose is 17.1q indicating much lower proportion in the total paddy cultivation of the ADO circle. The highest producer is the one who is a large farmer and produces 75q of auose; there are a few farmers producing more than 30q. However most of the farmers sell their auose produce in the market. The farmers producing very low amt.like 3q-4q-5q are subsistence farmers.

- The mean output of potato is 5.6q showing deficiency and therefore dependence on outside supply. The highest producer is with 25q while most of them sell it in village market or through traders. Those who produce more than 2q-3q can sell.

- The sugarcane is an important source of earning for the farmers. They sell it in village market and district haedquarter for molases. Sugarcane is a cash crop and thus an important source for the farmers to earn some extra money. Most of the farmers produce sugarcane to some extent. The highest producer is with 78.15q of sugarcane and the lowest is with 3.8q. The mean prduction is 18.32q which is good as it is sold entirely by the farmers.

- However the condition of summer and winter vegetables is not at all satisfactory. Most of the farmers are subsistence farmers. Only a few large farmers produce vegetables commercially. The mean produce of the summer vegetables is 1.09q while the highest output is 6q, the condition of winter vegetables is little better as the mean produce is 5.5q and maximum is 28.5q while the minimum is 0.7q.

Productivity statistics

Table-122

	TOTAL	AREA UNDER PRODUCTION	WORKERS APPLIED	OUTPUT PER BIGHA	OUTPUT PER WORKER
Mean	105.322	25.460	2.27	4.068	45.147
Minimum	24.01	6.5	1	2.9	24.0
Maximum	371.15	90.0	6	4.7	72.3
Sum	7899.04	1909.5	170		

Source : Calculated by the scholar from 75 samples.

- Total crop is calculated by taking in to account output of all products. The mean volume is 105.32q which is not at all bad. The highest producer produces 371.15 who is the only large scale farmer taken from Arunachal ADO. The most poor one produces only 24.01q. The mean area under cultivation in Arunachal ADO is 25.4 Bigha. From land holding table we know that most of the farmers belong to the class of small, marginal and semi medium farmers while medium and large farmers are a few. The workers applied in the production varies in between 1/2/3 for the small farmers and 3/4/5 for the medium and large farmers. The mean observation is 2 and a maximum of 6 has been used in the land.
- The most important parameter to understand the productivity are output per worker and output per bigha i.e. labour productivity and fertility of the land. The output per bigha varies in between 3/4/5q paddy per bigha . The mean value is 4.0q and the maximum one is 4.7q while the minimum one is 2.9q per bigha. The labour productivity varies largely from 24q to 72.3q per worker. As the table depicts the

mean productivity is 45.14q per worker. Actually it is largely determined by the size of land.

Performance in marketing (Based on % of output sold)

Table-123

Indicator	Amt sold	% of output sold	Indicator	Number of farmers	Percentage of farmers
Mean observation	74q	55.19	Excellent (80% & above)	13	17%
Max. observation	339q	91.38	Very good (60%- 80%)	29	39%
Min. observation	0q	0.0	Good/medium/average (40%- 60%)	13	17%
			Poor/ Less than average (20%- 40%)	8	11%
			Very Poor/Negligible (Below 20%)	12	16%
			Total	75	100

Source : Calculated by the scholar from 75 samples.

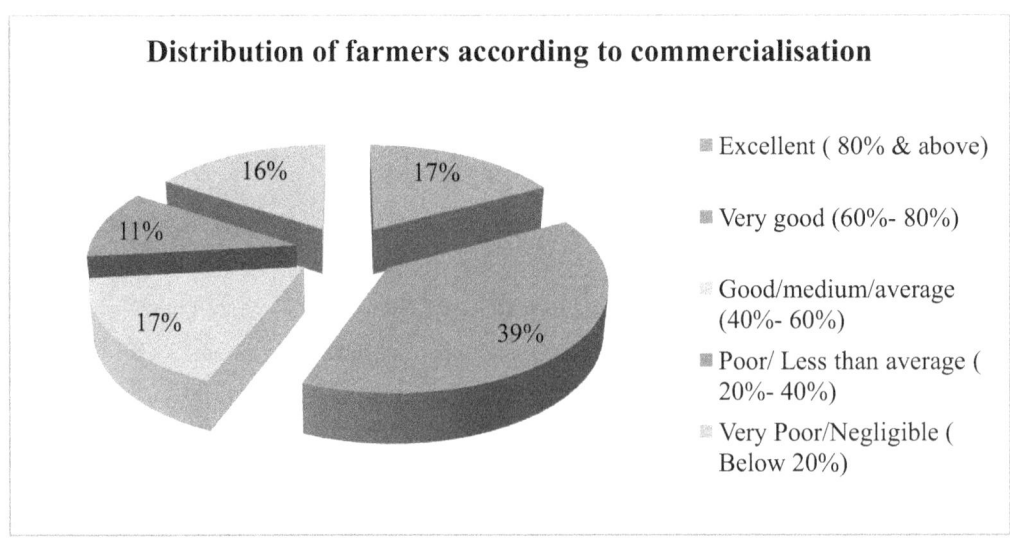

- The marketing performance in Arunachal ADO circle is of mixed one. The mean sale of crop is 74 quintals and the mean % of output sold is 55.19% thus showing moderate level of performance in selling the output. The highest producer is selling 339q of output or 91.18% of the total, he is the only one large scale farmer in the Sadarashi ADO. The minimum or the worst performer are those who sold nothing or they are the subsistence farmers.
- The farmers who have sold more than 80% of their output are 13 in number or 17% of the study samples. They are the best performer in commercialisation of agriculture. Very good farmers are those who have sold 60% to 80% of their crop. They constitute 39% of the ADO or 29 in number. The medium or average farmers contribute largely to the marketable surplus. The good or average farmers constitute 17% of the ADO and they sell 40% to 60% of their output.
- The poor or less than average farmers are also large in Arunachal. They form 11% of the total samples. If they could utilize their resource properly the performance would certainly increase. They are poor performers and that is mainly caused by deficiency in capacity to use the existing resources. Very poor or bad performers are those who could sell only below 20% of the crop. They are mainly subsistence farmers and their land holding is mostly marginal and small. They constitute 16% of the samples.

Statistical Evaluation of Arunachal ADO

Table-124

Major variables		Intra-QLI		Intra- API	
Indicator	Arunachal	Indicator	Arunachal	Indicator	Arunachal
Mean API	0.495	Mean WI	0.548	Mean LFI	0.507
Max API	0.765	Max WI	0.880	Max LFI	0.785
Min API	0.173	Min WI	0.260	Min LFI	0.012
Mean QLI	0.591	Mean EI	0.621	Mean MI	0.593
Max QLI	0.804	Max EI	1.00	Max MI	0.980
Min QLI	0.297	Min EI	0.00	Min MI	0.00
Mean MPI	0.246	Mean HI	0.622	Mean TAI	0.557
Max MPI	0.831	Max HI	0.930	Max TAI	1.000
Min MPI	0	Min HI	0.069	Min TAI	0.10
Correlation between API & QLI	0.524	Mean BMI	21.05	Mean LPI	0.324
Correlation between API & MPI	-0.551	Max BMI	35.8	Max LPI	0.568
		Min BMI	14.3	Min LPI	0.135
		Correlation between QLI & WI	0.695	Correlation between API & LFI	0.530
		Correlation between QLI & EI	0.851	Correlation between API & MI	0.919
		Correlation between QLI & HI	0.375	Correlation between API & TAI	0.825
				Correlation between API & LPI	0.627

Source : Calculated by the scholar from 75 samples.

- In Arunachal ADO circle the Agricultural Performance Index is found moderate with index value of 0.495. The maximum value is 0.765 and the minimum one is 0.173. The average performance in API shows the condition of agriculture in this ADO. The productivity and marketing along with technology has been reflected in this performance.

- The Quality of Life Index is a little higher than the average level with index value of 0.591 which shows the level of human development in this ADO circle. It has been constructed with the wealth, education and health performance of the farmers of the ADO. It ranges in between the maximum of 0.804 to the minimum of 0.297.

- The ADO has performed in Multidimensional Poverty Index with a value of 0.246 thus showing the ADO circle as above the poverty level. The maximum one is 0.831 who is severly poor and the minimum one is 0.0 meaning no deprivation.

- The linkage between human development and agriculture or between API and QLI has been significant with correlation coefficient of 0.524 showing good positive relationship between these two. On the other hand there has been significant negative relationship between Multidimensional poverty and agriculture. The correlation coefficient is -0.551 thus showing inverse linkge i.e. when API increases, MPI decreases and vice-versa.

- Quality of Life Index is composed of three dimension indices. The Wealth index in this ADO is 0.548 indicating moderate value. The maximum one is 0.880 and the poorest one is 0.260 showing large variation in wealth. The Education index is 0.621, the moderate value and the maximum one is 1.00 who is educated as well as taking care of his children's enrolment while the lowest one is 0.00 who is illiterate and also not sending his child to the school. The Health index of this ADO is 0.622 which is good as well as denoting a little more than average performance. The maximum is 0.930 and the lowest is 0.069. the Body Mass Index is 21.05 which is normal and the highest value is 35.8 and the minimum score is 14.3.

- The correlation coefficient between Wealth index and Quality of Life index is quiet postive. It indicates strong positive linkage with the value of 0.695. The correlation coefficient between QLI and Education index is also quiet strong with 0.851 thus showing direct relation between education and human development. The correlation coefficient between Health index and QLI is also good with the value of 0.375, it shows the importance of good health for human development.

♣ Agricultural Performance Index is prepared with four dimensional index. The Land Fertility index in this ADO is 0.507 showing moderate. It ranges in between 0.785, the highest to 0.012, the lowest. The Market index is 0.602 and it ranges between 0.980, the highest seller to the subsistence one of index 0.00. The Technology Achievement index is 0.557 and ranges between 1.00 to 0.10. the Labour Productivity index is 0.324 and ranges in the maximum of 0.568 to the minimum of 0.135. The correlation coefficient between LFI and API is 0.530 denoting moderate value, but showing strong correlation between MI and API with 0.919, between TAI and API with 0.825 and between LPI and API with 0.627.

Sonai ADO: Villages-Govindanagar and Tulagram [Dist.- Cachar]

Output Statistics
Table-125

Indicator	Sali	Auose	Potato	Sugarcane	Summer veg.	Winter veg.	Total
Mean	54.8800	14.3733	4.8667	15.7901	.8980	4.1187	94.9275
Minimum	12.00	4.00	1.00	4.00	.18	.90	24.60
Maximum	190.00	100.00	25.00	99.20	6.00	30.00	450.20
Sum	4116.00	1078.00	365.00	1184.26	67.35	308.90	7119.56

Source : Calculated by the scholar from 75 samples.

- Gobindanagar and Tulaghram are two villages under Sonai ADO circle in Sonai subdivision of Cachar district. 38 samples from Govindanagar and 37 samples from Tulagram have been collected. Most of the farmers are small and medium farmers, some of them are marginal farmers and very few are large farmers. A common feature is that Sali paddy is the major crop produced by all farmers. The average production of Sali paddy is 54.8 quintals in Sonai ADO circle. The largest one has produced 190q of paddy who is the only large farmer and the poorest one produced 12q.

- Mean production of auose is 14.3q indicating much lower proportion in the total paddy cultivation of the ADO circle. The highest producer is the one who is a large farmer and produces 100q of auose; there are a few farmers producing more than 30q. However most of the farmers sell their auose produce in the market. The farmers producing very low amt.like 3q-4q-5q are subsistence farmers.

- The mean output of potato is 4.8q showing deficiency and therefore dependence on outside supply. The highest producer is with 25q while most of them sell it in village market or through traders. Those who produce more than 2q-3q can sell.

- The sugarcane is an important source of earning for the farmers. They sell it in village market and district haedquarter for molases. Sugarcane is a cash crop and thus an important source for the farmers to earn some extra money. Most of the farmers produce sugarcane to some extent. The highest producer is with 99q of sugarcane and the lowest is with 4q. The mean prduction is 15.7q which is good as it is sold entirely by the farmers.

- However the condition of summer and winter vegetables is not at all satisfactory. Most of the farmers are subsistence farmers. Only a few large farmers produce vegetables commercially. The mean produce of the summer vegetables is 0.89q while the highest output is 6q, the condition of winter vegetables is little better as the mean produce is 4.11q and maximum is 30q while the minimum is 0.90q.

Productivity Statistics
Table-126

INDICATOR	TOTAL	AREA UNDER PRODUCTION	WORKERS APPLIED	OUTPUT PER BIGHA	OUTPUT PER WORKER
Mean	94.9275	23.0200	2.2133	4.0600	41.4667
Minimum	24.60	6.00	1.00	3.40	24.60
Maximum	450.20	110.00	6.00	5.00	75.00
Sum	7119.56	1726.50	166.00		

Source : Calculated by the scholar from 75 samples.

- Total crop is calculated by taking in to account output of all products. The mean volume is 94.9q which is not at all bad. The highest producer produces 450.2 who is the only large scale farmer taken from Sonai ADO. The most poor one produces only 24.6q. The mean area under cultivation in Sonai ADO is 23.02 Bigha. From land holding table we know that most of the farmers belong to the class of small, marginal and semi medium farmers while medium and large farmers are a few. The workers applied in the production varies in between 1/2/3 for the small farmers and 3/4/5 for the medium and large farmers. The mean observation is 2 and a maximum of 6 has been used in the land.

- The most important parameter to understand the productivity are output per worker and output per bigha i.e. labour productivity and fertility of the land. The output per bigha varies in between 3/4/5q paddy per bigha . The mean value is 4.06q and the maximum one is 5q while the minimum one is 3.4q per bigha. The labour productivity varies largely from 24.6q to 75q per worker. As the table depicts the mean productivity is 41.4q per worker. Actually it is largely determined by the size of land.

Performance in marketing (Based on % of output sold)

Table-127

Indicator	Amt sold	% of output sold	Indicator	Number of farmers	Percentage of farmers
Mean observation	63q	52.81	Excellent (80% & above)	7	9%
Max. observation	418q	92.89	Very good (60%- 80%)	32	43
Min. observation	0q	0.0	Good/medium/average (40%- 60%)	15	20
			Poor/ Less than average (20%- 40%)	11	15
			Very Poor/Negligible (Below 20%)	10	13
			Total	75	100

Source : Calculated by the scholar from 75 samples.

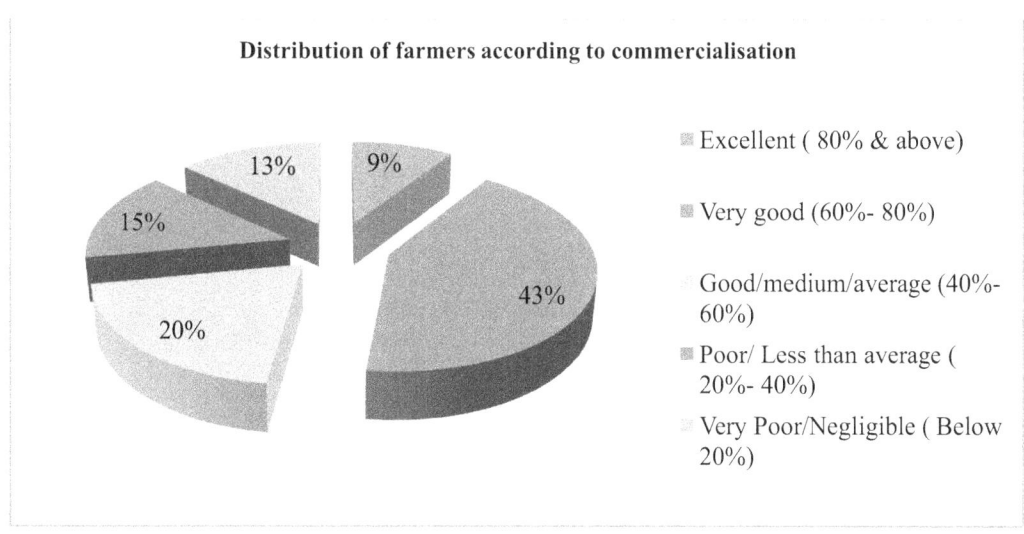

Distribution of farmers according to commercialisation

- The marketing performance in Sonai ADO circle is of mixed one. The mean sale of crop is 63 quintals and the mean % of output sold is 52.81% thus showing moderate level of performance in selling the output. The highest producer is selling 418q of output or 92.8% of the total, he is the only one large scale farmer in the Sonai ADO. The minimum or the worst performer are those who sold nothing or they are the subsistence farmers.
- The farmers who have sold more than 80% of their output are 7 in number or 9% of the study samples. They are the best performer in commercialisation of agriculture. Very good farmers are those who have sold 60% to 80% of their crop. They constitute 43% of the ADO or 32 in number. The medium or average farmers contribute largely to the marketable surplus. The good or average farmers constitute 20% of the ADO and they sell 40% to 60% of their output.
- The poor or less than average farmers are also large in Sonai. They form 15% of the total samples. If they could utilize their resource properly the performance would certainly increase. They are poor performers and that is mainly caused by deficiency in capacity to use the existing resources. Very poor or bad performers are those who could sell only below 20% of the crop. They are mainly subsistence farmers and their land holding is mostly marginal and small. They constitute 13% of the samples.

Statistical Evaluation of Sonai ADO

Table-128

Major variables		Intra-QLI		Intra- API	
Indicator	Sonai	Indicator	Sonai	Indicator	Sonai
Mean API	0.463	Mean WI	0.556	Mean LFI	0.506
Max API	0.778	Max WI	0.980	Max LFI	0.926
Min API	0.174	Min WI	0.320	Min LFI	0.218
Mean QLI	0.599	Mean EI	0.633	Mean MI	0.567
Max QLI	0.828	Max EI	1.00	Max MI	0.980
Min QLI	0.336	Min EI	0.00	Min MI	0.00
Mean MPI	0.189	Mean HI	0.627	Mean TAI	0.496
Max MPI	0.554	Max HI	0.887	Max TAI	1.00
Min MPI	0	Min HI	0.055	Min TAI	0.10
Correlation between API & QLI	0.509	Mean BMI	20.6	Mean LPI	0.291
Correlation between API & MPI	-0.209	Max BMI	33.2	Max LPI	0.593
		Min BMI	14.3	Min LPI	0.141
		Correlation between QLI & WI	0.592	Correlation between API & LFI	0.581
		Correlation between QLI & EI	0.894	Correlation between API & MI	0.885
		Correlation between QLI & HI	0.403	Correlation between API & TAI	0.752
				Correlation between API & LPI	0.635

Source : Calculated by the scholar from 75 samples.

♣ In Sonai ADO circle the Agricultural Performance Index is found moderate with index value of 0.463. The maximum value is 0.778 and the minimum one is 0.174. The average performance in API shows the condition of agriculture in this ADO. The productivity and marketing along with technology has been reflected in this performance.

- ♣ The Quality of Life Index is a little higher than the average level with index value of 0.599 which shows the level of human development in this ADO circle. It has been constructed with the wealth, education and health performance of the farmers of the ADO. It ranges in between the maximum of 0.828 to the minimum of 0.336.

- ♣ The ADO has performed in Multidimensional Poverty Index with a value of 0.189 thus showing the ADO circle as above the poverty level. The maximum one is 0.554 who is severly poor and the minimum one is 0.0 meaning no deprivation.

- ♣ The linkage between human development and agriculture or between API and QLI has been significant with correlation coefficient of 0.509 showing good positive relationship between these two. On the other hand there has been significant negative relationship between Multidimensional poverty and agriculture. The correlation coefficient is -0.209 thus showing inverse linkge i.e. when API increases, MPI decreases and vice-versa.

- ♣ Quality of Life Index is composed of three dimension indices. The Wealth index in this ADO is 0.556 indicating moderate value. The maximum one is 0.980 and the poorest one is 0.320 showing large variation in wealth. The Education index is 0.633, the moderate value and the maximum one is 1.00 who is educated as well as taking care of his children's enrolment while the lowest one is 0.00 who is illiterate and also not sending his child to the school. The Health index of this ADO is 0.627 which is good as well as denoting a little more than average performance. The maximum is 0.887 and the lowest is 0.055. the Body Mass Index is 20.6 which is normal and the highest value is 33.2 and the minimum score is 14.3.

- ♣ The correlation coefficient between Wealth index and Quality of Life index is quiet postive. It indicates strong positive linkage with the value of 0.592. The correlation coefficient between QLI and Education index is also quiet strong with 0.894 thus showing direct relation between education and human development. The correlation coefficient between Health index and QLI is also good with the value of 0.403, it shows the importance of good health for human development.

- ♣ Agricultural Performance Index is prepared with four dimensional index. The Land Fertility index in this ADO is 0.506 showing moderate. It ranges in between 0.926, the highest to 0.218, the lowest. The Market index is 0.566 and it ranges between 0.980, the highest seller to the subsistence one of index 0.00. The Technology Achievement index is 0.496 and ranges between 1.00 to 0.10. the Labour Productivity index is 0.291

and ranges in the maximum of 0.593 to the minimum of 0.141. The correlation coefficient between LFI and API is 0.581 denoting moderate value, but showing strong correlation between MI and API with 0.885, between TAI and API with 0.752 and between LPI and API with 0.635.

Motinagar ADO: Villages- Binnakandi and Kaptanpur [Dist.- Cachar]

Output Statistics
Table-129

Indicator	Sali	Auose	Potato	Sugarcane	Summer veg.	Winter veg.	Total
Mean	52.6533	12.1267	4.7867	13.0861	.9237	4.2840	87.8609
Minimum	10.00	3.00	.00	2.48	.00	.90	18.10
Maximum	195.00	80.00	29.00	90.00	6.00	28.50	421.50
Sum	3949.00	909.50	359.00	981.46	69.28	321.30	6589.57

Source : Calculated by the scholar from 75 samples.

➤ Binnakandi and Kaptanpur are two villages under Motinagar ADO circle in Lakhipur subdivision of Cachar district. 38 samples from Binnakandi and 37 samples from Kaptanpur have been collected. Most of the farmers are small and medium farmers, some of them are marginal farmers and very few are large farmers. A common feature is that Sali paddy is the major crop produced by all farmers. The average production of Sali paddy is 52.6 quintals in Sonai ADO circle. The largest one has produced 195q of paddy who is the only large farmer and the poorest one produced 10q.

➤ Mean production of auose is 12.1q indicating much lower proportion in the total paddy cultivation of the ADO circle. The highest producer is the one who is a large farmer and produces 80q of auose; there are a few farmers producing more than 30q. However most of the farmers sell their auose produce in the market. The farmers producing very low amt.like 3q-4q-5q are subsistence farmers.

- The mean output of potato is 4.7q showing deficiency and therefore dependence on outside supply. The highest producer is with 29q while most of them sell it in village market or through traders. Those who produce more than 2q-3q can sell.
- The sugarcane is an important source of earning for the farmers. They sell it in village market and district haedquarter for molases. Sugarcane is a cash crop and thus an important source for the farmers to earn some extra money. Most of the farmers produce sugarcane to some extent. The highest producer is with 90q of sugarcane and the lowest is with 2.4q. The mean prduction is 13.08q which is good as it is sold entirely by the farmers.
- However the condition of summer and winter vegetables is not at all satisfactory. Most of the farmers are subsistence farmers. Only a few large farmers produce vegetables commercially. The mean produce of the summer vegetables is 0.92q while the highest output is 6q, the condition of winter vegetables is little better as the mean produce is 4.28q and maximum is 28.5q while the minimum is 0.90q.

Productivity Statistics
Table-130

INDICATOR	TOTAL	AREA UNDER PRODUCTION	WORKERS APPLIED	OUTPUT PER BIGHA	OUTPUT PER WORKER
Mean	87.8609	20.5667	2.1867	4.1853	37.4707
Minimum	18.10	4.50	1.00	3.00	18.10
Maximum	421.50	95.00	6.00	4.80	70.30
Sum	6589.57	1542.50	164.00		

Source : Calculated by the scholar from 75 samples.

- Total crop is calculated by taking in to account output of all products. The mean volume is 87.8q which is not at all bad. The highest producer produces 421.5 who is the only large scale farmer taken from Motinagar ADO. The most poor one produces only 18.1q. The mean area under cultivation in Motinagar ADO is 20.56 Bigha. From land holding table we know that most of the farmers belong to the class of small, marginal and semi medium farmers while medium and large farmers are a few. The workers applied in the production varies in between 1/2/3 for the small farmers and

3/4/5 for the medium and large farmers. The mean observation is 2 and a maximum of 6 has been used in the land.

> The most important parameter to understand the productivity are output per worker and output per bigha i.e. labour productivity and fertility of the land. The output per bigha varies in between 3/4/5q paddy per bigha . The mean value is 4.18q and the maximum one is 4.8q while the minimum one is 3q per bigha. The labour productivity varies largely from 18.1q to 70.3q per worker. As the table depicts the mean productivity is 37.4q per worker. Actually it is largely determined by the size of land.

Performance in marketing (Based on % of output sold)

Table-131

Indicator	Amt sold	% of output sold	Indicator	Number of farmers	Percentage of farmers
Mean observation	57q	45.12	Excellent (80% & above)	8	11%
Max. observation	390q	92.41	Very good (60%- 80%)	26	34%
Min. observation	0q	0.0	Good/medium/average (40%- 60%)	9	12%
			Poor/ Less than average (20%- 40%)	15	20%
			Very Poor/Negligible (Below 20%)	17	23%
			Total	75	100

Source : Calculated by the scholar from 75 samples.

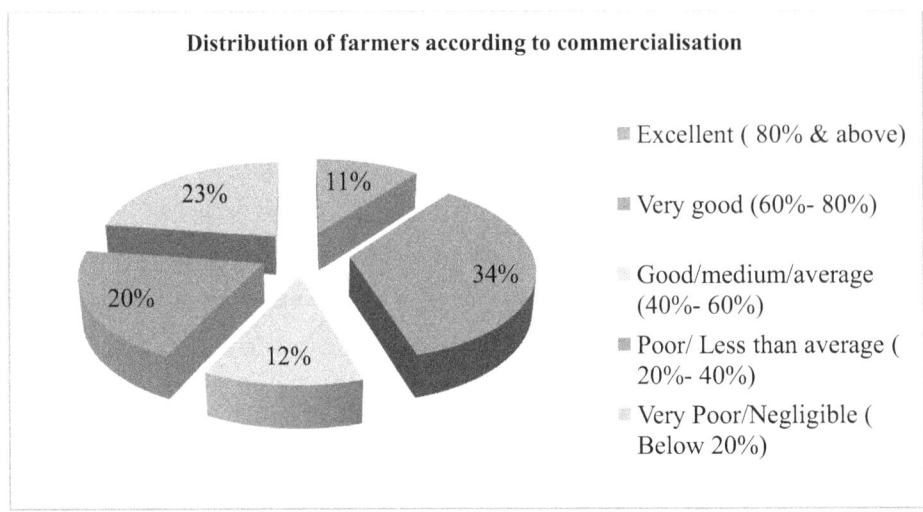

- ➤ The marketing performance in Motinagar ADO circle is of mixed one. The mean sale of crop is 57 quintals and the mean % of output sold is 45.1% thus showing moderate level of performance in selling the output. The highest producer is selling 390q of output or 92.4% of the total, he is the only one large scale farmer in the Motinagar ADO. The minimum or the worst performer are those who sold nothing or they are the subsistence farmers.

- ➤ The farmers who have sold more than 80% of their output are 8 in number or 11% of the study samples. They are the best performer in commercialisation of agriculture. Very good farmers are those who have sold 60% to 80% of their crop. They constitute 34% of the ADO or 26 in number. The medium or average farmers contribute largely to the marketable surplus. The good or average farmers constitute 12% of the ADO and they sell 40% to 60% of their output.

- ➤ The poor or less than average farmers are also large in Motinagar. They form 20% of the total samples. If they could utilize their resource properly the performance would certainly increase. They are poor performers and that is mainly caused by deficiency in capacity to use the existing resources. Very poor or bad performers are those who could sell only below 20% of the crop. They are mainly subsistence farmers and their land holding is mostly marginal and small. They constitute 23% of the samples.

Statistical Evaluation of Motinagar ADO

Table-132

Major variables		Intra-QLI		Intra- API	
Indicator	Motinagar	Indicator	Motinagar	Indicator	Motinagar
Mean API	0.450	Mean WI	0.554	Mean LFI	0.559
Max API	0.791	Max WI	0.940	Max LFI	0.841
Min API	0.071	Min WI	0.300	Min LFI	0.061
Mean QLI	0.613	Mean EI	0.668	Mean MI	0.478
Max QLI	0.817	Max EI	0.867	Max MI	0.99
Min QLI	0.318	Min EI	0.00	Min MI	0.00
Mean MPI	0.231	Mean HI	0.635	Mean TAI	0.493
Max MPI	0.886	Max HI	0.987	Max TAI	1.00
Min MPI	0	Min HI	0.079	Min TAI	0.10
Correlation between API & QLI	0.608	Mean BMI	21.3	Mean LPI	0.255
Correlation between API & MPI	-0.567	Max BMI	38.2	Max LPI	0.550
		Min BMI	14.4	Min LPI	0.082
		Correlation between QLI & WI	0.617	Correlation between API & LFI	0.661
		Correlation between QLI & EI	0.810	Correlation between API & MI	0.911
		Correlation between QLI & HI	0.523	Correlation between API & TAI	0.737
				Correlation between API & LPI	0.741

Source : Calculated by the scholar from 75 samples.

- In Motinagar ADO circle the Agricultural Performance Index is found moderate with index value of 0.450. The maximum value is 0.791 and the minimum one is 0.071. The average performance in API shows the condition of agriculture in this ADO. The productivity and marketing along with technology has been reflected in this performance.

- The Quality of Life Index is a little higher than the average level with index value of 0.613 which shows the level of human development in this ADO circle. It has been constructed with the wealth, education and health performance of the farmers of the ADO. It ranges in between the maximum of 0.817 to the minimum of 0.318.

- The ADO has performed in Multidimensional Poverty Index with a value of 0.231 thus showing the ADO circle as above the poverty level. The maximum one is 0.886 who is severly poor and the minimum one is 0.0 meaning no deprivation.

- The linkage between human development and agriculture or between API and QLI has been significant with correlation coefficient of 0.608 showing good positive relationship between these two. On the other hand there has been significant negative relationship between Multidimensional poverty and agriculture. The correlation coefficient is -0.567 thus showing inverse linkge i.e. when API increases, MPI decreases and vice-versa.

- Quality of Life Index is composed of three dimension indices. The Wealth index in this ADO is 0.554 indicating moderate value. The maximum one is 0.940 and the poorest one is 0.300 showing large variation in wealth. The Education index is 0.668, the moderate value and the maximum one is .867 who is educated as well as taking care of his children's enrolment while the lowest one is 0.00 who is illiterate and also not sending his child to the school. The Health index of this ADO is 0.635 which is good as well as denoting a little more than average performance. The maximum is 0.987 and the lowest is 0.079. the Body Mass Index is 21.3 which is normal and the highest value is 38.2 and the minimum score is 14.4.

- The correlation coefficient between Wealth index and Quality of Life index is quiet postive. It indicates strong positive linkage with the value of 0.617. The correlation coefficient between QLI and Education index is also quiet strong with 0.810 thus showing direct relation between education and human development. The correlation

coefficient between Health index and QLI is also good with the value of 0.523, it shows the importance of good health for human development.

♣ Agricultural Performance Index is prepared with four dimensional index. The Land Fertility index in this ADO is 0.559 showing moderate. It ranges in between 0.841, the highest to 0.061, the lowest. The Market index is 0.478 and it ranges between 0.990, the highest seller to the subsistence one of index 0.00. The Technology Achievement index is 0.493 and ranges between 1.00 to 0.10. the Labour Productivity index is 0.255 and ranges in the maximum of 0.550 to the minimum of 0.082. The correlation coefficient between LFI and API is 0.661 denoting moderate value, but showing strong correlation between MI and API with 0.911, between TAI and API with 0.737 and between LPI and API with 0.741.

Hailakandi ADO: Villages- Kanchanpur and Narainpur [Dist.- Hailakandi]

Output Statistics
Table-133

Indicator	Sali	Auose	Potato	Sugarcane	Summer veg.	Winter veg.	Total
Mean	47.3813	10.7600	3.6533	11.1083	.7107	4.1307	77.7448
Minimum	9.00	4.00	.00	2.00	.00	.40	17.70
Maximum	193.00	60.00	30.00	63.00	8.40	22.80	377.20
Sum	3553.60	807.00	274.00	833.13	53.30	309.80	5830.86

Source : Calculated by the scholar from 75 samples.

➤ Kanchanpur and Narainpur are two villages under Hailakandi ADO circle in Hailakandi subdivision of Hailakandi district. 38 samples from Kanchanpur and 37 samples from Naraipur have been collected. Most of the farmers are small and medium farmers, some of them are marginal farmers and very few are large farmers. A common feature is that Sali paddy is the major crop produced by all farmers. The average production of Sali paddy is 47.3 quintals in Hailakandi ADO circle. The largest one has produced 193q of paddy who is the only large farmer and the poorest one produced 9q.

- Mean production of auose is 10.7q indicating much lower proportion in the total paddy cultivation of the ADO circle. The highest producer is the one who is a large farmer and produces 60q of auose; there are a few farmers producing more than 30q. However most of the farmers sell their auose produce in the market. The farmers producing very low amt.like 3q-4q-5q are subsistence farmers.
- The mean output of potato is 3.65q showing deficiency and therefore dependence on outside supply. The highest producer is with 30q while most of them sell it in village market or through traders. Those who produce more than 2q-3q can sell.
- The sugarcane is an important source of earning for the farmers. They sell it in village market and district haedquarter for molases. Sugarcane is a cash crop and thus an important source for the farmers to earn some extra money. Most of the farmers produce sugarcane to some extent. The highest producer is with 63q of sugarcane and the lowest is with 2q. The mean prduction is 11.1q which is good as it is sold entirely by the farmers.
- However the condition of summer and winter vegetables is not at all satisfactory. Most of the farmers are subsistence farmers. Only a few large farmers produce vegetables commercially. The mean produce of the summer vegetables is 0.71q while the highest output is 8.4q, the condition of winter vegetables is little better as the mean produce is 4.13q and maximum is 22.8q while the minimum is 0.40q.

Productivity Statistics
Table-134

INDICATOR	TOTAL	AREA UNDER PRODUCTION	WORKERS APPLIED	OUTPUT PER BIGHA	OUTPUT PER WORKER
Mean	77.7448	18.2611	2.1200	4.2133	34.1680
Minimum	17.70	4.50	1.00	3.50	17.60
Maximum	377.20	88.00	6.00	5.00	62.90
Sum	5830.86	1369.58	159.00		

Source : Calculated by the scholar from 75 samples.

- Total crop is calculated by taking in to account output of all products. The mean volume is 77.7q which is not at all bad. The highest producer produces 377.2q who is the only large scale farmer taken from Hailakandi ADO. The most poor one produces only 18.1q. The mean area under cultivation in Hailakandi ADO is 18.26 Bigha. From land holding table we know that most of the farmers belong to the class of small, marginal and semi medium farmers while medium and large farmers are a few. The workers applied in the production varies in between 1/2/3 for the small farmers and 3/4/5 for the medium and large farmers. The mean observation is 2 and a maximum of 6 has been used in the land.
- The most important parameter to understand the productivity are output per worker and output per bigha i.e. labour productivity and fertility of the land. The output per bigha varies in between 3/4/5q paddy per bigha . The mean value is 4.21q and the maximum one is 5q while the minimum one is 3.5q per bigha. The labour productivity varies largely from 17.6q to 62.9q per worker. As the table depicts the mean productivity is 34.1q per worker. Actually it is largely determined by the size of land.

Performance in marketing (Based on % of output sold)

Table-135

Indicator	Amt sold	% of output sold	Indicator	Number of farmers	Percentage of farmers
Mean observation	47q	40.24	Excellent (80% & above)	5	7%
Max. observation	345q	91.52	Very good (60%- 80%)	26	35%
Min. observation	0q	0.0	Good/medium/average (40%- 60%)	10	13%
			Poor/ Less than average (20%- 40%)	4	5%
			Very Poor/Negligible (Below 20%)	30	40%
			Total	75	100

Source : Calculated by the scholar from 75 samples.

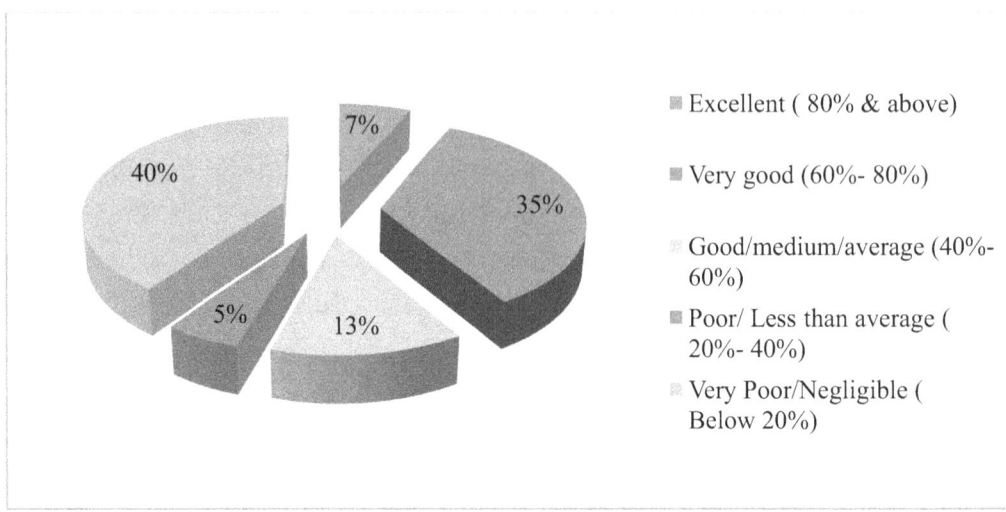

- The marketing performance in Hailakandi ADO circle is of mixed one. The mean sale of crop is 47 quintals and the mean % of output sold is 40.24% thus showing a little less than moderate level of performance in selling the output. The highest producer is selling 345q of output or 91.5% of the total, he is the only one large scale farmer in the Hailakandi ADO. The minimum or the worst performer are those who sold nothing or they are the subsistence farmers.

- The farmers who have sold more than 80% of their output are 5 in number or 7% of the study samples. They are the best performer in commercialisation of agriculture. Very good farmers are those who have sold 60% to 80% of their crop. They constitute 35% of the ADO or 26 in number. The medium farmers contribute largely to the marketable surplus. The good or average farmers constitute 13% of the ADO and they sell 40% to 60% of their output.

- The poor or less than average farmers are also there in Hailakandi. They form 5% of the total samples. If they could utilize their resource properly the performance would certainly increase. They are poor performers and that is mainly caused by deficiency in capacity to use the existing resources. Very poor or bad performers are those who could sell only below 20% of the crop. They are mainly subsistence farmers and their land holding is mostly marginal and small. They constitute a sizable part and 40% of the samples.

Statistical Evaluation of Hailakandi ADO

Table-136

Major variables		Intra-QLI		Intra- API	
Indicator	Hailakandi	Indicator	Hailakandi	Indicator	Hailakandi
Mean API	0.441	Mean WI	0.536	Mean LFI	0.569
Max API	0.743	Max WI	0.900	Max LFI	0.896
Min API	0.170	Min WI	0.260	Min LFI	0.273
Mean QLI	0.608	Mean EI	0.676	Mean MI	0.432
Max QLI	0.843	Max EI	1.00	Max MI	0.98
Min QLI	0.313	Min EI	0.00	Min MI	0.00
Mean MPI	0.229	Mean HI	0.630	Mean TAI	0.538
Max MPI	0.831	Max HI	0.990	Max TAI	0.930
Min MPI	0	Min HI	0.043	Min TAI	0.10
Correlation between API & QLI	0.662	Mean BMI	21.4	Mean LPI	0.226
Correlation between API & MPI	-0.467	Max BMI	38.4	Max LPI	0.484
		Min BMI	14.4	Min LPI	0.078
		Correlation between QLI & WI	0.660	Correlation between API & LFI	0.507
		Correlation between QLI & EI	0.762	Correlation between API & MI	0.936
		Correlation between QLI & HI	0.439	Correlation between API & TAI	0.783
				Correlation between API & LPI	0.674

Source: Calculated by scholar from 75 samples of each ADO circle

- In Hailakandi ADO circle the Agricultural Performance Index is found moderate with index value of 0.441. The maximum value is 0.743 and the minimum one is 0.170. The average performance in API shows the condition of agriculture in this ADO. The productivity and marketing along with technology has been reflected in this performance.

- The Quality of Life Index is a little higher than the average level with index value of 0.608 which shows the level of human development in this ADO circle. It has been constructed with the wealth, education and health performance of the farmers of the ADO. It ranges in between the maximum of 0.843 to the minimum of 0.313.

- The ADO has performed in Multidimensional Poverty Index with a value of 0.229 thus showing the ADO circle as above the poverty level. The maximum one is 0.831 who is severly poor and the minimum one is 0.0 meaning no deprivation.

- The linkage between human development and agriculture or between API and QLI has been significant with correlation coefficient of 0.662 showing good positive relationship between these two. On the other hand there has been significant negative relationship between Multidimensional poverty and agriculture. The correlation coefficient is -0.467 thus showing inverse linkge i.e. when API increases, MPI decreases and vice-versa.

- Quality of Life Index is composed of three dimension indices. The Wealth index in this ADO is 0.536 indicating moderate value. The maximum one is 0.900 and the poorest one is 0.260 showing large variation in wealth. The Education index is 0.676, the moderate value and the maximum one is 1.00 who is educated as well as taking care of his children's enrolment while the lowest one is 0.00 who is illiterate and also not sending his child to the school. The Health index of this ADO is 0.630 which is good as well as denoting a little more than average performance. The maximum is 0.990 and the lowest is 0.043. the Body Mass Index is 21.4 which is normal and the highest value is 38.4 and the minimum score is 14.4.

- The correlation coefficient between Wealth index and Quality of Life index is quiet postive. It indicates strong positive linkage with the value of 0.660. The correlation coefficient between QLI and Education index is also quiet strong with 0.762 thus showing direct relation between education and human development. The correlation

coefficient between Health index and QLI is also good with the value of 0.439, it shows the importance of good health for human development.

♣ Agricultural Performance Index is prepared with four dimensional index. The Land Fertility index in this ADO is 0.569 showing moderate. It ranges in between 0.893, the highest to 0.273, the lowest. The Market index is 0.432 and it ranges between 0.980, the highest seller to the subsistence one of index 0.00. The Technology Achievement index is 0.538 and ranges between 0.930 to 0.10. the Labour Productivity index is 0.226 and ranges in the maximum of 0.484 to the minimum of 0.078. The correlation coefficient between LFI and API is 0.507 denoting moderate value, but showing strong correlation between MI and API with 0.936, between TAI and API with 0.783 and between LPI and API with 0.674.

7.4 Agriculture and Poverty Interface

Rural development is a process that aims at reducing poverty and improving living standards through sustainable and broad based growth and investment in the people who reside in the countryside. For economies whose mainstay is agriculture, efforts directed at sustainable rural development contribute to poverty reduction. Agriculture can play a substantial role in reducing poverty especially in those areas where agriculture is the most important source of living. In Barak Valley Multidimensional Poverty Index has been prepared to assess the poverty. The methodology has been borrowed from Sabina Alkire and Maria Emma Santos. MPI uses the household as a unit of analysis. Moreover four Millenium Development Goals have been connected with it. They are- MDG1 is to Eradicate Extreme Poverty and Hunger; MDG2 is to Achieve Universal Primary Education; MDG4 is to Reduce Child Mortality; MDG7 is to Ensure Environmental Sustainability.

There are total three dimensions and ten indicators. Dimensions are deprivation in Education, deprivation in Health and deprivation in Living Standard. Education has two indicators a) Years of schooling and b) Child school attendance. They are defined as- he/she is deprived if a) No household member has completed five years of schooling and b) Any school-aged child is not attending school up to class 8. They are related to MDG2. Health has also two indicators- a) Child mortality and b) Nutrition. Anyone will be deprived if a) Any child has died in the family and b) Any adult for whom nutritional information is malnourished or their BMI is less than 18.5 kg/m^2. They are related to MDG4 and MDG.

The dimension is Living standard and the indicators are measured as- anyone is deprived if

a) The household has no electricity, b) The household's sanitation facility is not improved (according to MDG guidelines), or it is improved but shared with other households, c) The household does not have access to safe drinking water (according to MDG guidelines) or safe drinking water is more than a 30-minute walk from home roundtrip, d) The household has a dirt, sand or dung floor, e) The household cooks with dung, wood or charcoal, f) The household does not own more than one radio, TV, telephone, bike, motorbike or refrigerator and does not own a car or truck. They are linked with MDG7.

Multidimensional Poverty Index

Table-137

			Statistic	Std. Error
MPI	Mean		.25045	.009229
	95% Confidence Interval for Mean	Lower Bound	.23232	
		Upper Bound	.26859	
	5% Trimmed Mean		.23820	
	Median		.22200	
	Variance		.038	
	Std. Deviation		.195785	
	Minimum		.000	
	Maximum		.886	
	Range		.886	
	Interquartile Range		.277	
	Skewness		.636	.115
	Kurtosis		-.289	.230

- The mean of Multidimensional Poverty Index is 0.250 in Barak Valley which is moderate amd below the cut-of levelof 0.33 however falls in vulnerable zone. The Standard Error of the Mean indicates how much the value of the mean may vary from repeated samples of the same size taken from the same distribution and the value is .0092.
- The 95% Confidence Interval for Mean are two numbers that we would expect 95% of the means from repeated samples of the same size to fall between. The 5% Trimmed Mean is .238 in Barak Valley i.e. the mean after the highest and lowest 2.5% of the values have been removed.
- The vriance is .038 and the standard deviation of Health Index is .195.
- Skewness measures the degree and direction of asymmetry which is negative with 0.636 in Barak Valley as the value of median (.621) is lower than the mean.

♣ Kurtosis is a measure of the heaviness of the tails of a distribution while the kurtosis is -0.289. Kurtosis is positive if the tails are "heavier" than for a normal distribution and negative if the tails are "lighter" than for a normal distribution.

Distribution of farmers according to score in MPI

Table-138

Indicator	Multidimensional Poverty Index	Sample	Indicator	Number of farmers	Percentage of farmers
Mean observation	0.250		Excellent (Scored zero)	17	4%
Max. observation	0.886	s-338	Above poverty level (0.1-0.2)	180	40%
Min. observation	0.00	s-446	Vulnerable/ at risk of being poor (0.2-0.33)	35	8%
			Multidimensionally Poor (above 0.3)	181	40%
			Severly Poor (above 0.5)	37	8%
			Total	450	100

Source: Calculated by scholar from 450 samples

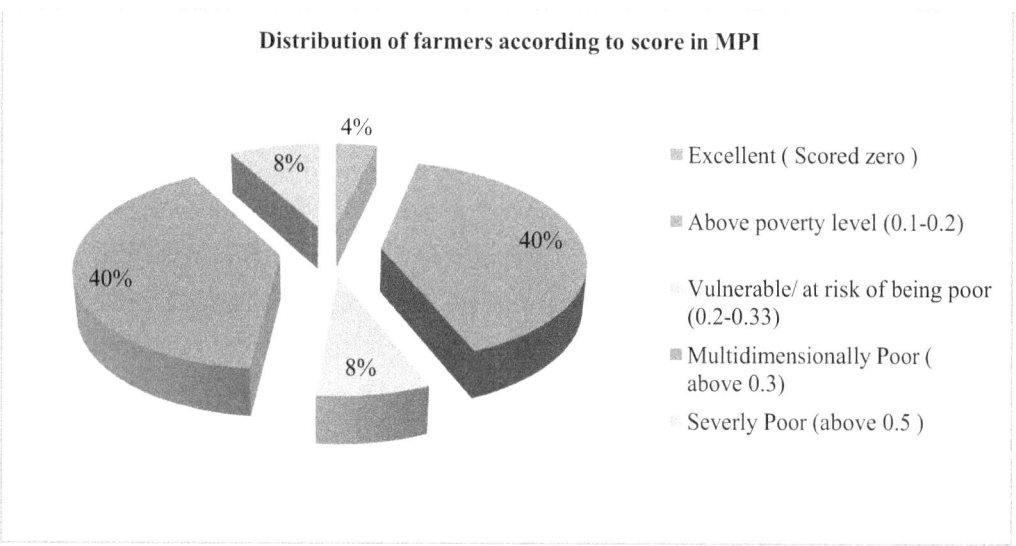

- Multidimensional poverty endeavours to include deprivation in all aspects of human life. The adoption of MPI in Barak Valley by the given guidelines show that the mean performance is below the cut-off level. But it does not mean that the size of poverty striken people are low rather the result shows that a huge portion of the people are poor.

- The mean performance of Barak Valley is 0.250 MPI while the maximum or the worst performer is s-338 with the index of 0.886 and the minimum or the best performer has achieved 0.00. The farmers who have scored zero or index value of 0.00 mean no deprivation at all. They have qualified in all ten indicators of deprivation. They are 17 in number or only 4% of the total samples under study. The best performer are mostly rich people, having big land holdings or better performer in wealth index, education and health index etc.

- Those farmers who have scored in between 0.100 to 0.200 are regarded as safe or above poverty line. They are sizable in number in Barak Valley as 180 farmers or 40% of the total farmers. These farmers are well-off and they have deprivation in some of the indicators but qualified in most of the others. However it is clear that these 40% farmers are neither deprived in both the health indicators nor deprived in both the education indicators. Out of six indicators of living standard, hardly they may be deprived in 2/3 indicators.

- Those farmers who have scored in between index value of 0.200 to 0.33 are vulnerable. Though they are not referred as poor yet deprivation score is such that they are close to risk. They constitute 8% of the farmers in my study area or 35 in all.
- The farmers who are multi dimensionally poor scored more than index of 0.33. This cut-off has been set by experts earlier (2011- HDR). In Barak Valley the performance is really alarming. They are 181 in number which is huge or 40% of the total samples. Just imagine if 40% of the farmers are found multi dimensionally poor by the international standards out of 450, what could be the actual situation if the methodology is applied for entire population. All government claim about poverty reduction and schemes will be put before question.
- There are farmers found during my survey that they are heavily affected by poverty. By MPI methods they scored more than 0.500 index value and thus fall in the category of 'severely poor'. They constitute 8% of the total farmers under study or 37 in number.

Agricultural Performance and Poverty

Model Summary-17

Table-139

Model	R	R Square	Adjusted R Square	Std. Error of the Estimate
1	-.451[a]	.203	.202	.174947

a. Predictors: (Constant), API

Dependent Variable: MPI

In the Model Summary-17, a linear regression model, we find that the coefficient of multiple correlations(R) is .451, indicating a good negative linear relationship between the predictor Agricultural Performance Index and the dependent variable- Multidimensional Poverty Index in Barak Valley. The coefficient of determination r2 (R Square) of .203 indicates that for the sample, 20% of the variation in Multidimensional Poverty can be explained by the variation in Agricultural Performance. But this may be an overestimate for the population from which the sample is drawn, so we use the Adjusted R Square as a better estimate for the population i.e .202. Finally the Std. Error of the Estimate is 0.174947.

Model Summary-18 and Parameter Estimates

Table-140

Dependent Variable: MPI

Equation	Model Summary					Parameter Estimates	
	R Square	F	df1	df2	Sig.	Constant	b1
Linear	.203	114.330	1	448	.000	.513	-.539

The independent variable is API.

The relationship between two variables is explained with the help of R square 0.203 i.e. 20% of the variation in Multidimensional Poverty is explained by variation Agricultural Performance Index in Barak Valley. The value of F 114.330 is the quotient of Mean Square Regression and the Mean Square Residual -MSR and MSE respectively.

The following diagram shows the negative linear relation between Multidimensional Poverty index and Agricultural Performance Index.

Curve Estimation

Negative correlation between Agricultural Performance and Multidimensional Poverty.

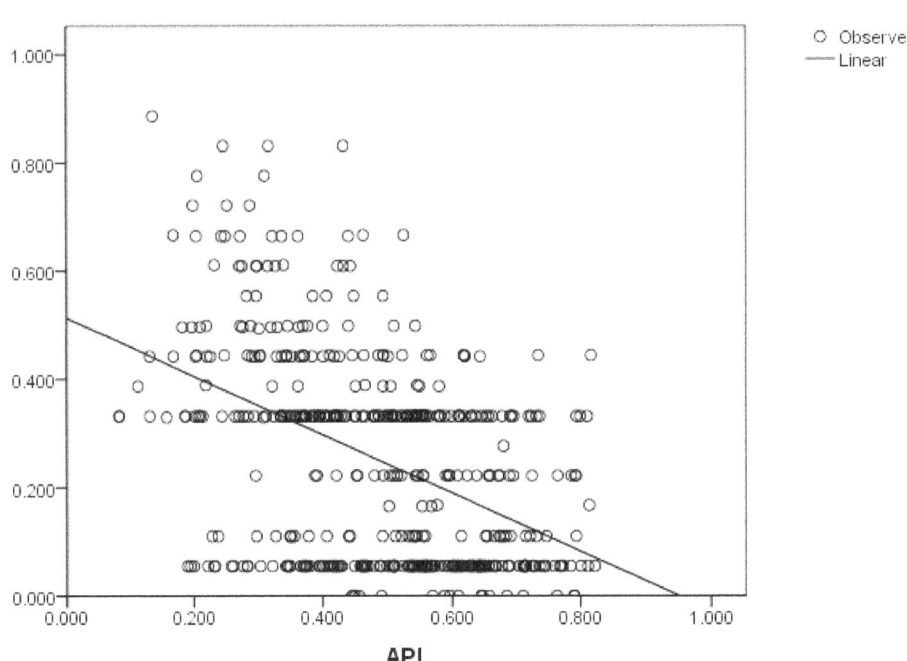

Human Development and Poverty

Model Summary-20

Table-141

Model	R	R Square	Adjusted R Square	Std. Error of the Estimate
1	-.677[a]	.458	.457	.144281

a. Predictors: (Constant), QLI

In the Model Summary-19, a linear regression model, we find that the coefficient of multiple correlations(R) is -.677, indicating a good negative linear relationship between the predictor Quality of Life Index and the dependent variable- Multidimensional Poverty Index in Barak Valley. The coefficient of determination r^2 (R Square) of .458 indicates that for the sample, 45% of the variation in Multidimensional Poverty can be explained by the variation in Quality of Life Performance. But this may be an overestimate for the population from which the sample is drawn, so we use the Adjusted R Square as a better estimate for the population i.e. .457. Finally the Std. Error of the Estimate is 0.144281.

Model Summary-21 and Parameter Estimates

Table-142

Dependent Variable: MPI

Equation	Model Summary					Parameter Estimates	
	R Square	F	df1	df2	Sig.	Constant	b1
Linear	.458	378.780	1	448	.000	.882	-1.066

The independent variable is QLI.

The relationship between two variables is explained with the help of R square 0.458 i.e. 45% of the variation in Multidimensional Poverty is explained by variation Quality of Life Index in Barak Valley. The value of F 378.780 is the quotient of Mean Square Regression and the Mean Square Residual -MSR and MSE respectively.

The following diagram shows the negative linear relation between Multidimensional Poverty index and Quality of Life Index.

Curve Estimation

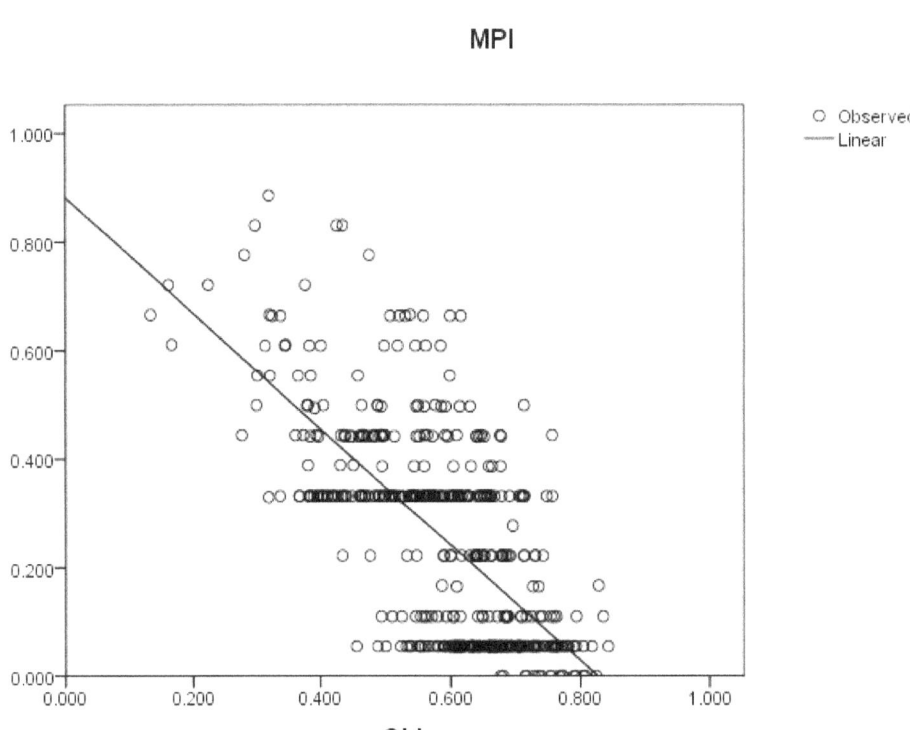

Negative correlation between Quallity of Life Performance and Multidimensional Poverty.

Number of farmers deprived in various indicators
Table-143

Indicator	Number of farmers	% of farmers
Deprived in BMI	126	28%
Deprived in Child mortality	18	4%
Deprived in schooling	75	16.6%
Deprived in enrolment	119	26.4%
Deprived in electricity	25	5.5%
Deprived in sanitation	166	36.88%
Deprived in drinking water	98	21.77%
Deprived in flooring	57	12.66%
Deprived in cooking fuel	248	55.11%
Deprived in asset ownership	229	50.88%

Source: Calculated by scholar from 450 samples

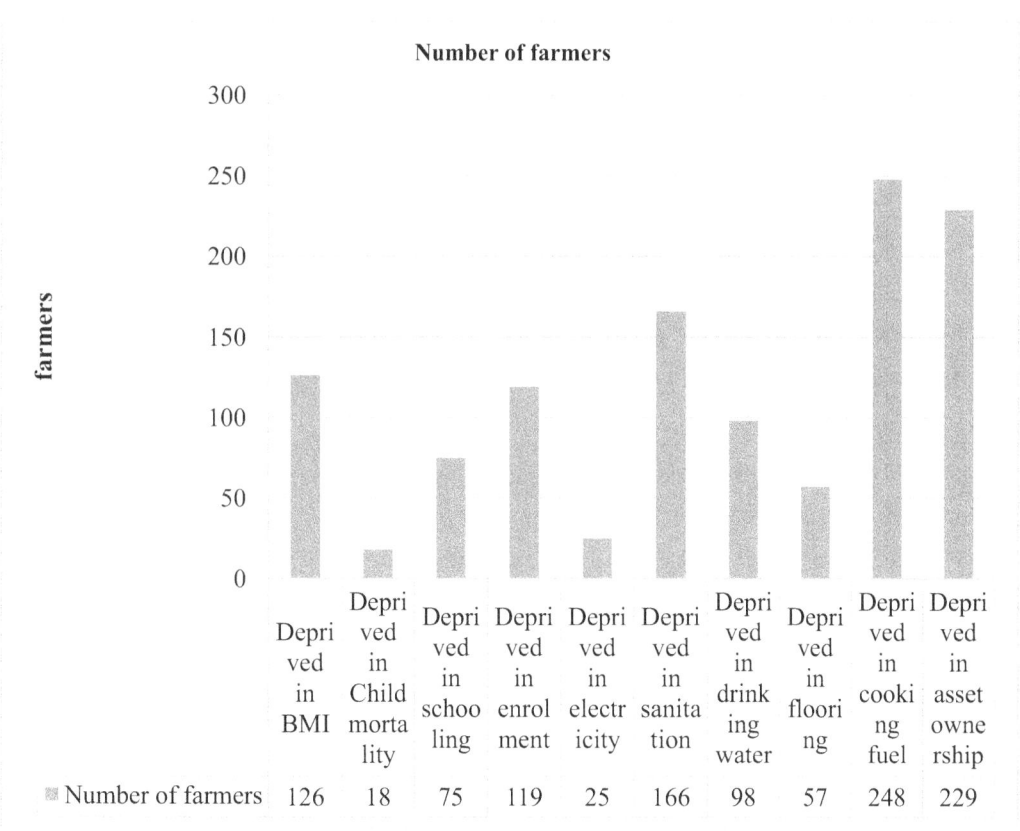

The number of farmers deprived in different indicators of poverty show that there is large variation in the performance in facets of muldimensional poverty index in Barak Valley for the sample farmers. The Body Mass Index is an important indicator of nutritional status of the people. If BMI is found below the cut-off level of 18.5 kg/m^2, they are regarded as poor. The number of farmers deprived in BMI is 132 or 29% of the total farmers which shows an alarming level of nutritional intake of the farmers. Certainly it reduces the productivity of the labour and output in Barak Valley. Those famers who experienced child mortality in their family are 18 in number. Child mortality is found to decline if compared with the state. 4% of the farm household is deprived in this indicator. 21% of the farmers are deprived in schooling or 87 in total out of 450 farmers. The farmers' family in which no one has completed 5 years of schooling is 87. The number of farmers deprived in school enrolment is 119 or 26.4% of the total sample households. The criterion is that any school aged child who is not attending school up to class 8. The number farm households found to be deprived in electricity is 25 or 5.5% of the total. The number of farm family deprived in sanitation is very high with 166 or 36.88% of the total. According to MDG guideline, a household is considered to have access to improved sanitation if it has some type of flush toilet or latrine, or ventilated improved pit or composting toilet, provided that they are not shared. The number of farmers deprived in access to safe drinking water is 21.77% of the total or 98 in number. The criteria of safe drinking water according to MDG is- a household has access to clean drinking water if the water source is any of the following types: piped water, public tap, borehole or pump, protected well, protected spring or rainwater, and it is within a distance of 30 minutes' walk (roundtrip). The number of farmers deprived in flooring of the house is 57 or 12.66% of the total. Someone is poor in flooring if the household has a dirt, sand or dung floor. The poor household is one which cooks with dung, wood or charcoal and the number of farmers deprived in cooking fuel is really alarming as the figure is 248 out of 450 farmers or 55.11%. Thus access to cooking fuel is still in deplorable condition is this Valley. The number of farmers deprived in asset ownership is 229 or 50.88% of the total which shows the level of asset poverty for the farmers. The criterion is- a deprived household does not own more than one radio, TV, telephone, bike, motorbike or refrigerator and does not own a car or truck.

Correlations

		LFI	LPI	MI	TAI	API	EI	WI	HI	QLI	BMI	MPI
LFI	Pearson Correlation	1	.182**	.380**	.243**	.544**	.150**	.457**	.180**	.352**	.098*	-.240**
LPI	Pearson Correlation	.182**	1	.608**	.448**	.697**	.092	.596**	.087	.334**	.016	-.259**
MI	Pearson Correlation	.380**	.608**	1	.598**	.910**	.245**	.727**	.158**	.517**	.025	-.502**
TAI	Pearson Correlation	.243**	.448**	.598**	1	.804**	.166**	.736**	.086	.441**	-.010	-.282**
API	Pearson Correlation	.544**	.697**	.910**	.804**	1	.232**	.847**	.167**	.560**	.035	-.452**
EI	Pearson Correlation	.150**	.092	.245**	.166**	.232**	1	.259**	.138**	.833**	.004	-.473**
WI	Pearson Correlation	.457**	.596**	.727**	.736**	.847**	.259**	1	.120*	.623**	.021	-.406**
HI	Pearson Correlation	.180**	.087	.158**	.086	.167**	.138**	.120*	1	.505**	.696**	-.529**
QLI	Pearson Correlation	.352**	.334**	.517**	.441**	.560**	.833**	.623**	.505**	1	.263**	-.677**
BMI	Pearson Correlation	.098*	.016	.025	-.010	.035	.004	.021	.696**	.263**	1	-.338**
MPI	Pearson Correlation	-.240**	-.259**	-.502**	-.282**	-.452**	-.473**	-.406**	-.529**	-.677**	-.338**	1

**. Correlation is significant at the 0.01 level (2-tailed).

Chapter 8

Findings and Policy Recommendation

Major findings and policy implications on 1ˢᵗ and 2ⁿᵈ chapters

Land, Environment and Natural Resources

Land

Experience from other countries/states indicates that land reform is costly and requires significant political support. However, there are two general concerns. Many poor farmers do not understand what their legal rights to land are, and this deters them from investing in infrastructure, perennial crops and trees, or soil conservation technologies. Where people do understand their rights under the law, they may have no faith in local juridical systems to enforce these. Secondly, rights to land are still highly disputed, even though they may provide the major labour input on the land. Attempts to address this have proved controversial and have not had sufficient political support.

Recommendation

Land reform, as well as improved management and administration are seen as contributing to the increase in production by (i) enhancing food security through redistributing land to the landless and land poor, thus giving them opportunities to be directly productive; (ii) facilitating investment and enhancing efficiency in the use of factors of production; and (iii) contributing to resource conservation by providing up-to-date inventories of natural resources and improving allocation of land to its optimal use.

Water

Water and its sustainable management and utilisation are crucial factors in agricultural production. The vision for water for production encourages availability of water all year round for increased and sustainable commercial agricultural production without degrading the environment. This is expected to involve simple water harvesting techniques, improved rainwater management and effective use of early warning systems and meteorological forecasts, rather than heavy investment in irrigation systems.

Recommendation

1. A Water for Production Strategy and Investment Plan should be drafted which sets out its principles as having: a poverty reduction focus; demand-responsive approaches; sustainability; cost-efficiency; decentralisation and management at the lowest level; private sector involvement; a gender-responsive approach; incorporation of environment and health concerns; and a sector-wise approach to planning.

2. Water resources management: Exploring and costing optional technologies (e.g. boreholes, dug wells) for increasing water supply at the household level; installing and training the community in rain-water harvesting and collection from rooftops and storage tanks in schools, medical facilities and other appropriate buildings; providing material and training to filter and/or disinfect all collected water depending on the raw water quality; and promoting the creation of ventilated improved pit latrines.

Environment and Natural resources with Policy Recommendations

1. Increasing agricultural productivity without degrading the environment is one of the challenges of the government. To do this will require greater mainstreaming of the environment, improving the linkages between, in particular, environment committees and agricultural services and research, appropriate monitoring etc.

2. Land tenure is very important for the commercialisation of agriculture, both in terms of providing collateral for finance and allowing larger-scale production. At present it is difficult to consolidate the increasingly fragmented landholdings. Internationally equitable access to land is increasingly recognised as a necessary prerequisite for pro-poor growth in agriculture. For all of these reasons, the medium term impact of investment in agriculture is likely to be constrained unless the land issue is addressed more expeditiously.

3. There are several issues that affect agricultural performance and rural development. These relate to land, the environment and disease. As the agricultural sector becomes modernised and land becomes scare, labour is expected to be released to the industrial

sector and urban areas for wage employment. Cash remittances from urban areas are important to the rural poor while food from rural areas is vital to the urban poor. The importance of urban migration and wage employment as a coping strategy for the rural poor implies that better competitiveness and information in rural areas about urban economic opportunities can help the poor.

4. Water, biomass, land, soil and weather are critical factors in supporting the sustainability of agriculture, enhancing rural livelihoods and reducing the vulnerability of the poor. The quantity and quality of natural resources are, however, declining as a result of inappropriate use of arable land, excessive cultivation, population pressure, inadequate fertilisation or soil erosion through removal of crop residues. This is aggravated by drought conditions, wetland encroachment and reclamation and use of hazardous chemicals in a manner that is harmful to the bio-diversity and well-being of the communities.

Land, Water and Sustainable Development

➢ The integration of agriculture with land and water management, and with ecosystem conservation is essential for both environmental sustainability and agricultural production. An environmental perspective must guide the evaluation of all development projects, recognizing the role of natural resources in local livelihoods. This recognition must be informed by a comprehensive understanding of the perceptions and opinions of local people about their stakes in the resource base.

➢ To ensure the sustainability of the natural resource base, the recognition of all stakeholders in it and their roles in its protection and management is essential. There is need to establish well-defined and enforceable rights (including customary rights) and security of tenure, and to ensure equal access to land, water and other natural and biological resources. It should be ensured that this applies, in particular, to indigenous communities, women and other disadvantaged groups living in poverty. Water governance arrangements should protect ecosystems and preserve or restore the ecological integrity of all natural water bodies and their catchments. This will maintain the wide range of ecological services that healthy ecosystems provide and the livelihoods that depend upon them.

- Biomass is, and will continue for a long time to be, a major source of fuel and energy, especially for the rural poor. Recognizing this fact, appropriate mechanisms must be evolved to make such consumption of biomass sustainable, through both resource management and the promotion of efficient and minimally polluting technologies, and technologies which will progressively reduce the pressures on biomass, which cause environmental degradation. The traditional approaches to natural resource management such as sacred groves and ponds, water harvesting and management systems, etc., should be revived by creating institutional mechanisms which recapture the ecological wisdom and the spirit of community management inherent in those systems.

- With increasing purchasing power, wasteful consumption linked to market driven consumerism is stressing the resource base of developing countries further. It is important to counter this through education and public awareness. In several areas, desirable limits and standards for consumption need to be established and applied through appropriate mechanisms including education, incentives and legislation. Several traditional practices that are sustainable and environment friendly continue to be a regular part of the lives of people in developing countries. These need to be encouraged rather than replaced by more 'modern' but unsustainable practices and technologies. Development decisions regarding technology and infrastructure are a major determinant of consumption patterns. It is therefore important to evaluate and make development decisions which structurally lead to a more sustainable society. Technologies exist through which substantial reduction in consumption of resources is possible. Efforts to identify, evaluate, introduce and use these technologies must be made.

- Poverty and a degraded environment are closely inter-related, especially where people depend for their livelihoods primarily on the natural resource base of their immediate environment. Restoring natural systems and improving natural resource management practices at the grassroots level are central to a strategy to eliminate poverty. The survival needs of the poor force them to continue to degrade an already degraded environment. Removal of poverty is therefore a prerequisite for the protection of the environment. Poverty magnifies the problem of hunger and malnutrition.

- The problem is further compounded by the inequitable access of the poor to the food that is available. It is therefore necessary to strengthen the public distribution system to overcome this inequity. Diversion of common and marginal lands to economically useful purposes deprives the poor of a resource base which has traditionally met many of their sustenance needs. Market forces also lead to the elimination of crops that have traditionally been integral to the diet of the poor, thereby threatening food security and nutritional status.

- While conventional economic development leads to the elimination of several traditional occupations, the process of sustainable development, guided by the need to protect and conserve the environment, leads to the creation of new jobs and of opportunities for the reorientation of traditional skills to new occupations. Women, while continuing to perform their traditional domestic roles' are increasingly involved in earning livelihoods. In many poor households they are often the principal or the sole breadwinners. A major thrust at the policy level is necessary to ensure equity and justice for them. Literacy and a basic education are essential for enabling the poor to access the benefits offered by development initiatives and market opportunities. Basic education is therefore a precondition for sustainable development.

- If no single practice by itself secures sustainability, what can be done to reduce the negative impacts of agriculture while maintaining or improving its productivity and sustainability? This is a major challenge with no easy, single solution. However, answers may present themselves if we are willing to re-think our approach to farming.

- Making the transition to sustainable agriculture is a process that requires a series of steps. In this process, three issues should be recognized. First, we must be aware that agro ecosystems are ecologically complex units where soil, water, air, wildlife, insects, pathogens, plants and humans interact. When farmers make management decisions, they influence interactions among crops, livestock, beneficial organisms, pests and the physical environment. While biological and ecological considerations play a role in these decisions, so do a number of economic, social and legal considerations. To achieve sustainability, farmers should be aware of the short-, mid- and long-term consequences of these management decisions. In a sustainable farming framework, external inputs such as synthetic fertilizers and pesticides may supplement ecological processes, but should not supplant them. In this context, producers should be aware of the importance of ecological processes such as nutrient cycling, crop-weed competition, host-parasitic and predator-prey relationships in determining crop yields and system stability in the design of sustainable farming systems.

- Because of the ecological complexity of agricultural systems, sustainable farming requires the adoption of a systems-level and interdisciplinary perspective. As with any system, farms consist of a set of parts acting in coordination to achieve desired actions or results for the whole. In addition, a farm exists in a landscape where adjacent land use and community objectives should be considered. Consequently, one should clearly define the goals of the production system and search for the actions that will achieve those goals.

- Finally, sustainable farming aims at maximizing many ecosystem services including yields, clean water and air, the presence of wildlife and other organisms valued by society, carbon sequestration, and recreation. Clearly, these goals can compete with each other at times. Thus, achieving sustainability must, in reality, be considered an optimization process that engages all participants including farmers, labourers, policy makers, retailers, consumers and researchers. For example, better water quality in an agricultural ecosystem can reduce the cost and need for drinking water treatment of those living in the region as well as more distant communities. Likewise, water is one of the most valued resources for livestock, so saving and protecting water quality can enhance livestock production.

Increasing the sustainability of the Farmers in Assam

The road to sustainability is long and complex. Each farm represents a unique combination of biological, climatic, soil and management conditions such that no single "silver bullet" exists to secure sustainability. However, there are principles that will help farmers move in the direction of more sustainable agro ecosystems. Among them:

a. Use cover crops and green manure and/or animal manure to build soil quality and fertility
b. Protect water quality
c. Develop ecologically-based pest management programs
d. Integrate crop and livestock production
e. Increase energy efficiency in production and food distribution
f. Maintain profitability
g. Use water and nutrients efficiently
h. Keep soil covered throughout the year
i. Reduce or eliminate tillage in a manner consistent with effective weed control
j. Diversify your farming enterprise to spread agronomic and economic risk

Major findings and policy implications on 3rd, 4th and 5th chapters

- ♣ Fertiliser use, irrigation and rainfall were found to cause significant variation in productivity across districts. The highest coefficient was that of rainfall which shows that on 1% increase in rainfall between districts results in 0.43 percent increase in agriculture productivity. Fertiliser comes next with coefficient of 0.277. This implies that productivity increased by 0.27 percent in response to 1 percent increase in use of fertiliser.

- ♣ Elasticity of productivity with respect to irrigation across districts was 0.11. These results indicate the importance and need to manage rainfall water to raise productivity particularly in low productivity districts. Another very interesting result from the cross section data of districts was agricultural productivity is very powerful in reducing rural poverty. A 1 percent increase in land productivity reduces poverty by as much 0.51 percent. The effect of dependence of workers on agriculture was reverse. A 1 percent reduction in labour force in agriculture resulted in 0.49 percent decline in rural poverty.

- ♣ There are significant variations across districts. Only seven districts have HDI values higher than the State average. The remaining 16 districts have HDI values lower than the State average, reflecting considerable inequality.

- ♣ When human development is dependent variable and agricultural development index, % of rural poor, human poverty index are independent variables, the coefficient of multiple correlation r(R) is .532, indicating a good positive linear relationship. Similarly when agricultural development index is replaced by productivity i.e. output per worker it comes out to be .546.

- ♣ Alternatively agricultural development largely depends on human development. The coefficient of multiple correlation r(R) is .677, indicating a high level of positive linear relationship between agricultural development index and HDI+HPI+% of rural poor.

- ♣ When production per worker is dependent variable and human development index is independent variable, the coefficient of multiple correlation r(R) is .920, indicating a high positive linear relationship between the predictor HDI and the dependent variable PPW-production per worker. In the Model Summary-2, we see that the coefficient of multiple correlation r(R) is .989, indicating a good positive linear relationship between the predictor ADI-Agricultural Development Index and the dependent variable HDI-human development index. In the Model Summary-3, we see that the coefficient of multiple correlation r(R) is .954, indicating a strong linear negative relationship between the predictor % of Rural Poor and the dependent variable PPW-production per worker.

♣ There are significant variations across districts. Cachar and Hailakandi district fall in medium human development zone while Karimganj is a low human development district. Regarding literacy rate the position of Barak Valley is better than the state average. But regarding household characteristics like access to electricity, toilet facility, television, mobile phone etc the performance of Barak Valley is not much improved along with the entire state.

♣ Interesting result from the data of districts was agricultural productivity is very powerful in reducing rural poverty. A 1 percent increase in land productivity reduces poverty by as much 0.51 percent. The effect of dependence of workers on agriculture was reverse. A 1 percent reduction in labour force in agriculture resulted in 0.49 percent decline in rural poverty.

Thus we find that there exists a vital relation between factors of human development and agricultural development. Human development expands the productivity of the farmers in the form of raising the skill of farming, giving access to modern technology, more market information, extension services etc. Both issues are interlinked heavily to raise the growth rate, reduce the poverty and improve the human development situation. Economic development in true sense of the term requires the reinforcing effect of both agrarian and human development policies.

Major findings and policy implications on 6th chapter

- Low public sector spending on health services results in over-dependence on private sector for getting health services. In India the share of private sector on health care expenditure constitutes around 72 % and household sector being the major constituent of the private sector claims 68.8% of expenditure on health care. In other words out-of-pocket expenditure comprises major share of expenditure on health care. There exists wide gap among the states of NER regarding expenditure on health. So public health services must be widened in various regards.

- India has entered a high growth rate trajectory of 9 per cent. This high rate of growth, however, is not accompanied by a high level of social development. The social sectors particularly health and education have been accorded a very low priority in terms of the allocation of resources. For example, public expenditure on health services as a percentage of Gross Domestic Product (GDP) in India is less than 1.5 per cent. So health expenditure by both central and state governments must increase.

- It is a well known fact that the children from the economically and socially backward states face higher risks of mortality compared to the advanced ones. The examination of the NFHS data indicates that this is the case for most of the states of this region. The nature and degree of disparity varied for all the segments of anaemia. The existence of large disparities in states with relatively low levels of mortality is a matter of great concern; clearly, the weaker sections have been deprived of recent advances and improvements in child survival.

- There is wide gap in the health outcomes among the northeast states. Though Mizoram has performed better in IMR, sex ratio, child sex ratio etc but there is a long way to go regarding nutrition, anaemia, safe drinking water, toilet facility etc. All other states including Assam must increase expenditure on health and nutritional facility, especially for women and children.

- Education, health, living conditions, awareness, etc are important factors of rural development. Most importantly the future of the nation depends on healthy mothers and children and there our state has achieved lopsided development. Thus we conclude that there is wide rural-urban gap in women, child and reproductive health care.

- The women and child health is still poor regarding achievement in nutrition, health care in rural areas and health awareness.

- Human health in its broadest sense of physical, mental and spiritual wellbeing is to a great extent dependent on the access of the citizen to a healthy environment. For a healthy, productive and fulfilling life every individual should have the physical and economic access to a balanced diet, safe drinking water, clean air, sanitation, environmental hygiene, primary health care and education. Access to safe drinking water and a healthy environment should be a fundamental right of every citizen.

- Citizens of developing countries continue to be vulnerable to a double burden of diseases. Traditional diseases such as malaria and cholera, caused by unsafe drinking water and lack of environmental hygiene, have not yet been controlled Many of the widespread ailments among the poor in developing countries are occupation-related, and are contracted in the course of work done to fulfil the consumption demands of the affluent, both within the country and outside. The strong relationship between health and the state of the environment in developing countries is becoming increasingly evident. This calls for greater emphasis on preventive and social medicine, and on research in both occupational health and epidemiology. Because of the close link, there needs to be greater integration between the ministries of Health and Environment, and effective coordination and cooperation between them. Basic health and educational facilities in developing countries need to be strengthened.

- The role of public health services must give preventive health care equal emphasis as curative health care. People should be empowered through education and awareness to participate in managing preventive health care related to environmental sanitation and hygiene. Most developing countries are repositories of a rich tradition of natural resource-based health care. This is under threat, on the one hand from modern mainstream medicine, and on the other from the degradation of the natural resource base.

- Traditional medicine in combination with modern medicine must be promoted while ensuring conservation of the resource base and effective protection of IPRs of traditional knowledge. Developing countries should also strive to strengthen the capacity of their health care systems to deliver basic health services and to reduce environment-related health risks by sharing of health awareness and medical expertise globally.

Major findings and policy implications on 7th chapter

Major Factors Influencing Agricultural Performance and Human Development along with Policy Recommendations

Markets

1. The major marketing problems in Barak Valley are due mainly to limited access to finance by many small traders, the small amounts that most farmers have to sell and the high costs and availability of transport. Government interventions are designed to gradually overcome these constraints. Otherwise, even with these limitations, the marketing system is moving, although farmers complain of low and variable prices, these reflect the costs and risks of the current market system. Sometimes the market is unfairly blamed for an inability to cope with sudden production surges caused by encouragement of farmers to diversify into, or expand production of, specific products without consideration of the whole value chain, the size of the final market, agro-processing capacity and the financing and risk costs involved.

2. As emphasised earlier, the realisation of the vision and mission will hinge on the capacity of rural producers and processors to deliver the results. The link between performance and human development is clear – the farmers and processors must have the knowledge and skills necessary for improved performance. While strategy for growth only states that the target beneficiaries are 'small-scale farmers', within this very broad group actual benefits are likely to vary widely. For example, the criteria used for road development and maintenance, the selection criteria used in providing marketing training to farmers' groups, the presence of agro-processing facilities in the locality, the farmers' ability to generate a marketable surplus, are just a few of the parameters that will determine the actual beneficiaries within the farming community. Some of the components also target traders, although there should be indirect benefits for all those marketing produce through the new sources of finance that are mobilised. From a gender perspective, the majority of players in rural market chain are male.

Recommendations

1. Based on the foregoing, the agriculture and rural development sector remains the key to socio-economic transformation, and consequently to poverty reduction in the country. Poverty reduction and human development strategies must therefore be based on approaches that link agriculture to other sectors at all levels, from the farmer up to the grocery shelf.

2. The marketing network along with rural infrastructure like pucca roads, access to regulated markets for all farmers, corruption free co-operative society, warehousing facility etc can definitely improve the marketing of local products.

Knowledge and Innovation

The task of increasing agricultural performance is directly linked to building human capacity through the enhancement of farmers' knowledge and skills. There are three key factors that contribute to building this human capacity, namely: research and technology adoption, agricultural advisory and technical services, and agricultural education and training.

A. Research and technological adoption

Government realised the need to reformulate the national agricultural research system, including putting in place a policy and legal framework that responds to the needs of human development in the agriculture and rural development sector. The vision of the new agricultural research system and policy is "a farmer-responsive research system that generates and disseminates problem-solving, profitable and environmentally sound technologies on a sustainable basis". The mission for research is "generation, adoption and dissemination of appropriate technologies, knowledge and information through an effective, efficient, sustainable, decentralised and well coordinated agricultural research system".

Recommendations

1. Support should be extended to technology development and multiplication, where emphasis should be placed on responsive commercial orientation and customised packaging and dissemination of agricultural best practices to poor rural farmers. Government should support socio-economic and strategic research, which would meet the needs of poor farmers, incorporate gender analysis and address biotechnology and genetic resource conservation. Appropriate farm power and post-harvest technologies, including agricultural transport and marketing, should be accorded high priority in funding and institutional support. In order to restore and increase soil fertility in a sustainable manner, appropriate land and water resources management practices and technologies should be identified, developed and disseminated to the rural masses.

2. The key strategies to achieve a more farmer-responsive research system are: the decentralisation of research by establishing Agricultural Research and Development Centres in key agro-ecological zones away from the central region; these should have autonomy to address indigenous knowledge and technology in their local areas; greater stakeholder involvement in priority-setting, planning-implementation and evaluation of research; subsistence farmers, processors, traders, NGOs would play a part here, and particular emphasis should be placed on developing technologies which address the needs of small and semi-medium farmers; and greater involvement of the private sector in both financing and conducting research; an Agricultural Research Fund could be established as a conduit for private sector funds.

Five major themes that can contribute to human development:

1. Understanding people, their livelihood systems, demands and the impact of innovations
2. Enhancing the innovation process and partnerships
3. Enhancing integrated management of natural resources
4. Technological options which respond to demands and market opportunities

5. Enabling policies and linking producers to markets

B. Extension and technical services

Until the end of the 1990s, the Government of Assam provided extension services using top-down approaches that were not responsive to farmers' needs. Most of the research and extension lacked relevance and reached less than 5 per cent of the farming population.

Recommendations

Like research and technology development, the government should adopt a decentralised idea ushered a complete review and reformulation of the extension approach geared to ensuring a system that was more directly responsive to farmers' needs, and a shift towards private sector service delivery. The new approach would result in decentralised, farmer-owned and private sector delivered advisory services, contributing to the realisation of objectives of the agricultural sector.

C. Agricultural education

Agricultural education is a priority area of efficiency, which requires it as the primary tool of human development to achieve agricultural modernisation. The vision of agricultural education is one in which "agriculture is treated as a business and an honourable profession, and farmers acquire knowledge and skills that enable them to increase productivity, profits so as to improve their quality of life". The rationale for including agricultural education has arisen from: (i) lack of a coherent policy for agricultural education and training; (ii) insufficient funding for agricultural education and training; (iii) ineffective institutional framework for the delivery of agricultural education and training; (iv) inappropriate curricula and teaching and learning methodologies in agricultural education and training; and (v) negative attitudes towards agriculture in general and agricultural education and training in particular.

Recommendation

At the primary school level, more pupil friendly posters, tapes, videos, and informative materials should be developed and widely circulated in schools. Facilitation mechanisms to informal education approaches, such as visits to model farms, should be applied to stimulate interest in pupils. Functional adult literacy is a affirmative action strategy for the people with disabilities, women and other vulnerable groups should be formulated.

Linkage with Human Development

Critical Linkage and Recommendation

1. The linkage between agricultural performance with rural development and human development arises from the fact that: (i) substantial land and human resources are tied to this sector; and (ii) the sector contributes significantly to food security, national income and the balance of payments. Agriculture is still a major source of livelihood for the majority of Barak Valley's population and remains the engine of growth. More importantly, the growth of other economic and social sectors is heavily dependent on the agriculture and rural sector, including those which contribute most to human development. Arising from previous analyses improved and sustained agricultural performance/ development and progression in the knowledge and skill of farmers are directly related.

2. Human development in the agriculture and rural development sector entails the acquisition and building of scientific knowledge and farming skills by farmers, and is a sine qua non for sustained agricultural performance. As farmers increases their knowledge and skills, they increase their agricultural performance, and as their performance increase they not only become more confident but they also extend their horizon toward the outside world through increased transactions and contacts with traders and government agents. The knowledge and skills that result in increased production performance also bring about changes in people's attitude towards agriculture and the environment. In addition, improved health and nutrition is associated with improved agricultural performance and transformation.

3. In the long run this transformation generates positive backward and forward linkages with other sectors such as research, extension services, trade, agro-processing, transport, finance and education, among others.

Time poverty and relationship with agricultural performance and human development

In Barak Valley, rural women work between 12 and 18 hours per day compared to men's 8 to 10 hours and thus experience time poverty. Women many times make several journeys a day to fetch water and spend an average of 1.5 hours daily in the performance of this task. This is aggravated by long waiting times at the source, poor footpaths and the labour-and energy-intensive methods of carrying. In an attempt to reduce their time burden, a number of women have resorted to limiting household water usage to 12-14 litres per person, which is less than the recommended 20 litres, or collecting unsafe water that is nearer – both of which increase health risks for household members. Similar challenges are evident in the collection and the consumption of fuel wood. More than 90 per cent of the total energy is biomass, mainly collected by women, a labour-and time-consuming. Environmental degradation has exacerbated the magnitude of this task for rural women and children, who have to walk longer distances and to more isolated places to collect fuel wood.

Recommendation

Rural development program should emphasize on building rural utility services by Government. As a result of time poverty, women face many more trade-offs than men, and these impose restrictions on their economic choices and the enhancement and exercise of their capabilities. Time poverty hinders women's capacity to benefit from poverty-reducing programmes. The two key underlying issues behind women's time poverty are mobility and access. Bringing water, health, education, market, credit and energy services nearer to households would be the ideal.

Food and Nutrition Security

A study of the planted area shows Sali paddy takes up 70% per cent of the total area planted with crops. The rate of growth of Barak Valley's population is undermining agricultural growth by putting more pressure on land through land fragmentation and on the environment in general.

Recommendation

It is also necessary for the government to enhance labour productivity, foster diversification of the economy for industry and services to absorb the excess population from agriculture and take other measures to curb unemployment, which is the main cause of poverty. The poor performance of the food subsector has resulted in continued problems of malnutrition. The prevailing levels of childhood and adult under-nutrition and malnutrition are high. Nevertheless, there are some significant imports, especially of vegetable products and cereals.

Rural Infrastructure and Recommendations

1. The failure to link commodity production and the market using appropriate infrastructure has been considered one of the biggest omissions in the current approach to fighting poverty. There are many potentially productive areas of the country that are essentially not part of the productive economy simply because of lack of access infrastructure (roads, rail and telecommunication services). Because of the infrastructural deficiencies that have constrained smallholder producers from participating in supply chains, there has been a proliferation of exploitative middlemen taking advantage of the inadequacies of small producers in accessing markets. Integrating producers into new supply chains is critical if poverty is to be reduced.

2. Four infrastructural elements are identified as critical to smallholder production and integration into supply chains: transportation, storage, communication and irrigation. In the effort to support rural development, Government is dividing the country into different ecological zones and, therefore, promoting the production of certain crops in

particular ecological zones. This effort, however, may not succeed without a strong infrastructural investment that will link the producers to the markets.

3. Schooling and health services must promote in rural areas for better human development.

Conclusion

Sustainable Development is the need of hour. Agricultural Performance is an essential strategy for increasing Human Development, achieving food self-sufficiency, increasing income of the rural mass, more access to basic amenities of life and alleviating poverty and food insecurity among smallholder farmers and thus ascertaining sustainable development. These farmers live and farm in areas where rainfall is low and erratic. In addition, infrastructure and institutions such as irrigation, input and product market, credit and extension services tend to be poorly developed. It is recommended that further research and rural development efforts should focus on the development of infrastructure and institutions in these areas. The technologies people use, play a significant role in determining how fast agricultural productivity grows and how that growth affects the poor and the condition of natural resources. The development of agricultural technology for both food and non-food crops, the dissemination of assets and information, developing agricultural research and extension facilities targeted towards the smallholder farmer, all work together to promote long-term agricultural productivity. Results show that emphasis over development and extension of rural services and enhancing production resources of the farming community that leads to improvement quality of life can have a considerable influence on agricultural sustainability.

The modelling results indicate that the Sustainable Agriculture and Human Development in Barak Valley are to be affected by policies that influence both economic and social factors. The study of factors determining the sustainability of agricultural system shows that social participation factors play the greatest role in the sustainability of agricultural system. By and large factors such as education, health, infrastructural support services, ecological etc have the greatest contribution to enhancement of sustainability in the agricultural system of the region under investigation.

Overall, the experience and evidence from research indicates that returns to agricultural development could be very high and far reaching, not only in the smallholder sector, but in the entire economy as well. They should emphasize certain variables which reduce the farmers' vulnerability to loss of income, bad health, natural disasters, and other factors. In addition, an understanding of local cultural practices and preferences is important if smallholder farmers are to benefit from agricultural technologies developed through research. All these form a potentially useful area of study for future research.

An Epilogue

Major Environmental & Man-Made Hazards in North-East India including Assam

A Hazard is a situation which poses a level of threat to life, health, property or environment. Most hazards are dormant or potential, with only a theoretical risk of harm, however, once a hazard becomes 'active', it can create an emergency situation. The unique geo-climatic conditions of the regions make Assam and the entire northeastern region of India very prone to natural disasters like flood, earthquake and landslide. The state of Assam experiences perennial floods, river bank erosion, landslide and other environmental catastrophes. Disasters cause sudden disruption to the normal life of a society along with enormous damage to property associated with high casualty of human life. A review of the past disasters indicates that the state had to bear the devastations of two natural disaster floods and earthquake. Natural Hazards:

- Earthquake
- Flood
- Landslides

1. Earthquake

Earthquakes in India are caused by the collision of the Indian Plate with the Eurasian Plate in the north. Every year the Indian Plate moves roughly 5 centimetres northward, pushing under the Eurasian Plate and forming the Himalayas and other great mountain chains in the northern part of the Indian peninsula. For great earthquakes the movement can be several meters and can covers several hundreds of square kilometres of the contact surface between the two plates. Most earthquakes in the northern part of the Indian Sub-continent are a result of this complex process. Earthquakes which occur at the margins of plates (or plate boundaries) are known as inter-plate earthquakes and account for 95% of the global seismic activity annually.

The North-eastern region of India is an earthquake prone area. The region has experienced a large number of earthquakes of tectonic origin. The risk probabilities of earthquake are less over the entire Brahmaputra valley. The region of Northeast India is seismically very active.

Two major earthquakes to the magnitude of 8.7 occurred in 1897 and 8.6 in 1950 causing large scale damage of lives and properties in this region. Sir Edward Gait (1933) has mentioned about the occurrence of destructive earthquakes in this region in 1548, 1596, 1607, 1642, 1663, 1696-1714, 1869, 1882, and in 1897. In the present century, destructive earthquakes occurred in 1918, 1923, 1930, 1932, 1938, 1943, 1947, 1950 and in 1988.

The 1897 earthquake caused great destruction to many towns in Assam and Meghalaya. 1500 people were killed and hundreds more hurt. In Shillong, where most of the structures like the Telegraph House, were demolished. Landslides were reported all across the Garo Hills. The towns of Dhubri, Goalpara, Guwahati and Kuch Bihar in Assam and West Bengal was heavily damaged. Earthquake fountains, some 4 feet high, were reported from Dhubri. At Goalpara, a 10-foot wave from the Brahmaputra, swept into the area, destroying the bazaar and many pukka buildings. Ground waves were reported from Nalbari, where the rice fields rise and fall as the waves passed under them. At Guwahati, the earth subsided along the Brahmaputra and several sand vents were formed. The Brahmaputra is also reported to have risen by 7.6 metres and even reversed its flow during the shock. The earthquake formed frozen earth waves of "jinamis" in a rice field in lower Assam, where the crest to trough difference was between 2 to 3 metres. Fissures and sand blows occurred over a wide area of Assam, Meghalaya, West Bengal and northern Bangladesh.

The entire state of Assam lies in Zone V. Here earthquakes of upto MM intensity IX can be expected. According to a hazard map by the Global Seismic Hazard Assessment Programme (GSHAP), the state can expect to have a peak gravitational acceleration (PGA) of 0.24g to 0.48g. The region where the highest PGA can be expected is along the state's border with Meghalaya, the site of the Great Indian earthquake of 1897.

January 1869 earthquake caused serious damage in the region of cachar and Surma Valley of undivided Bangladesh. The impact of the shock was felt over 6,50,000 square kilometres. There was heavy damage in the towns of Cherrapunji, Silchar, Shillong and Sylhet and also in Manipur. Fissures opened on the banks of the Surma river and sand vents threw up great amounts of sand and water. The epicentral tract was 30 - 45 kilometres long and 5 - 6 kilometres wide lying on the northern border of the Jaintia Hills. The hypocentre had a depth of 50 kilometres.

In 1950, there was widespread devastation in Upper Assam, the Abor Hills and the Mishmi Hills. Districts of Jorhat, Lahkimpur, Sibsagar and Sadiya, in Assam. Dibrugarh and Saikoaghat were among the worst affected areas. Railway communications were disrupted due to damage to tracks and bridges. However, the area that suffered damage and encompassed by the isoseist VIII was nearly 75,000 square miles. There were fissures in the earth, from which water and sand was emitted. These are called sand vents and represent liquefaction due to intense ground shaking. Vast areas of land either were elevated or subsided, altering the drainage of the region. There were huge landslides in the mountains and these dammed tributaries of the Bramaputra River, like the Dihang, Dihing and Subansiri. Dykes blocked the tributaries of the Brahmaputra; that in the Dibang valley broke without causing damage, but that at Subansiri opened after an interval of 8 days and the wave, 7 metres high, submerged several villages and killed 532 persons. The earthquake was followed by a large number of aftershocks, most of which were of magnitude 6.0 or greater. The aftershock zone extended from 900 east longitude to 970 east longitude.

In December 1984, in Cachar district, 20 persons were killed and 100 were injured. There was extensive damage in southern Assam. Underground pipes were broken and the ground was cracked. Sand, mud and water spewed forth and subsidence occurred along wide stretches of the Sonai River. Two bridges on the Sonai - Kachidharan road collapsed and others were damaged. An intensity of VI was recorded at Banskandi and Palanghat and intensity of V in Kumbhirgram, Lakhipur, Rajabazar, Silchar and Udarband.

2. Flood:

Flood the most frequent natural calamities faced by India. A relatively high flow or stage in river, marked by higher than the usual, causing inundation of low land or a body of water rising, swelling and over flowing land not usually covered by water is termed as flood. It is essentially a natural hydrologic phenomenon with a large volume of surplus water that inundates the flood plains, interfere greatly socio - economic condition. Studies shows that flood levels to the extent of 2 meters could be brought down and severity of floods could be substantially reduced in the rivers along with generation of hydropower of the order of 30,000 MW in N.E Region (M.U. Ghani).

The mean annual rainfall in the Brahmaputra basin is around 2300 mm. Internationally the Brahmaputra rank 10th in the world in terms of discharge. The water resources of NE Region has been assessed to be about 31 % of the country. However harnessing of water for irrigation and other beneficial purposes in Brahmaputra is 3%. Monsoon rainfall accounts for 75% to 80% of the annual rainfall. The flood problem has needlessly been continuing since time immemorial. This could have been overcome by the best utilization of huge water resources of the region for poverty alleviation and sustainable development which appear as disastrous flood in some part or other part of the region every year resulting in colossal damage.

Major river systems

The Brahmaputra is one of the largest rivers in the world. Another important river system of Assam is the Barak, the head stream of the Meghna, rises in the hills of Manipur in India and flows south-west for 250 Km. At Lakhipur, it emerges from hills and at Bhanga, it splits into the Surma and Kushiyara which cross into Bangladesh near Karimganj. Northern tributaries of the Brahmaputra and Barak are braided and unstable in their reach. The instability of the river is mainly attributed to high sediment charge, steep slopes and transverse gradient. Apart from these the entire area is in highly seismic zone and receives Earthquake shocks of severe intensity periodically. This is also one of the factors for unstable character of the river. The Earthquake that occurred in those periods considerably disturbed the drainage network of Assam in 1897 and 1950.

The Brahmaputra and Barak river system is subjected to frequent heavy floods, drainage congestion and bank erosion resulting in extensive submergence of land, loss of life and property as well as disruption in communication system. At times the period of floods above danger level is 40 to 70 days. The impact of floods was not felt to the same extent in the past as is felt now. This is due to rapid increase of population and subsequent increase in the all-round activities of man. The flood plain is gradually occupied to meet ever increasing requirements of food and fiber and consequently the flood problem has been accentuated.

Causes of flood

Floods in the region occur due to variety of causes such as:

- River channel carrying flows in excess of the transporting capacity within their banks. This is due to excessive precipitation that occurs in NE-India.
- Backwater in tributaries at their outfalls into the main river because of non-synchronization of peak floods in them.
- Heavy rainfall in short space of time.
- Storm
- Aggravation of river bed.
- Inadequate waterways at rail and road crossing and encroachment in the flood plains.
- Degradation of catchment area in forms of deforestation, jhuming and loss of soil mantle in Himalayan friable watershed.

The rainfall induces drainage problem occurs in naturally low land is severe and acute in this part of the country. The drainage congestion is caused due to heavy precipitation of short duration and higher flood level in the main river, which doesn't allow the water to drain into main river quickly. Drainage congestion is also caused due to construction of road, rail and embankments, which obstructs natural flow and encroachment in the river-side areas due to population pressure. The lack of sufficient capacity of drainage channel and natural bowel shape topography of land resulting from defunct river courses also contribute to drainage congestion problem.

Bank erosion of the Brahmaputra and its tributaries has become a matter of serious concern to both people and the Govt. consuming large annual exchequer of the Govt. in erosion control works. Along the valley specially in Dhemaji, Lakhimpur, Morigaon and Dhubri long reaches of river bank are eroded and consequently number of villages on record are seen left inside the Brahmaputra. The causes of heavy erosion are attributed to excessive sediment load, steep bed gradient, transverse bed slope, non cohesive erodible nature of bank material, formation of char island and consequent development of side channel. Majuli island and the Kaziranga National Park are also the worst victim of this erosion process. It is also observed below the confluence of major tributaries.

The extent and magnitude of flood problem is assessed in terms of different types of damages caused by flood. The floods of 1988 and 1998 of the Brahmaputra basin were unprecedented which completely shattered the economy of the state. Comprehensive studies have been undertaken to go into the various aspects of floods and flood control. Various aspects both structural and non-structural measures that are considered for formulation and implementation (M.U.Ghani).

Space Technology

Satellite Remote Sensing is found to be an effective tool to supplement this in near real time basis. Near Real time information is the key for the user departments in organizing the relief operations. For this flood inundation information has to be furnished to them as early as possible and space borne technology is found to be authentic and cost effective tool for dissemination of the same. For this State Remote Sensing Centre has to play an active role. Under the DMS programme as per guideline the digital flood map is generated at NRSA, Dept. of Space, Hyderabad and transmit the same to the State Remote Sensing Centre through internet for generation and dissemination of hard copy flood maps to the users. To use satellite remote sensing more effectively water level data of the rivers is necessary (source: CWC, Govt. of India). Since rising trend above danger level is indication of probable occurrence of flood, the water level information will facilitate to select proper satellite data during flood peak time. One limitation with operational Indian satellite is non-availability of microwave sensor which has cloud penetration capability, hence one has to depend on satellite having microwave sensor viz. RADARSAT SAR data. If the day happened to be a clear day just after occurrence of Peak flood, IRS series of data is good enough for analysis.

Another interesting area where remote sensing and Geographical Information System (GIS) can be used is in post flood damage assessment due to floods. The people in Assam strongly feel that floods are increasing and thereby the damages. The available data clearly shows the average area affected by floods during 1990's is higher than in 1980's. Floods in the Brahmaputra valley have been aggravated due to change of river course, change in bed topography, heavy landslides up stream, siltation, etc. In the recent past in 1988 the flood damage by the Brahmaputra and its tributaries have been considerable gravity as shown in the following estimates:

- Total area affected : 4.65 million ha
- Crop area affected : 1.33 million ha
- No. of houses damaged : 6,15,500
- Population affected : 1.2 million
- No. of heads of cattle- lost : 46,210

Flood damage assessment is required to identify and take up flood damage restoration works and to distribute the calamity relief fund to various agencies/ districts on more scientific basis. Detailed damage assessment is required by 15th September for the entire monsoon season i.e. from May to September. Out of 23 districts of Assam except the two hills districts all other are prone to floods every year. Nine districts are identified as worst affected areas in every year due to floods.

In 1998 as a 1st phase under DMS programme three districts viz. Dhubri, Dhemaji and Morigaon were taken to generate collateral information. User needs the information on inundation within 72 Hrs. If cloud free data is not available alternative is the RADARSAT for which request for acquisition of data require two days advance information and hence inundation data can be made available within 7 days for this specific case. Current IRS series satellites have enhance the temporal resolution in terms of revisit to same area almost alternate day. During floods in 1998 the available Indian satellite data are as follows.

Damage aspect for these three districts were taken up as usual as the requirement is towards mid of September. For achieving this objective a well knit institutional linkage had to be established among various agencies. For damage assessment pre flood satellite data was procured and rectified using topomaps. Rectified data was used as master image for rectifying other data sets. Pre flood landuse classification is made. Satellite data procured during flood season is geometrically rectified and enhanced. Subsequently the image is classified for extent of inundation and flood inundation maps are prepared. Now the extracted landuse, flood layer and other existing layer such as village were integrated in GIS environment for analysis of damage to crops and number of village affected.

Few technological constraint as seen during the task are cloud cover, temporal frequency of the data, inherent problems with microwave data, turn around time, close contour information, updated database, gaps in data (lack of monitoring network at appropriate locations), reliable historical database for modeling and lack of updated database of villages as per census record.

This acute problem is a major hindrance to the development of the region. The prosperity lies in regional co-operation, since crucial natural link among the states is provided by trans boundary rivers. Proper development and sharing of the water of these rivers could be an effective point for integrated development. There is in urgent need to create a conducive environment for co-operation and solution of the outstanding regional water and related issues and facilitate joint efforts for the benefit of all concerned. The region has chronic devastating flood, which could be mitigated, and development of rich hydropower could be undertaken through several multipurpose dams over rivers flowing through the territory.

3. Landslides

Landslide, the sudden and rapid down hill movement of soil along the hill slope is another dimension of slope instability. It now becomes a common environmental hazard all over the world. The rate of landslide is increasing day by day. Landslide being a natural hazard occurs either due to increase of load on its head or decrease of support in its toe. The nature of slope and the geomorphic processes induce landslides, but it became more hazardous as soon as the settlement process started on the hills. The landslide in the recent years was primarily man induced, the slopes of the hills of Guwahati in Assam are naturally prone to landslides for its structural peculiarities and prevailing climate of the region. The hills of the Guwahati city is coated with a thick layer of immature soil with low permeability which naturally became more landslide prone during rainy season. Growth of population and construction of houses on the steep slope zones and innumerable roads and footpaths caused removal of support at the toe of steeper part further deteriorate the situation.

The frequency of landslides increases with the increase of settlement. Unauthorized rapid growth of settlement on the hills is said to be the root cause of most of the landslides.

Man made hazards
Deforestation:

Causes of Deforestation

Forests in Assam are dwindling and the main reasons attributed to the gradual depletion of forests in Assam are:

- The hills and plateau of the two districts Karbi Along and N.C. Hills are populated by hill tribes having their own cultural life style intertwined with forests, wildlife and jhum (Shifting) cultivation. This particular process involves 'slash' and 'burn' of forest area and natural vegetation. Original jhum cultivation had a long jhum cycle of about 20-25 years, which was allowed to elapse before the same plot of land was cultivated. In this process, the forest cover remained intact. But the increase in population demanded more cultivable land, thus shortening the period to about 4-5 years. This greatly affected the vegetation of the area, as well as the total environment. A study using satellite mapping of forest degradation due to shifting cultivation in the hill districts of N. C. hills and Karbi Anglong district, carried out at the Assam Remote Sensing Application Centre, shows that out of 423885 hectares of land under Jhum cultivation in Karbi Anglong district, 6844 hectares, became degraded forest land. Similarly out of 292309 hectares in N.C. hills, 7938 hectares are degraded. The study further shows that indiscriminate felling of tries primarily for shifting cultivation in these two districts is causing certain serious environmental problems like loss of soil fertility, soil erosion, floods and siltation in the plains.
- Open rearing of domestic animals also contributes towards damage of the environment.
- Particularly in Karbi-Along district, from where the bamboo, required as the raw materials for the Nagaon Paper Mill at Jagiroad, is procured. As a result it loses its capacity for growth and a large areas in Karbi Anglong have undergone the evil process of deforestation.
- In other parts of Assam also, setting up of saw mills, veneer mills and plywood factories has caused rapid depletion of large forest areas, particularly during the last three decades. The data from National Remote Sensing Agency shows that within a period, of seven years (1975-82) about 64 million hectares of forest areas were depleted in the entire north east region.

- The growth of tea industry has caused depletion of a large forest area. The present spate of growth of small tea gardens, many forest covers have to give way to tea plantation, thus causing further shrinkage in the total forest area.

- Forests and grasslands have had to be shrunk by the expansion on settled agricultural practice.

- The link between human poverty and environmental degradation is also one of the important factor behind deforestation. Lack of alternative livelihood for some and greed on the part of unscrupulous traders has led to gradual denudation of the forest resources.

- Another poverty environment link is seen in the destruction of forest for collection of firewood. The demand for firewood being high, its supply is going on through illegal route. Even large trees are cut deep inside the forest, split into small pieces and supplied as firewood.

- Population pressure has led to encroachment of the forestland. Since the coming of the immigrants and their settlement in the forests, the process of capturing vote banks has been going on and the result is the gradual destruction of the forest land.

- Forest land becomes the first choice for rehabilitation of people affected by various natural calamities - thereby adds to further reduction.

- Use of the forest as a major revenue earner has also contributed much to the depletion of forests.

- Much destruction of forest occurs also due to building of roads, opening up new industrial towns, construction of communication towers and electrical lines.

- In illegally procuring coal from Karbi Anglong district, much forest is destroyed.

- For obtaining limestone from Karbi Anglong district for use in the cement factory at Bokajan, often large tracts of forests are destroyed in blasting. Another privately owned cement factory, due to start operation soon, is going to add to the depletion of forest.

- Further, the reserved forests along Assam's border with Nagaland, Meghalaya and Arunachal Pradesh were the worst victims of encroachment and about 12% of reserved forests are under border encroachment. This takes place because, with the developmental activities in the plains people who used to live in hilly areas came down to set up habitation .in the reserved forests in these areas to enjoy the benefits of development.

Solid Waste

From ancient time, waste has remained an inseparable part of the human society. The rapid population growth, growing urbanisation and proliferation of slums are all contributing to the generation of an ever increasing volume of garbage. The increasing pile of garbage has created health hazard and environmental problem.

Types of solid waste:

Solid waste can be classified into different types depending on their source:

1. Household waste is generally classified as municipal waste,
2. Industrial waste as hazardous waste, and
3. Biomedical waste or hospital waste as infectious waste.

Municipal solid waste

Municipal solid waste consists of household waste, construction and demolition debris, sanitation residue, and waste from streets. This garbage is generated mainly from residential and commercial complexes. With rising urbanization and change in lifestyle and food habits, the amount of municipal solid waste has been increasing rapidly and its composition changing.

Bio-Medical Waste:

Hospital waste is generated during the diagnosis, treatment, or immunization of human beings or animals or in research activities in these fields or in the production or testing of biologicals. It may include wastes like sharps, soiled waste, disposables, anatomical waste, cultures, discarded medicines, chemical wastes, etc. These are in the form of disposable syringes, swabs, bandages, body fluids, human excreta, etc. This waste is highly infectious and can be a serious threat to human health if not managed in a scientific and discriminate manner. During 1993 - 94, a survey was carried out in Guwahati, being the gateway of North- East India where attraction of lot of people to different parts of the country creates generation of wastes of different categories from household to commercial to study the aspects of Municipal solid waste management (MSW) and the associated problems along with the generation pattern, quality and quantity.

Storage of waste in community bins is found to be unsatisfactory in the whole city as people are often reluctant to walk to the community bins and therefore dump the waste on side walks, streets or open drains. This creates unhygienic condition in the locality and also creates problems for the Municipality Office to collect the waste for transportation. Lack of proper drainage facility and the large scale built up areas within the city leading to substantial increase in waste generation and flow of water and reduction in low lying areas within and around the city affecting the holding capacity or dumping of the drainage flow. In Guwahati, there is no mechanised recovery and recycling of solid waste, the manual recovery by individual scavengers at the city bins are carried out as well as at the dumping sites also. Hospital waste is not segregated and in the study it is found that three hospitals viz., Wintrobe, Down Town and Neurological Research Centre in the city, has adopted incinerator for disposal of hospital waste. In Down Town Hospital, the incinerator is used for providing hot water to the bathrooms during the morning and evening hours. Water collected in storage tanks is passed through the incinerator through pipes, which are connected, to the bathroom. The incinerator ash produced is disposed in a small dumping ground near Super Market. The kind of wastes fed into the incinerators are used cotton, bandages, disposable syringes, papers and other items including saline pipes. The incinerator in Wintrobe Hospital is not used for any other purpose other than burning the hospital waste. But there was no specific arrangement for disposing off the ash, as found in the survey.

Hazardous Waste:

Industrial and hospital waste is considered hazardous as they may contain toxic substances. Certain types of household waste are also hazardous. Hazardous wastes could be highly toxic to humans, animals, and plants; are corrosive, highly inflammable, or explosive; and react when exposed to certain things e.g. gases. Household wastes that can be categorized as hazardous waste include old batteries, shoe polish, paint tins, old medicines, and medicine bottles. Hospital waste contaminated by chemicals used in hospitals is considered hazardous. These chemicals include formaldehyde and phenols, which are used as disinfectants, and mercury, which is used in thermometers or equipment that measure blood pressure. In the industrial sector, the major generators of hazardous waste are the metal, chemical, paper, pesticide, dye, refining, and rubber goods industries. Direct exposure to chemicals in hazardous waste such as mercury and cyanide can be fatal.

Estimated solid waste generation in the major towns and cities in Assam, 2001

Sl. No.	Urban Center	Population, 2001	Estimated Solid Waste generation (kg/day)
1	Dhubri	63965	22388
2	Kokrajhar	31152	10903
3	Bongaigaon	60550	21193
4	Goalpara	48911	17119
5	Barpeta	41175	14411
6	Nalbari	23177	8112
7	Guwahati	814575	285101
8	Mangaldai	23854	8349
9	Tezpur	58240	20384
10	Lakhimpur	54262	18992
11	Dhemaji	11851	4148
12	Tinsukia	108102	37836
13	Dibrugarh	137879	48258
14	Sibsagar	54482	19069
15	Jorhat	135091	47282
16	Golaghat	33021	11557
17	Nagaon	123054	43069
18	Morigaon	20807	7282
19	Diphu	52062	18222

20	Haflong	35906	12567
21	Silchar	184285	64500
22	Karimganj	52316	18311
23	Hailakandi	29634	10372

Source- ASERB

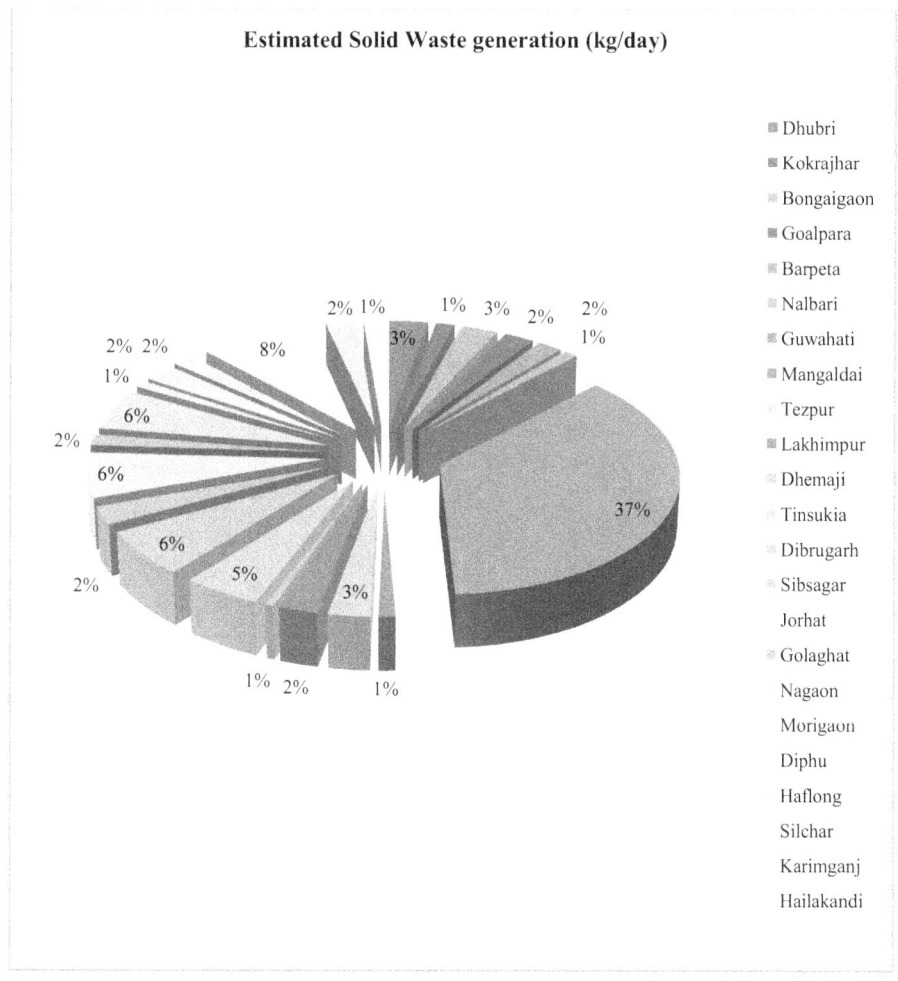

Maps

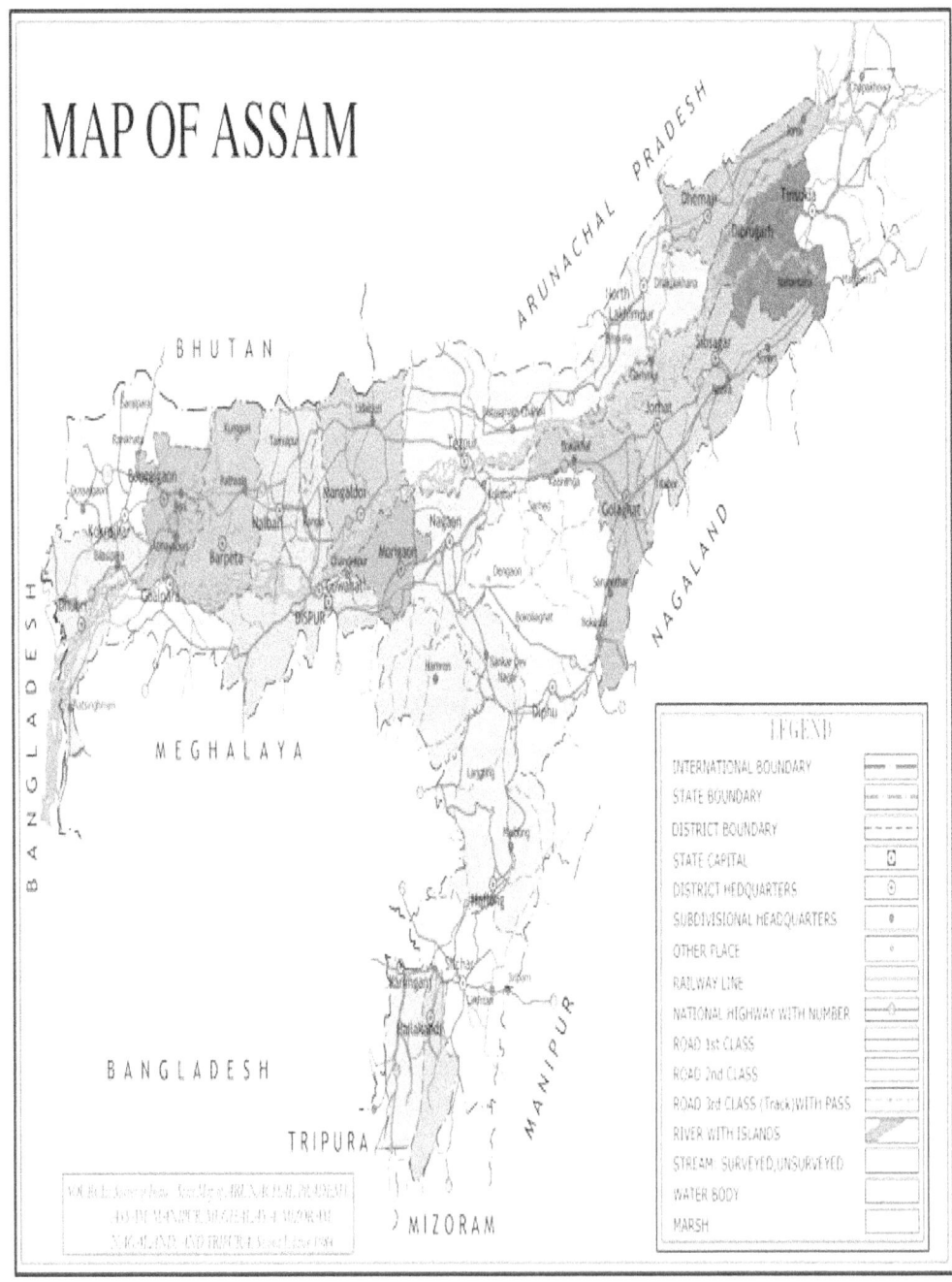

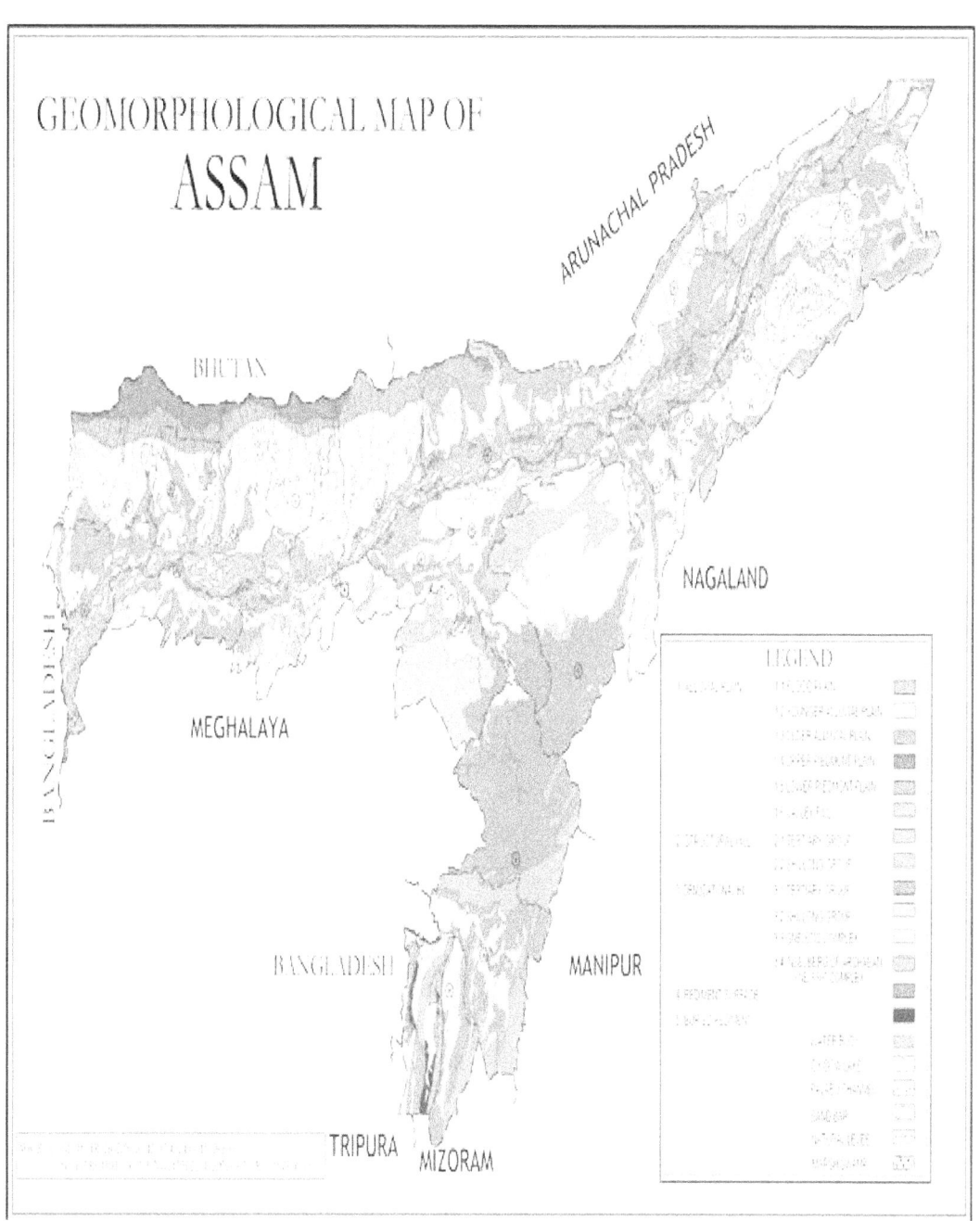

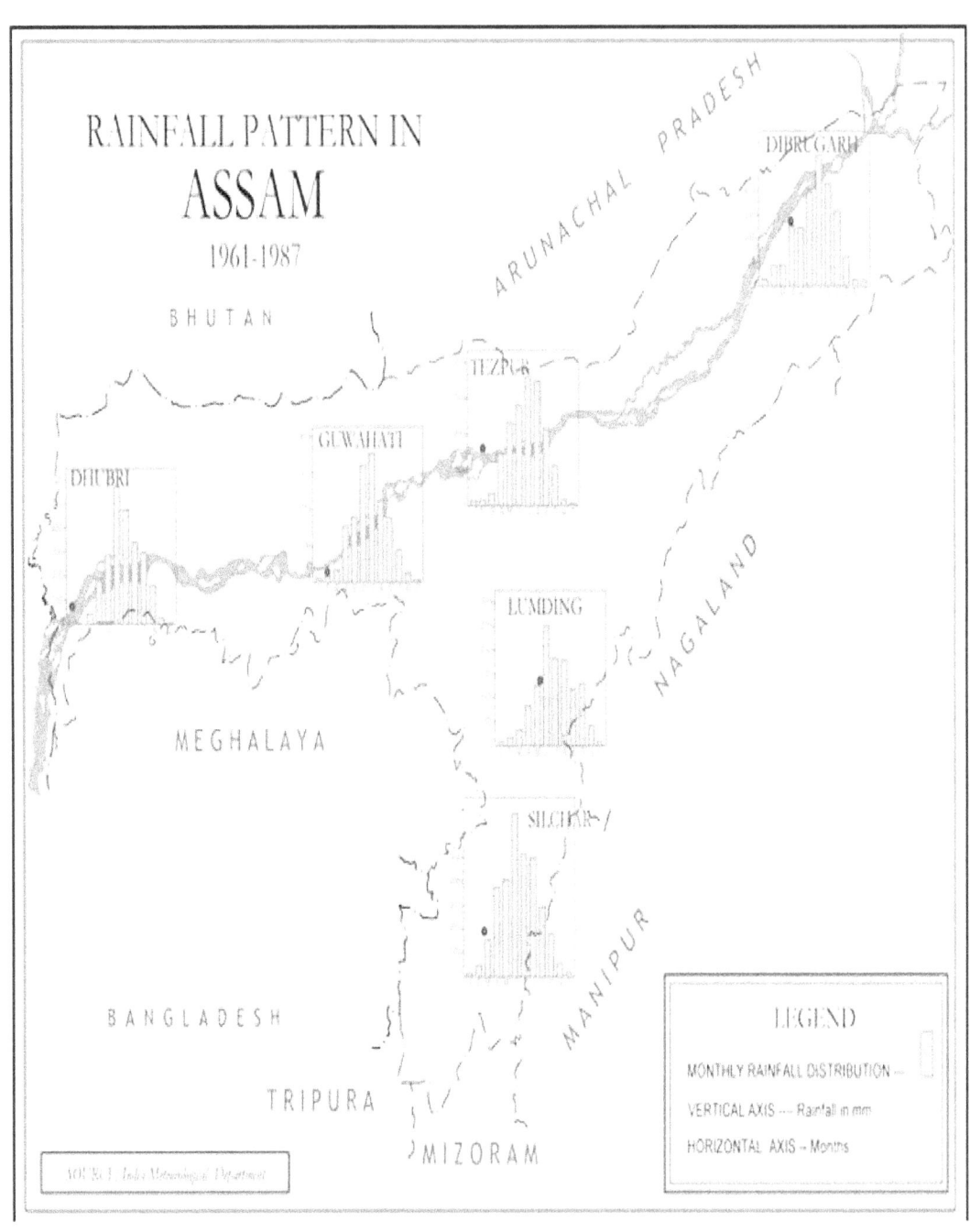

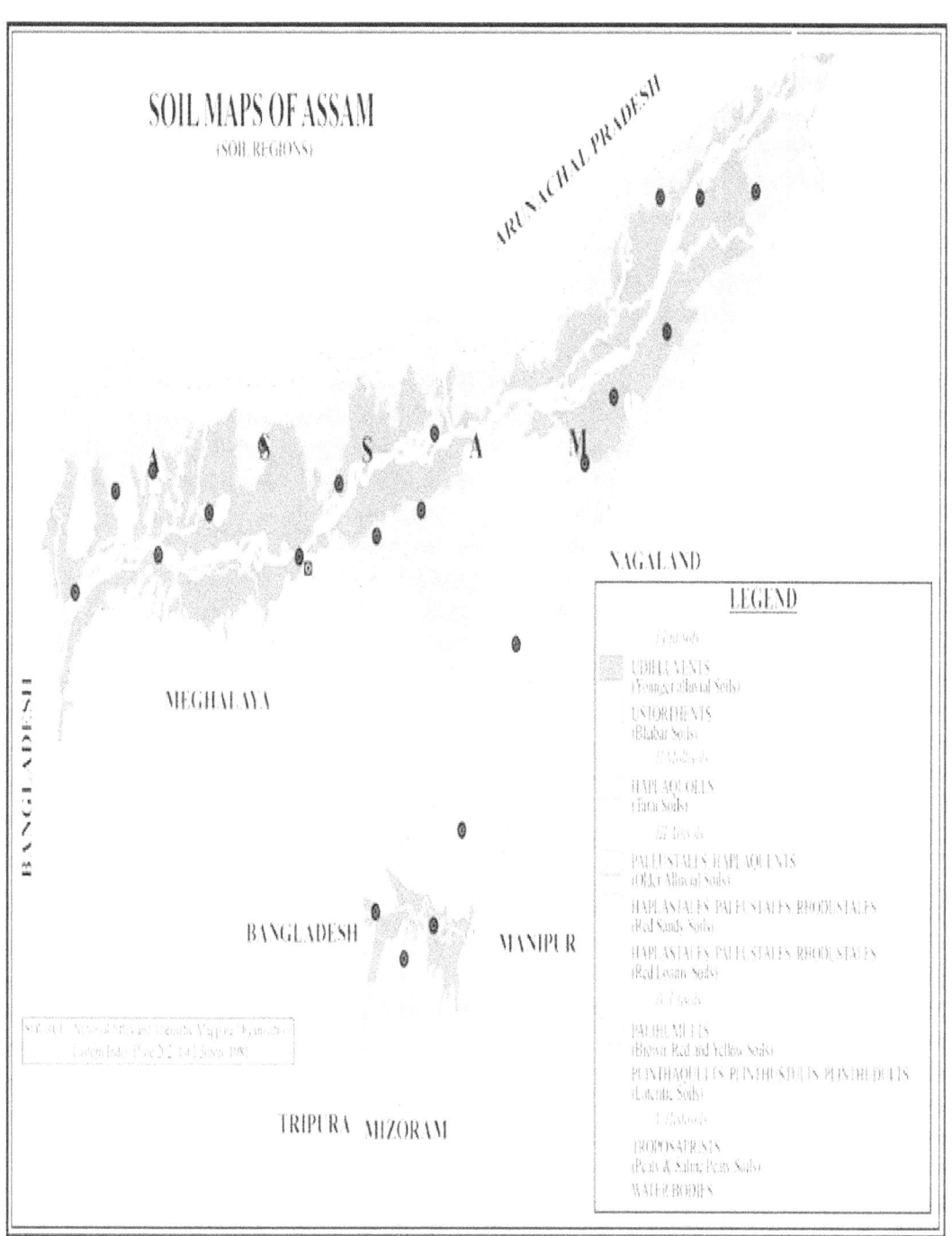

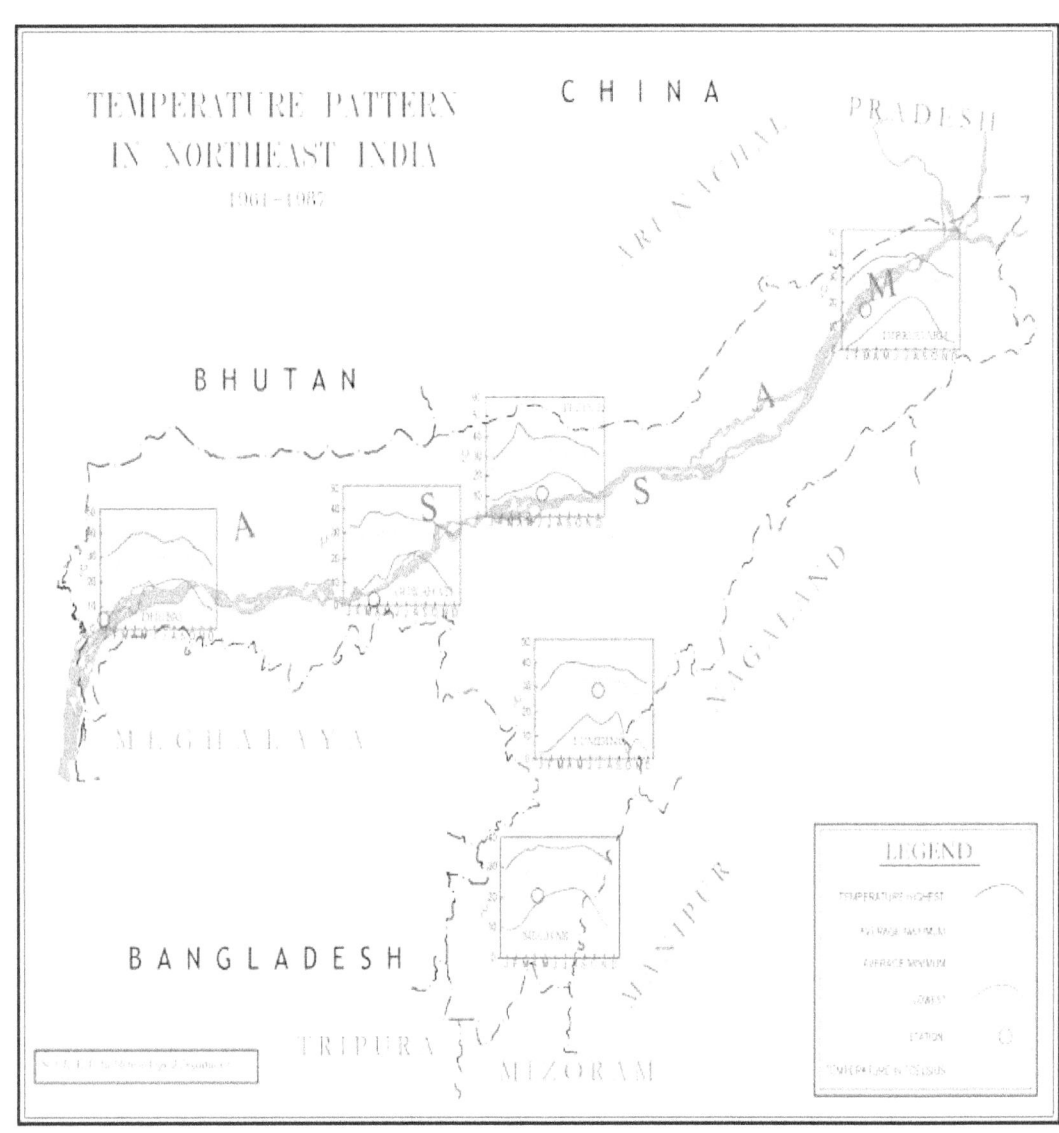

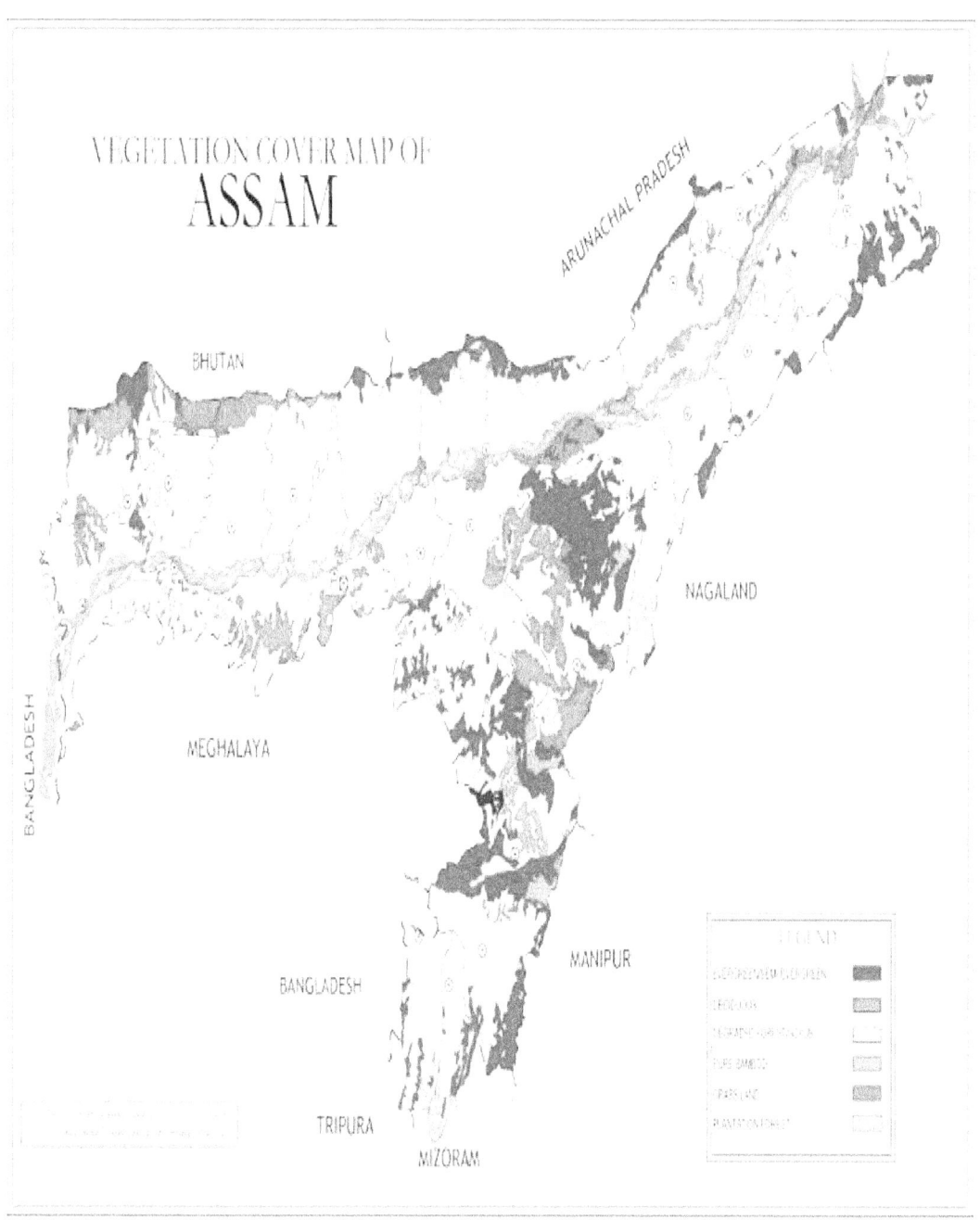

Bibliography

1. Ghatak, S. (1995): Introduction to Development Economics, Routledge, London.
2. Goswami, P.C. (1994): The Economic Development of Assam, Kalyani Publishers, Ludhiana.
3. Government of Assam (2009): Statistical Handbook, Directorate of Economics and Statistics, Guwahati.
4. Majumdar, et al (1998): Statistical Profile of Barak Valley, North Eastern Centre for Advanced Studies, Silchar.
5. Ministry of Environment & Forests, Govt. of India.
6. ENVIS Centre: Assam
7. Leopold Centre for Sustainable Agriculture. www.leopold.iastate.edu
8. McCauley, A., C. Jones, and J. Jacobsen. 2004. Sustainable Agriculture. Nutrient Management-Modulehttp://landresources.montana.edu/NM/Modules/Final%20NM15.pdf
9. National Sustainable Agriculture Information Service. www.attra.org
10. Minnesota Institute for Sustainable Agriculture. www.misa.umn.edu
11. Gibson, C & Fincham, R.(1993): Nutritional survey of Ezingolweni and
12. Nkandla. published report. Durban: University of Natal.
13. North Eastern Council (1995): Basic Statistics of North Eastern Region, NEC, Shillong.
14. Uganda Human Development Report (2007), Rediscovering Agriculture for Human Development, Kampala, UNDP.
15. Kenedy, E.T & Cogill, B.(1987) 'Income and nutritional effects of the
16. Commercialisation of Agriculture in south-western Kenya' Research Report No 63. Washington, DC: International Food Policy Research Institute.
17. Dasgupta, Partha (1998). The economics of poverty in poor countries. Scandinavian Journal of Economics, 100:1, 41-68.
18. Ahluwalia, M S (1978): 'Rural Poverty and Agricultural Performance in India', Journal of Development Studies, 14:13, pp 298-323.
19. Sen, A K (1981): Poverty and Famines: An Essay on Entitlement and Deprivation, Clarendon Press, Oxford.

20. Srinivasan, T N (2000): 'Growth and Poverty Alleviation: Lessons from Development Experience', Paper presented at the Symposium on Alternative Development Paradigms and Poverty Reduction, Asian Development Bank Institute, Tokyo.
21. Vyas, V S and V Sagar (1993): 'Alleviation of Rural Poverty in the States: Lessons of the 1980s' in K Parikh and R Sudarshan (eds), Human Development and Structural Adjustment, Macmillan.
22. Nayar, Gaurav (2005): 'Growth and Poverty in Rural India: An Analysis of Inter-State Differences' in 'Economic and Political Weekly' Vol. 40, No.16.
23. Datt, G and M Ravallion (1996a): 'Why have some Indian States Done Better than Others at Reducing Rural Poverty?' Economica, 65:257, pp 17-38. - (1998): 'Farm Productivity and Rural Poverty in India', Journal of Development Studies, April. - (1999): 'When is Growth Pro-Poor? Evidence from the Diverse Experiences of India's States', Policy Research Working Paper, World Bank, Washington, DC.
    - (2001): 'Why has Economic Growth Been More Pro-poor in Some States of India than Others?' Journal of Development Economics, 68.
24. Dreze J and Sen A.K. (2002): India: Development and Participation, Oxford University Press, New Delhi.
25. Food and Agricultural Organisation reports- 2006, 2002 and 1996.
26. Gallup, John, Steven Radelet and Andrew Warner (1997). Economic growth and the income of the poor. Harvard Institute for International Development, CAER II Discussion Paper No 36.
27. Ranis G and Fei J (1961), A Theory of Economic Development, American Economic Review, 51:4, 533-65.
28. Rosegrant, M., and Hazell. P.B.R. (1999), Rural Asia transformed: The quiet revolution. Oxford University Press, for the Asian Development Bank.
29. World Bank (1982a), World Development Report-1982, World Bank/Oxford University Press.
30. World Bank (2000), *World* Development Report 2000/01 'Attacking Poverty', World Bank/Oxford University Press.
31. Singh, J (1974) An agricultural atlas of India. Kurukshetra: Vishal-P.
32. Planning Commission. (2006). Towards Faster and More Inclusive Growth: An Approach to the 11th Five Year Plan (2007-2012). New Delhi: Government of India. December, p.9.
33. Census of India (2001, and 2011),

34. National Family Health Survey 2 (NFHS 2) (1998–9) and NFHS 3 (2005–6), Ministry of Health and Family Welfare and the National Sample Survey (NSS) 58th (2002) and 65th (2008–9) rounds-2.
35. India Human Development Report (2011)
36. Assam Human Development Report (2003) and NRHM Report-2010-11.
37. Central Bureau of Health Intelligence. Directorate General of Health Services, Ministry of Health and Family Welfare.
38. Health Information of India 2010 & 2011.
39. Garg S, Nath A. (2007). Current Status of National Rural Health Mission. Indian Journal of Community Medicine (Vol. 32, No. 3, pp. 171-172). Retrieved December 5, 2008, from: http://www.ijcm.org.in/text.asp?2007/32/3/171/36818.
40. Rao, Sujatha K.; Selvaraju, S.; Nagpal, Somil; and Sakthivel, S. (2005). Financing of Health in India. Financing and Delivery of Health Care Services in India. New Delhi: National Commission on Macroeconomics and Health, Ministry of Health & Family Welfare, Government of India.

Technical Appendix

Land Fertility Index

The calculation of land fertility index is shown below with the help of a Sample Farmer of Barak Valley-

Mr. Digendra Roy is a small farmer (as per govt. land holdings) having 14 Bigha of agricultural land in Fanairbond village under Dullabcherra ADO circle in Ram Krishna nagar subdivision of Karimganj district.

The results of the sample are-

Sample(S)	SALI	AUOSE	POTATO	SUGARCANE	S.VEG	W.VEG	TOTAL CROP	AREA UNDER PRODUCTION (In Bigha)	OUTPUT PER BIGHA (In Quintals)
S=1	40 Q	5 Q	1.5 Q	6 Q	0.38 Q	2.5 Q	55.38 Q	14	3.95 Q

Q- Quintals

The maximum observation is 5.2 Q per bigha in output per worker table and the minimum one is 2.9 per bigha.

Therefore Land Fertility Index $= \dfrac{\text{Actual value of the factor} - \text{Minimum value of the factor}}{\text{Maximum vaule} - \text{Minimum value}}$

$$= \dfrac{3.95 - 2.9}{5.2 - 2.9}$$

$$= 0.457$$

Thus the Land Fertility Index of sample-1 is 0.457 which is just below the average.

Market Index

The market index of the sample-1 is calculated as-

Sample(S)	SALI SOLD	AUOSE SOLD	POTATO SOLD	SUGARCANE SOLD	S.VEG SOLD	W.VEG SOLD	TOTAL CROP	TOTAL AMOUNT SOLD	% OF OUTPUT SOLD
S=1	24.5 Q	5 Q	50 Kg	6 Q	0 Q	2 Q	55.38	38	68.62

Q= Quintals

The maximum observation is 92.89 in the table of % of output sold and the minimum value is 0.00 who is a subsistence farmer or sold nothing.

Therefore market index $= \dfrac{\text{Actual value of the factor} - \text{Minimum value of the factor}}{\text{Maximum vaule} - \text{Minimum value}}$

$= \dfrac{68.62 - 0.00}{92.89 - 0.00}$

$= 0.74$

The sample-1 has scored 0.74, thus belong to the class of good seller.

Technology Achievement Index

The Technology achievement index is calculated by percentage of output by HYVseeds, use of tractor/powertiller, use of pumpset, use of sprayer, use of harvester/thresher and application of fertiliser & pesticides. All these six dimensions have been given weightage as- 50% for % of output by HYVseeds and 10% weightage for each of the other five dimensions. Thus Technology achievement index for 450 samples have been found out.

Let us take the case of our sample-1 again

Samples(S)	% of output by HYVseeds	Tractor/power tiller	Pumpset	Sprayer	Harvester/thresher	Fertilizer & pesticides
S=1	100%	1	0	1	0	1

Yes- 1 & No- 0

Therefore weighted factor score = HYVseed*50% + Tractor/powertiller*10% + Pumpset*10% + Sprayer*10% + Harvester/thresher*10% + Fertiliser & pesticide*10%

$$= 50 + 10 + 0 + 10 + 0 + 10$$

$$= 80$$

Technology Achievement Index = $\sum$ Factor index ÷ 100

$$= 80 \div 100$$

$$= 0.80$$

Thus the Technology Achievement Index for sample-1 is 0.80.

Labour Productivity Index

Labour Productivity Index is caculated on the basis of output per worker-

Sample(S)	Total output(In Quintals)	Workers applied	Output per worker(In Quintals)
S=1	55.375	2	27.7

Therefore Labour Productivity Index is

$$= \frac{\text{Actual value of the factor} - \text{Minimum value of the factor}}{\text{Maximum vaule} - \text{Minimum value}}$$

$$= \frac{27.7 - 8.9}{120.6 - 8.9}$$

$$= 0.168$$

Thus LPI of s-1 belongs to poor category value.

Agricultural Performance Index

For our sample-1, the Agricultural Performance Index (API) is calculated as

Agricultural Performance Index

$= ¼$(Land fertility index) $+ ¼$(Market index) $+ ¼$(Technical achievement index) $+ ¼$(Workers productivity index)

$= ¼ × 0.457 + ¼ × 0.74 + ¼ × 0.80 + ¼ × 0.169$

$= 0.111 + 0.180 + 0.200 + 0.040$

$= 0.541$

The Agricultural Performance Index of s-1 is 0.541 showing moderate performance.

Wealth Index: At first Wealth score of sample-1 is obtained from the questionnaire-

	Household characteristics	Scores				Answer of sample-1
1.	House type	Pucca =5	Semi pucca=3		Kachha=0	5
2.	Separate room for cooking/Kitchen	Yes=2			No=0	2
3.	Ownership of house	Yes=5			No=0	5
4.	Flooring	Pucca =2			Sand/dung/dirt=0	2
5.	Toilet facility	Own flush toilet=4	Public/ shared flush toilet/ own pit toilet=2	SHARED/PUBLIC PIT TIOLET=1	No facility=0	2
6.	Source of Lighting	Electricity=4	Kerosene, Gas, Oil=2		Other source of lighting=0	4
7.	Main fuel for cooking	Electricity, Liquid petroleum gas or Biogas=4	Coal, Charcoal or Kerosene=2		Other fuel=0	2
8.	Source of Drinking Water	Pipe, Hand pump, Well in residence/ yard/ plot=4	Public tap, Hand pump or Well=2		Other water source=0	4
9.	Car or Tractor	Yes=1			No=0	0
10.	Moped or Scooter	Yes=1			No=0	0
11.	Telephone	Yes=1			No=0	1
12.	Refrigerator	Yes=1			No=0	0
13.	Colour TV	Yes=1			No=0	1
14.	Black and white TV	Yes=1			No=0	0
15.	Bicycle	Yes=1			No=0	1
16.	Electric fan	Yes=1			No=0	1
17.	Radio	Yes=1			No=0	0
18.	Sewing machine	Yes=1			No=0	0
19.	Mattress	Yes=1			No=0	1
20.	Pressure cooker	Yes=1			No=0	1
21.	Chair	Yes=1			No=0	1
22.	Cot or bed	Yes=1			No=0	1
23.	Table	Yes=1			No=0	1
24.	Clock or watch	Yes=1			No=0	1
25.	Ownership of livestock	Yes=1			No=0	1
26.	Water pump	Yes=1			No=0	0
27.	Bullock cart	Yes=1			No=0	0
28.	Thresher	Yes=1			No=0	0
					Total	37

So he scored 37 out of total marks of 50. Wealth index is then calculated as-

$$= \frac{\text{Actual value of the factor} - \text{Minimum value of the factor}}{\text{Maximum vaule} - \text{Minimum value}}$$

$$= \frac{37 - 0}{50 - 0}$$

$$= 0.74$$

Therefore the sample farmer belongs to middle class with score of 0.74.

Education index

Education index is calculated by taking equal weights of the two indicators- literacy level and child enrolment (if any school-aged child is out of school in years 1 to 8). Our sample farmer has continued up to class 10 and he has three children. The eldest son of the family could go to class 10 and other two brothers finished at class 8. Both literacy level and enrolment have been found ok for them.

Their score in education is 10 and 1 for enrolment (0 if anyone failed to enrol). Here note that maximum score in schooling is 15 (Graduate has been found the highest level during survey) and the minimum is 0.

$$\text{The Literacy Index} = \frac{\text{Actual value of the factor} - \text{Minimum value of the factor}}{\text{Maximum vaule} - \text{Minimum value}}$$

$$= \frac{10 - 0}{15 - 0}$$

$$= 0.667$$

Therefore the Education Index = $50\% \times 0.667 + 50\% \times 1$

$$= 0.333 + 0.5$$

$$= 0.833$$

The farmer has achieved 0.833 which is really appreciable for a small farmer.

Health Index

Health is an important parameter of Human Development. Health Index is prepared with the help of two sub dimensions- Body Mass Index and Child Mortality, giving them equal weights. The data collected on the sample-1 is-

sample=1	weight(in kg)	height-Ft	Ft=MT	MT^2	BMI	Child mortality
s=1	50	5.1	1.55	2.4162	20.693	1

The above information is body weight of the farmer and height taken in ft. it was converted to metre^2. The BMI is obtained by dividing the weight in Kg by height in MT^2. The child mortality has not been found in the family.

Now Factor Index for BMI on Sample-1 = $\frac{\text{Actual value of the factor} - \text{Minimum value of the factor}}{\text{Maximum vaule} - \text{Minimum value}}$

$$= \frac{20.69 - 14.3}{38.4 - 14.3}$$

$$= 0.266$$

Therefore Health Index = 50% × BMI + 50% × Child Mortality

$\qquad$ = 50% × 0.266 + 50% × 1

$\qquad$ = 0.129 + 0.5

$\qquad$ = 0.629

The Health Index for s-1 is found 0.629 which is moderate and BMI of 20.69 shows normal nutrition.

Quality of Life Index

Quality of Life for our sample-1 is calculated simply as Human Development Index by equally weighted three dimension indices- wealth index, education index and health index-

Quality of Life Index = 1/3 (wealth index) + 1/3 (education index) + 1/3 (health index)

$$= 1/3 \times 0.740 + 1/3 \times 0.833 + 1/3 \times 0.629$$

$$= 0.727$$

Multidimensional Povrtey Index

A household is identified as multidimensionally poor if, and only if, it is deprived in some combination of indicators whose weighted sum exceeds 30 percent of deprivations. The dimensions and indicators are presented below with an example.

Our sample-1 farmer has performed as-

1. Health (each indicator weighted equally at 1/6)

Child Mortality: If any child has died in the family. Answer- No. Score- 0

Nutrition: If the adult in the family is malnourished. Answer- No. Score- 0

2. Education (each indicator weighted equally at 1/6)

Years of Schooling (if no household member has completed 5 years of schooling). Answer- No. Score- 0

Child Enrolment (if any school-aged child is out of school in years 1 to 8). Answer- No. Score- 0

3. Standard of Living (each of the six indicators weighted equally at 1/18).

Electricity (no electricity is poor) Score- 0

Drinking water (MDG definitions) Score- 0

Sanitation (MDG definitions, including that toilet is not shared) Score- 0.55.

Flooring (dirt/sand/dung are poor). Score- 0

Cooking Fuel (wood/charcoal/dung are poor). Score- 0.55

Assets (poor if do not own more than one of: radio, tv, telephone, bike, motorbike). Score- 0.55

The total deprivation score = 0 + 0 + 0 + 0 + 0 + 0 + 0.55 + 0 + 0.55 + 0.55

$$= 1.65$$

The score of 1.65 < 3 or MPI of 0.165 < 0.33 is not multidimensionally poor. Any result > 0.33 is poor.

www.ingramcontent.com/pod-product-compliance
Lightning Source LLC
Chambersburg PA
CBHW080235180526
45167CB00006B/2291